Cultivating Teacher Renewal

Guarding Against Stress and Burnout

Barbara Larrivee

ROWMAN & LITTLEFIELD EDUCATION

A division of
ROWMAN & LITTLEFIELD PUBLISHERS, INC.
Lanham • New York • Toronto • Plymouth, UK

Published by Rowman & Littlefield Education
A division of Rowman & Littlefield Publishers, Inc.
A wholly owned subsidary of The Rowman & Littlefield Publishing Group, Inc.
4501 Forbes Boulevard, Suite 200, Lanham, Maryland 20706
www.rowman.com

10 Thornbury Road, Plymouth PL6 7PP, United Kingdom

British Library Cataloguing in Publication Information Available

Library of Congress Cataloging-in-Publication Data

Library of Congress Cataloging-in-Publication Data Available

ISBN 978-1-4758-0109-5 (cloth : alk. paper) – ISBN 978-1-4758-0110-1 (paper : alk. paper)
ISBN 978-1-4758-0111-8 (electronic)

∞™ The paper used in this publication meets the minimum requirements of American National Standard for Information Sciences—Permanence of Paper for Printed Library Materials, ANSI/NISO Z39.48-1992.

Printed in the United States of America

To all my students who have cultivated my renewal
To all those in my life who sustain my well-being
To Chuck who supports and nurtures me in so many ways

Contents

Introduction

The call to help teachers take a more proactive stance to insulate themselves from the onset of burnout is just beginning to be heard. Although every job has its own set of demands and available resources to buffer those demands, the nature of the teaching profession places unrelenting demands on a teacher while offering diminishing resources. It is no wonder teachers are more stressed than ever.

Teachers are choosing to leave the profession at alarming rates, with nearly half of new teachers leaving the profession within their first five years of teaching. Given this dire set of circumstances, many are now realizing the need for teacher education programs and ongoing professional development to develop an awareness of the stress exposure in the teaching profession as well as explicitly teach stress management strategies.

Teachers need to be prepared in order to keep the potentially destructive effects of stress at bay. Job demands such as massive workload, time pressure, and lack of control of their teaching tasks are making it more difficult for teachers to exercise much autonomy. As a teacher's creative talents are stifled, the job becomes more mundane. It is easy to see how frustration and disenchantment can set in. Increasing demands with imposed federal and state mandates often lead to disillusionment and a sense of alienation that can leave teachers feeling like mere pawns in the system.

Because every day is unpredictable and full of new demands and challenges, many teachers experience ongoing stress, and with that stress comes a range of negative health outcomes affecting teacher motivation, performance, and zeal for teaching. When lack of ability to cope reaches a peak, teachers experience an extreme form of stress—burnout. It is crucial that teachers develop the tools necessary to preserve their well-being to keep from falling prey to burnout.

Mounting constraints imposed by current high-stakes testing coupled with the emotional outlay teaching requires render teachers more susceptible to burnout than those in other professions. When teachers are overwhelmed and emotionally exhausted they have fewer personal resources to invest. Signs of imbalance due to burnout can take the form of being completely spent by the end of the day, lack of motivation to go to work, preoccupation with negative thoughts, and feelings of anger and resentment.

When passion and enthusiasm wither, it can be the marker for the early stages of burnout. Feeling demoralized periodically throughout one's teaching career is normal and predictable. Burnout doesn't happen all of a sudden; rather, it results from a long-term pattern of self-neglect, a slow disintegration that eventually erodes both a teacher's passion and compassion.

Cultivating Teacher Renewal: Guarding Against Stress and Burnout offers the antidote to teacher burnout by facilitating the development of the attitudes, habits, and practices that will keep teachers from surrendering to burnout. It provides the knowledge and skills for counteracting early signs of burnout.

This book is both evidence based and multidisciplinary, providing an extensive review of the abundant research on stress and burnout and specifically applying it to the teaching profession. There is a vast amount of research coming from a variety of disciplines that taken together provide a multidimensional approach to teacher stress and burnout. Such an approach paints a complete picture of the relevant issues and the range of resources that can be tapped.

The book is divided into two parts. Part 1 lays out the many facets of the teacher's job that make it one of the most stressful professions. Work environment characteristics that are common sources of stress and burnout and the personal traits and behaviors that can head a teacher down the path to burnout are identified. The first section of the book also helps teachers find ways to maintain work-life balance, get the vital support they need, and navigate the total spectrum of emotions that teaching elicits. When teachers are more conscious of the conditions that induce stress and are able to notice the symptoms of distress early, they can begin to take specific steps to vigorously counteract the effects of stress.

Part 2 offers numerous strategies to help teachers become stress hardy. The research and resulting strategies presented span the fields of education, the social sciences, and the neurosciences. Included in these domains are behavior and classroom management, stress management, general coping skills, emotion regulation, and stress-related growth, the personal growth that often stems from highly stressful situations such as teacher burnout.

Topics covered in the newer domain of positive psychology include building character strengths, resilience, optimism, and hope. In the sociocultural domain, research on emotional labor is very pertinent to teachers' work. In the neurosciences, brain research has important implications for understanding and managing emotions and enhancing learning capacity. And lastly, the topics of well-being and mindfulness, which seem to be everywhere these days, are very relevant to the topic of teacher renewal.

Addressing teacher stress and burnout requires not only individual solutions but also measures that change the work environment. The route to offsetting teacher stress needs to be twofold—teachers helping themselves as well as schools becoming better places to work. Actively confronting teacher stress and preventing burnout should be an integrated part of life and work in schools. Yet, realistically, with many competing agendas it is not likely that preserving teacher well-being will be a high priority any time soon, leaving teachers to fend for themselves. Teachers can't afford to wait. They have to take action on their own behalf.

Teachers need access to social and organizational resources that will help support them. There is little doubt of the importance of a collegial and collaborative school culture in the prevention of burnout. Successful schools operate in a mutually supportive spirit, putting in place a variety of collaboration structures. Research clearly indicates that teachers who have such supportive resources are more resistant to the harmful effects of stress as well as cope better when they do experience stress. It would be ideal for such support to be in place, but when it isn't teachers need to be industrious in constructing opportunities to support each other.

Pressed for time, teachers often fail to engage in daily lifestyle practices that might reduce stress. Understandably, teachers may fall into habits that exacerbate stress. Healthy diet, adequate rest, and regular exercise are obviously essential for sustaining well-being. Yet, busy, stressed-out teachers may choose harmful palliative practices, such as overeating or drinking and avoidance behavior as ways to reduce stress. Such poor choices have deleterious effects, resulting in slow and insidious biochemical cascades that can lead to chronic illness.

Reactions to stress affect nearly every system in the body. Chronic stress weakens the immune system, our natural defense for fending off disease, increasing the likelihood of getting sick. In the quest to do their job effectively and meet their students' needs, teachers often ignore their own physical and mental health.

Teachers must constantly be on guard to heed the signs of stress so that they can be vigilant in keeping from succumbing to burnout. The comprehensive approach this book takes offers an array of strategies to address burnout on many fronts. A variety of reflective personal exercises are incorporated to enhance implementation and integration of these strategies.

Cultivating Teacher Renewal offers many intentional practices to help teachers stay in a renewal cycle. These stress management coping strategies include:

- Minimizing conditions that induce stress
- Maintaining work-life balance
- Activating a support network
- Implementing classroom management strategies that reduce stress
- Being a reflective practitioner
- Building teacher self-efficacy
- Engaging in respectful dialogue and authentic communication
- Becoming stress hardy
- Creating on-the-job stressbusters
- Challenging self-defeating beliefs and expectations
- Modifying destructive thought patterns
- Curbing stress-producing self-talk
- Recognizing emotional triggers
- Expressing anger in sane ways
- Keeping negative emotions from cascading
- Developing mindfulness practices
- Using relaxation techniques
- Building on character strengths
- Cultivating optimism and hope

Part I

UNDERSTANDING THE MANY FACETS OF TEACHER STRESS AND BURNOUT

Chapter One

The Consequences of Stress and Burnout

Stress has received much attention in the psychological literature because of its well-established relationship to emotional, behavioral, and physiological problems. The physical and emotional manifestations of stress are taking a toll on the health of the nation, with close to half of Americans reporting increased stress over the past five years in the most recent American Psychological Association *Stress in America* survey (APA, 2012). With teaching considered one of the most stressful professions, the problem among teachers is acute.

STRESS AND ITS IMPACT

Stress is the physical, mental, and emotional response to life's changes and demands. Stress occurs when your usual way of doing things is inadequate for the demands of the situation. Simply stated, stress is what happens when life hands you more than you can handle. For teachers, this often happens when they have to deal with challenging student behavior and they have exhausted their repertoire of strategies.

Some stress is normal and can be useful. Selye (1974) labeled the rush of adrenaline that is felt in the form of excitement or enthusiasm *eustress*. This kind of physiological arousal generates productive and vital energy. Although stress is most often seen in a negative light, a certain level of stress can result in improved performance and help you focus on the work at hand, like getting a report done by the deadline. As long as the stress is temporary, it is not necessarily harmful. It becomes problematic, however, when the stress is long-term and ongoing. This is often the case for teachers because every day is unpredictable and full of new demands and challenges.

Stress is experienced in levels. Low levels may not be noticeable at all. Occasional, moderate stress can be positive and challenge you to act in creative and resourceful ways. A certain level of discomfort is healthy and can lead to taking necessary action. The goal is not to be stress free but rather to keep the harmful effects of cumulative stress at bay. When stress becomes chronic, it can take over your life. Luskin and Pelletier (2005) refer to this type of stress as Type 2 stress—the kind that doesn't just go away, it's unrelenting. It keeps sending out signals to you that you are exceeding the limits of your mind and body. If you don't pay attention early and take corrective action and keep ignoring these early warning signs, the symptoms of the body will continue to worsen until you pay attention, or eventually become immobilized by a stress-related disease.

Transactional View of Stress

The literature on stress offers a number of definitions and conceptualizations. The most comprehensive and widely accepted view of stress is a dynamic *transaction* between personal resources and environmental demands. When a person encounters life demands, a transaction occurs in which the person weighs perceived demands of the event against his/her perceived capabilities for coping with it (Lazarus & Folkman, 1984). In this transactional scheme, stress occurs when there is a perceived shortfall of resources needed to deal with the problem.

Researchers who study stress have consistently identified perceptions of the balance between perceived demands and perceived coping resources for dealing with such demands as the critical variables in determining whether or not a person will experience harmful stress levels (Sapolsky, 1998). Because stress results from an imbalance between what you have to do and the resources you have available at any given time (for example, energy, skill, patience, money), something stressful on Friday may not be stressful on Saturday when you may have more time and more help and support.

This transactional approach to stress emphasizes the active role of the individual in mediating potential stressors in the environment. When lack of ability to cope reaches a peak, those in helping professions, such as teaching, experience an extreme form of stress—burnout.

Applying this transactional model, teachers become susceptible to stress if they perceive an imbalance between the demands they face in their jobs and the resources they have for coping with these demands. The actual impact of the stress will be mediated by the perception that job demands are a threat and by coping mechanisms used to reduce the threat (Kyriacou & Sutcliffe, 1978). Potential stressors become actual stressors if a teacher perceives them as a threat to well-being or self-esteem.

Because stress is a subjective response to potentially stressful events, different teachers function more or less effectively with varying amounts of stress. Some teachers seem to be able to manage great amounts of stress while others become overwhelmed with modest amounts. A teacher's coping skills will determine how successful he or she will be in managing the stress. Burnout is the end product of cumulative unsuccessful attempts to deal with classroom demands.

Within this transactional view, individual teacher variables and job-related features are not independent contributors to burnout; rather, they generate a dynamic, reciprocal mix. When a teacher perceives the imbalance to be in favor of demands, burnout is a likely result. Integral to the production of stress and burnout are the underlying conscious processes that lie between the comparison of existing demands and available resources, such as perceptions, judgments, and appraisals. With regard to teacher burnout, appraisals made of student misbehavior are perhaps the most significant of these transactional factors. This topic is discussed in greater detail in a later chapter.

The Impact of Stress

The early work of Selye (1956, 1974) highlighted the links between stress and the body's physiological response, and he was one of the first to focus attention on the value and importance of stress prevention. Given the physiological changes that accompany a stress response, it is not surprising that 50 to 80% of all visits to a doctor are estimated to be for medical conditions related to stress (Luskin & Pelletier, 2005).

Physiologically, a lot happens when you are experiencing the stress response. Your heart pumps faster to get more blood to your muscles, your breathing becomes faster to move more oxygen to your blood, and your muscles tense up to get ready for action. This response diminishes blood flow to the reasoning center of the brain as blood flows to the more primitive part of the brain. Your blood pressure rises, your digestion stops so that more blood is available for your brain and muscles, you sweat more to cool off your body, your arteries around your heart become strained, and your immune system is diminished.

Stress is associated with negative health in a bewildering array of illnesses, ranging from headaches and backaches to heart disease, and perhaps even cancer (Aldwin & Gilmer, 2004; Duijts, Zeegers, & Borne, 2003; Krantz & McCeney, 2002; Vitaliano, Zhang, & Scanlan, 2003). Stress affects nearly every system in the body, including the immune (Schneiderman, Ironson, & Siegel, 2005; Segerstrom & Miller, 2004), cardiovascular (McEwen, 1998; Dimsdale, 2008), and respiratory systems (Chen et al., 2006). Stress is also associated with a higher risk of mortality in healthy as well as chronically ill samples (Matthews & Gump, 2002; Nielsen, Kristensen, Schnohr, & Gronbaek, 2008; Rosengren, Orth-Gomer, Wedel, & Wilhelmsen, 1993; Turrell, Lynch, Leite, Raghunathan, & Kaplan, 2007).

Psychologically, life stress is associated with subsequent depression (Brown & Harris, 1989; Hammen, 2005) and other forms of psychopathology (Dohrenwend, 2000; Johnson & Roberts, 1995). Additionally, continuous stress can adversely affect mental health and undermine resilience, hope, and the capacity to forgive (Ong et al., 2006; Lopez, Snyder, & Pedrotti, 2003; Harris & Thoresen, 2005).

If stress happens too often or lasts too long, it can have serious effects. The immune system is the body's natural defense system that helps fight infections. When you are stressed, your body responds as though you are in danger. A high level of stress weakens your immune system, making it harder to fight off disease. Chronic stress makes you more likely to get sick more often. If you already have a health problem, stress makes it worse.

Consequences of Stress for Teachers

Some degree of stress in the school environment is inevitable. Chronic stress has both physical and mental side effects. Research has shown a clear relationship between stressors inherent in teaching and physiological symptoms (Dunham & Varma, 1998). The most prevalent symptom is a feeling of being totally spent by the end of the day. Signs of imbalance due to stress, which may ultimately lead to burnout, can take the form of preoccupation with negative thoughts, lack of motivation to go to work, and general irritability. Typical reactions to teacher stress include some of the following symptoms.

Physical Symptoms Associated with Teacher Stress

Somatic Complaints
Physical exhaustion
Feeling nervous or tense
Headache
Back pain
Difficulty getting to and staying asleep
Becoming easily fatigued
Swelling or aching joints and muscles
Stomach pain
Difficulty breathing
Voice loss
Illnesses and Chronic Conditions
High blood pressure
Kidney or bladder trouble
Arthritis
Respiratory or breathing problems
Gallbladder disorders
Cardiovascular disorders
Insomnia
Gastritis
Stomach ulcers
Colitis
Psychological Effects Associated with Teacher Stress
Emotional exhaustion
Frustration
Anxiety
Job dissatisfaction
Depression
Burnout
Lack of self-confidence
Hypersensitivity to criticism
Excessive worry and guilt
Inability to relax
Feelings of alienation, anger, and resentment
Moodiness
Difficulty concentrating
Cynical attitude toward students, parents, and other school staff

How Stress Affects Your Thoughts and Emotions

Signs of stress are not only physical and psychological. Reactions to stress permeate the way you think, feel, and act. You may:

- Feel cranky, yelling at others for no reason
- Feel frustrated, losing your temper often
- Feel jumpy, wanting to run away
- Seem unable to deal with even small problems
- Imagine that bad things are about to happen

FACTORS CONTRIBUTING TO TEACHER STRESS AND BURNOUT

Due to the unrelenting pressures and demands on teachers not only from others but also from self, teaching is among the most stressful professions (Blase & Kirby, 1991; Farber, 1991; Friedman, 2000; Goddard, O'Brien, & Goddard, 2006; Montgomery & Rupp, 2005; Smylie, 1999). Because teachers answer to so many different people, a number of factors contribute to their stress. In an early comprehensive review of sources of teacher stress, seven problem areas were consistently identified: school environment, student misbehavior, poor working conditions, personal concerns of the teacher, relationships with parents, time pressures, and inadequacy of training (Turk, Meeks, & Turk, 1982). Poor school environment was identified most frequently in the 49 studies reviewed, with student misbehavior as the second contributor to teacher stress. More recent research moves student behavior to the top position, especially for early career teachers.

Stress and burnout are common among teachers as they struggle to cope with an increasingly bureaucratic system, with more students who are needy and troubled, and with ever-increasing responsibilities. Some of the challenges teachers today face include:

- The constant threat of teacher accountability for student performance
- Unsettling changes due to school transfers, building closings, and loss of jobs
- Loss of autonomy and control over the curriculum
- Excessive workload leading to lack of spontaneity and creativity
- Perpetual changes and expectations that are in constant flux with school reform efforts
- Conflict between school policy and one's own professional beliefs that can compromise a teacher's integrity
- Increase in the workflow they must manage
- Quantity replacing quality as the job becomes more bureaucratic than professional

In addition to the big stresses there are the "little" stresses—those tiny, almost unrecognized events that can accumulate rapidly in a teacher's day. A small stressor may be rain that confines students and the teacher to the classroom all day, the knock at the door interrupting a lesson at a critical point, or the student arriving late to class.

In a given day, a lot of small hassles can add up. A cascade of little annoyances can easily gather momentum.

Summarizing the results of numerous teacher stress surveys, Truch (1980) found that up to 90% of teachers reported experiencing job-related stress, and 95% indicated the need for a stress management course. Surveying teachers regarding stress, Humphrey (1992) found that 49% indicated they were at a loss about how to deal with their stress. He noted that teachers are highly ineffective in coping with stress as they often have no strategies other than to simply tolerate the stress. Even though teacher stress has been a concern for decades, it is not until recently that it has come to the forefront.

Increasing demands with recently imposed federal and state mandates often lead to disillusionment and a sense of alienation that can leave teachers feeling like mere pawns in the system. Teachers need to take control of their teaching lives and become empowered decision makers who act on their world to effect change.

Multiple Arenas of Teacher Stress

Stress is not simply attributed to long hours and too much work. Rather, problems seem to appear for teachers when their own needs begin to conflict with the demands of the school environment. The causes of these problems generally emerge from three broad bases linked to stress research.

1. Systemic factors that are part of the institutional and political organization of schools
2. Job-specific factors that are intrinsic to the teaching profession
3. Factors that affect the individual vulnerability of a teacher

There are innumerable stressors that may emerge from outside issues distinct from the job itself. Teachers' personal lives can change their perspective, motivation, and job performance. Financial, family, or spousal stressors may seep into the classroom, and when such problems become acute they can render a teacher preoccupied and distracted.

In their research, Clausen and Petruka (2009) found that if a teacher was experiencing stress in one area, for example, a conflict with administration, he or she could still reasonably perform the job. A teacher only approached burnout when there was a prolonged period of exposure to the stress, or a combination of stressors emerged simultaneously from several sources.

Burnout

Burnout refers to the physical, mental, and emotional exhaustion that results from chronic job stress and frustration. Whereas a new job has energizing effects with the excitement of learning new things and mapping out new territory, as the job becomes familiar, enthusiasm and energy can begin to wane. Burnout often sets in when two conditions prevail: Certainties start to characterize the workday, and demands of the job make workers lose a sense of control. If, in addition, an organization is characterized by rigid rules, problems that arise feel insurmountable because creative problem solving seems too risky. When bureaucratic work settings are of the "we've always done it this way" mentality, burnout is common (Langer, 1989). When mature adults are forced to work in any environment where they seem to be losing control, stress results (Argyris, 1964).

The concept of burnout is most usually applied to the work of human service professionals. The concept was coined by Freudenberger (1974) to describe the "wearing out" of human service professionals whose clients, patients, or students seem not to improve, recover, or learn. The workers no longer perform their roles effectively and sometimes even become hostile or uncaring about those they are charged to serve. According to Freudenberger, those who are the most dedicated and committed are the ones more prone to burnout. His original idea of burnout was that workers would find themselves under increasing pressure to help others, would demand more of themselves than they were able to give, and would ultimately exhaust themselves. (Does this sound familiar?)

Those in helping professions, such as teaching, often fall prey to burnout as a "consequence of caring," or the emotional response to the chronic strain of dealing with others. The following are typical characteristics of burnout victims (Maslach, 1982).

1. Reluctance to discuss work with others
2. High incidence of daydreaming to escape current plight
3. Attitude of cynicism and negativity toward constituents
4. Loss of excitement and interest in daily activities
5. Emotional exhaustion and feelings of being spent
6. Decreased effectiveness in job performance
7. Blaming others for unhappiness
8. Feeling powerless to change the situation

Burnout in Teachers

Research on burnout in teachers emerged in the early 1980s. Since then, the concept of burnout has come to be used more in connection with teachers than with any other group. This is not surprising given the intrinsic characteristics of the teaching profession. Teachers are prone to the effects of excessive stress, which if unattended can result in burnout. School, like any workplace, can be a hub of maladies and health problems as a result of job-related stress.

Because burnout is a process that develops over time, there has been interest in discovering the paths through which burnout develops. Research has demonstrated the existence of two paths to burnout: a cognitive path, manifested in personal and professional feelings of lack of accomplishment, and an emotional path, reflected in a sense of overload and emotional exhaustion. The process generally begins to develop with external stressors such as disruptive student behavior, excessive paperwork, and conflicting demands, which then lead to emotional exhaustion.

Researchers have found that burnout manifests in three major dimensions: (1) emotional exhaustion, (2) depersonalization, and (3) lack of personal accomplishment

(Friesen, Prokop, & Sarros, 1988; Maslach, 1982). Emotional exhaustion is considered to be the core dimension of burnout (Maslach, Leiter, & Schaufeli, 2008). Research findings indicate that emotional exhaustion has the most consistent relationship to job-related stressors (Maslach, Schaufeli, & Leiter, 2001).

- *Emotional exhaustion* is the draining of mental energy caused by interpersonal demands. Emotional exhaustion is characterized by feelings of frustration, anger, depression, and dissatisfaction. With emotional exhaustion, a teacher can feel a lack of emotional resilience.
- *Depersonalization* involves a dehumanized and impersonal view of others, resulting in blaming others. Teachers suffering from depersonalization develop negative attitudes toward those they work with and become cynical and critical.
- *Lack of personal accomplishment* signifies a loss of self-efficacy on the job and results in the tendency to evaluate oneself negatively, devaluing his or her own work and that of others. When teachers feel a lack of personal accomplishment it leads to disillusionment because they are not satisfying their own needs for challenges, recognition, and appreciation.

Teachers are particularly at risk for experiencing stress due to depersonalization because of the sense of isolation they often experience. Teachers may spend their entire day in their lonely classroom without any opportunity to interact with peers. Spending most of their day behind a closed door strengthens teachers' risk for burnout because they have no opportunity to decompress accumulated stressors of the day by talking with their peers. The risk of teachers developing burnout looms large because much of their daily work occurs in professional isolation (McCarthy, Lambert, O'Donnell, & Melendres, 2009). The sense of isolation is exacerbated by the configuration of classrooms combined with scheduling constraints of the workday. To address this issue, in particular, it is important for teachers to strategically seek out opportunities for positive interactions with their colleagues.

Burnout signifies an erosion of a sense of engagement such that what started out as important, meaningful, and challenging work becomes unpleasant, meaningless, and unfulfilling (Maslach & Leiter, 1997). Burnout happens when exhaustion replaces feeling energized, cynicism replaces being hopeful and involved, and disillusionment replaces self-efficacy.

Feeling demoralized periodically throughout one's teaching career is normal and predictable. Burnout doesn't happen all of a sudden; rather, it results from a long-term pattern of self-neglect, a slow disintegration that eventually erodes both a teacher's passion and compassion. Teachers must constantly be on guard to heed the signs of stress so that they can be vigilant in keeping stress at bay.

Rustout: When Teachers Cease to Be Enthusiastic Learners

Gmelch (1983) coined the term *rustout* to describe a type of professional burnout that afflicts teachers in the form of waning enthusiasm. Rustout is operating when teachers temporarily or permanently cease to be enthusiastic learners. Seeing oneself as a lifelong learner promotes risk taking, inventing, and exploring—all vital to sustaining excitement about learning.

When the desire to keep learning withers, the teacher merely goes through the motions of teaching. Every teacher makes the choice to seek growth or resist growth as a learner. If the choice is to stop learning, then students' learning will atrophy as well, and one of the major satisfactions of teaching will be lost. By seeking perpetual growth, a teacher strives to become the best that he or she can be—what Maslow referred to as self-actualization.

Teachers need to access resources and develop the skills for counteracting early signs of burnout. When frustration and disenchantment set in, it's easy to fall into habits that can exacerbate stress. Becoming more conscious of the conditions that induce stress, teachers can begin to notice the symptoms of distress sooner and take specific steps to vigorously counteract the effects of stress.

Three-Stage Model of Burnout

One way to understand burnout is as a three-stage process (Girdin, Everly, & Dusek, 1996). These stages shown in Table 1.1 usually occur sequentially from Stage 1 to Stage 3, although the process can be stopped at any point. Unfortunately, it is often not until the exhaustion stage that most teachers finally get a sense that something may be wrong. Remember, burnout is a process that usually occurs sequentially, progressing through stages, so you have the opportunity to recognize symptoms and take necessary action early in the process.

Table 1.1.   Three Stages of Burnout

Stage 1: Stress Arousal*

1. Persistent irritability	6. Forgetfulness
2. Persistent anxiety	7. Heart palpitations
3. Periods of high blood pressure	8. Unusual heart rhythms
4. Grinding your teeth at night	9. Inability to concentrate
5. Insomnia	10. Headaches

Stage 2: Energy Conservation*

1. Lateness for work	7. Social withdrawal from friends and/or family
2. Procrastination	8. Cynical attitude
3. Needed three-day weekends	9. Resentfulness
4. Decreased sexual desire	10. Increased coffee/tea/cola consumption
5. Persistent tiredness in the mornings	11. Increased alcohol consumption
6. Turning work in late	12. Apathy

Stage 3: Exhaustion*

1. Chronic sadness or depression	5. Chronic headaches
2. Chronic stomach or bowel problems	6. The desire to "drop out" of society
3. Chronic mental fatigue	7. The inclination to move away from work/friends/family
4. Chronic physical fatigue	8. Perhaps even the wish to commit suicide

*At each stage, any two of these symptoms may signal you are in this stage of the burnout cycle.

TEACHERS MOST LIKELY TO EXPERIENCE BURNOUT

Some teachers given their specific personality tendencies are more likely to experience teaching demands as more emotionally stressful. Certain personalities predispose some teachers to greater risk of stress and burnout. The two personality characteristics most often studied in relationship to burnout are neuroticism and introversion. Neuroticism is characterized by high anxiety and emotional instability. Those with neurotic tendencies express more negative emotions and have greater stress reactions, making them more vulnerable not only to the majority of psychopathological disturbances, but to burnout as well (Watson, Clark, & Harkness, 1994). Introversion is characterized by passivity and lack of interest in social exchanges. Because those who are introverted are less disposed toward positive emotionality, they are more prone to emotional exhaustion and depersonalization. Specific research findings substantiate the following relationships.

- Having a personality trait of being neurotic is significantly related to burnout (Burisch, 2002; Cano-García, Padilla-Muñoz, & Carrasco-Ortiz, 2005; Fontana & Abouserie, 1993; Kokkinos, 2007; Mills & Huebner, 1998; Swider & Zimmerman, 2010; Teven, 2007; Zellars, Perrewe, & Hochwarter, 2000; Zellars, Hochwarter, Perrewe, Hoffman, & Ford, 2004).
- Being introverted predicts burnout (Cano-García et al., 2005; Dunham & Varma, 1998; Fontana & Abouserie, 1993; Mills & Huebner, 1998; Swider & Zimmerman, 2010).
- A tendency to feel unpleasant feelings, including hostility and irritability, termed negative affectivity, is strongly correlated with burnout (Brotheridge & Grandey, 2002; Carson et al., 2011; Houkes, Janssen, de Jonge, & Bakker, 2003; Kahn, Schneider, Jenkins-Henkelman, & Moyle, 2006; Thoresen, Kaplan, Barsky, Warren, & DeChermont, 2003).
- Having a Type-A personality predicts burnout (Maslach et al., 2001; Montgomery & Rupp, 2005).
- Being competitive and impatient, needing to be perfect, and not feeling in control of emotions put teachers at greater risk of burnout (Mills, Powell, & Pollack, 1992).
- Those most likely to experience burnout are teachers with the tendency to be ambitious and driven, likely to be loners, and with a propensity to be depressed (Gold, 1988).
- Teachers who think others hold highly positive opinions of them experience a greater degree of burnout because these teachers become emotionally exhausted trying to live up to others' expectations and standards (Mazur & Lynch, 1989).
- Socially anxious teachers have exaggerated stress responses to the task of teaching (Dunham & Varma, 1998).
- Teachers with little experience hold more irrational or illogical beliefs, leading them to make unreasonable demands on themselves as well as their students, which produces stress (Bernard, 1988).
- Having a tendency to blame oneself for difficulties predicts burnout (Bibou-Nakou, Stogiannidou, & Kiosseoglou, 1999).

- Those who cope in passive and defensive ways are more vulnerable to burnout (Schaufeli & Enzmann, 1998; Semmer, 2003).
- Timid teachers who habitually think about fear-producing situations are the most prone to feeling inadequate and lack coping skills, which exacerbates their stress (Dunham & Varma, 1998).
- Teachers who have low frustration tolerance are likely to become extremely stressed by time and workload pressures (Forman, 1990).
- The lower a teacher's self-image, the more intense the feeling of burnout (Friedman & Farber, 1992).

Teachers who have a tendency toward any of these personality characteristics will need to be more diligent in their efforts to reduce stress. You are especially at risk if you have neurotic tendencies, such as being anxious, insecure, or nervous, or often feel irritable or hostile. Likewise, if you are passive, introverted, worry about what others think, or perseverate about feeling inadequate as a teacher, your risk for burnout is greater. If you tend to be hard on yourself, have little teaching experience, or have a low frustration tolerance level, you will need to be especially on guard to ward off burnout.

Teacher Stress and Self-Efficacy

The concept of self-efficacy has particular relevance to teacher burnout. Self-efficacy is your own judgment regarding the degree to which you are capable of coping effectively and realistically with a specific task in the future (Bandura, 1997). Teacher self-efficacy refers to a teacher's perceived ability to be effective, find reasonable solutions to classroom problems, and maintain a belief in one's own capacity to effect positive change in their students. Teachers with a strong sense of self-efficacy quickly regain their confidence after facing stumbling blocks, and they attribute such impediments to lack of knowledge, skills, or effort on their part—all of which they can control by acknowledging such shortcomings and striving to overcome them. Believing that you are capable of finding reasonable solutions to the day-to-day problems you face helps keep you actively engaged and enthusiastic about your work.

Teachers facing job-related hurdles and setbacks who believe they have what it takes to overcome challenges develop not only stress hardiness but also physical hardiness, as barriers to stress. Researchers have found that teachers high in self-efficacy exhibit lower stress hormones (Schwerdtfeger, Konermann, & Schonhofen, 2008).

The effort needed for creativity, problem solving, and self-management that characterize feelings of self-efficacy obviously run counter to the feelings of emotional emptiness, exhaustion, and reduced self-fulfillment that characterize burnout. Burnout is the antithesis of feelings of control and self-direction.

Teacher Stress and Idealism

Another major contributor to teacher stress and burnout results from a perceived discrepancy between idealistic professional expectations and the harsh reality of the classroom (Friedman, 2006). Asked to identify the characteristics of a good teacher, 92% of teachers responded in idealistic, absolute terms that were later associated with high levels of stress (Chorney, 1998). Researchers consistently find that discrepancies between ideals of what it means to be a good teacher and school reality are significantly related to burnout (Dworkin, 1986; Brown & Ralph, 1998; Esteve, 2000; Troman & Woods, 2001).

For female teachers, the media has created an image that consistently portrays female teachers as saintly mother figures capable of saving even students who are the most difficult (Vanslyke-Briggs, 2010). Such stereotypes give shape to the notion of "teacher hero," which those just entering the profession attempt to emulate (Joseph & Burnaford, 2001). Popular culture plays a formative role in the developing teacher's identity (Weber & Mitchell, 1995). Attempting to balance such socialized expectations with the actual reality of the classroom is another source of stress for beginning female teachers as they try to cope with reconciling an internalized stereotypic image of what it is to be a teacher.

Teacher Stress and Lack of Meaning

Burnout occurs in teachers when they no longer find significance in their work and feel powerless to define their professional roles (Pines, 2002). Burnout can be experienced as a feeling of a lack of meaning that teachers expect to achieve through their work. When individuals feel that their job performance is failing or that the way in which their job "ought to be performed" is not the way they actually perform it, and when work no longer gives their lives a sense of purpose, they become burned out (Malach-Pines, 2000).

When teachers perceive that there is no connection between their effort and the outcomes achieved, a feeling of hopelessness can set in. Such feelings lead to lack of motivation, stress, and ultimately, burnout. When teachers lose their belief that they can make a difference in the lives of their students, they are taking steps down the path to burnout. As Schoeberlein and Sheth (2009) describe it, teacher burnout occurs when there is a net loss—when the costs outweigh the benefits, with the energy going out greatly outpacing the energy coming in and leaving a teacher feeling that he/she has little or nothing left to give.

Teacher Stress and Sense of Identity

Burnout is also linked to threats to one's sense of identity because teachers often derive their self-concept and self-esteem from their work roles (Pines, 1993). Some teachers are so intrinsically motivated by their work that their well-being and home life suffer because they are so highly focused on doing their job well. Paradoxically, some of the satisfaction from teaching depends on worrying more about others than about themselves (Nias, 1996). In their willingness to make sacrifices for the needs of their students, teachers often ignore their own physical and emotional health, increasing their susceptibility to stress and burnout.

Teacher Stress and Classroom Behavior Management

The interactions teachers have in their work environment and the relationships with the people they work with—students, fellow teachers, administrators, parents, and the community—comprise the most prevalent sources of stress and burnout for teachers. While contending with demanding and sometimes irate parents is a source of stress, there is consensus that the most common cause of teachers' work stress stems from their interactions with students.

Although burnout involves societal, organizational, and individual factors, for teachers, burnout is often triggered by the stress inflicted by students' challenging behavior. The relationship of classroom behavior management to teacher stress has been substantiated over several decades of research. Handling student inappropriate and unproductive behavior along with workload are often identified as the two most common contributors to teacher stress and burnout (Billingsley & Tech, 1993; Clunies-Ross, Little, & Klenhuis, 2008; Cooper & Kelly, 1993; Geving, 2007; Griffith, Steptoe, & Cropley, 1999; Whitehead & Ryba, 1995). One of the main reasons teachers report leaving the profession is stress related to classroom management (Beaman & Wheldall, 2000; Ingersoll, 2001).

Managing student behavior is an important demand of the job of teaching and an essential part of teachers' role identity. Disruptive behaviors prevent teachers from feeling professionally effective and satisfied and reduce their status in their own eyes over time (Farber, 1991; Travers & Cooper, 1996). Because of the preponderance of research evidence validating the relationship of classroom management and relationships with students to teacher stress and burnout, a later chapter is devoted to this topic.

Beginning Teachers and Burnout

Research has shown that because of the excessive initial work demands many beginning teachers experience, they are especially susceptible to burnout (Cano-García et al., 2005; Carlson & Thompson, 1995; Conderman & Stephens, 2000; Friedman, 2000; Goddard et al., 2006; Gold, Roth, Wright, & Michael, 1991; Kokkinos, 2007; Leung & Lee, 2006; McCarthy, Kissen, Yadley, Wood, & Lambert, 2006). Studies of burnout also indicate that younger teachers, those aged 30 and younger, have a higher propensity for burnout (Farber, 1984; Friedman & Farber, 1992). Early career teachers often lack the behavior management skills to successfully address challenging and unproductive student behavior, which contributes to their stress level.

Beginning teachers need explicit support in equipping themselves with the tools to dissipate stress and deal more effectively with the early signs of burnout. Developing teachers need to be prepared for the challenges they will face by having strategies to vigorously counteract the potentially destructive effects of stress. It is essential that new teachers take a proactive stance to insulate themselves from the onset of burnout by developing the attitudes, habits, and practices early on that can keep them from surrendering to burnout.

Who Leaves the Profession

Public school teacher attrition, especially among new teachers, has become an issue of major concern. This concern has been fueled by reports indicating that nearly half of new teachers "flee" the profession within their first five years of teaching (Alliance for Excellent Education, 2005; National Commission on Teaching and America's Future, 2003).

Teachers who enter the profession at a younger age, usually defined as up to 30 years old, are more likely to leave teaching (Feng, 2006; Kirby, Berends, & Naftel, 1999; Quartz et al., 2008; Theobald & Laine, 2003). A number of studies show that female teachers are more likely to leave early than their male counterparts, although this difference has become much less pronounced in recent years (Grissmer & Kirby, 1992; Imazeki, 2005; Quartz et al., 2008; Stinebrickner, 1998, 2002; Theobald & Laine, 2003). For example, Grissmer and Kirby reported a gender difference of 7 to 12 percentage points for new teacher cohorts entering the profession between 1965 in 1982, whereas Theobald and Laine found only about a 4 percentage point difference for teacher cohorts from the mid-1990s.

With increasing emotional demands being placed on teachers with minimal, if any, support, it is not surprising that both the rate of teacher burnout is increasing as well as the rate at which teachers are leaving the profession (Ingersoll, 2001; Ingersoll & Smith, 2003; MetLife, 2004; Provasnik & Dorfman, 2005). More than ever, teachers are succumbing to burnout and choosing to leave the profession at alarming rates. Excessive work demands coupled with the emotional investment required render teachers highly susceptible to burnout if they do not develop the tools necessary to stay on the path of continual renewal.

Chapter Two

Job Characteristics and Their Impact on Burnout and Well-Being

Researchers since the 1970s have put forth several models for understanding and interpreting stress and burnout as well as their counterparts, well-being and engagement.

MULTIPLE MODELS FOR UNDERSTANDING BURNOUT AND WELL-BEING

Taken together, these varying models paint a clear picture as to why teaching is a profession especially vulnerable to stress and burnout. These models also define what it takes to embark on the alternative path, cultivating engagement and renewal.

Job Demand-Control (JDC) Model

Karasek (1979) introduced a now seminal model outlining the impact of adverse job characteristics on health and well-being, the Job Demand-Control (JDC) model. He identified job demands and job control as essential job characteristics influencing well-being. Combining these two dimensions, jobs high on demands and low on control are considered to be "high strain" jobs, bearing the highest risk of illness and reduced well-being, with burnout being the most serious long-term impairment in job-related well-being. These two characteristics definitely define a teacher's job.

This model is particularly relevant for studying teacher well-being given the highly demanding nature of a teacher's job. Additionally, the expectation to teach to imposed standards along with escalating pressure to raise students' test scores clearly limits a teacher's job control. With this realization, many are calling for both teacher training as well as professional development programs to not only develop an awareness of the stress exposure in the teaching profession but also to explicitly teach stress management strategies.

Job demands are typically perceived in terms of quantitative aspects such as workload and time pressure, role conflict and ambiguity, as well as physical and emotional demands (Karasek et al., 1998). Although role conflict and role ambiguity can occur independently, they both refer to the uncertainty about what one is expected to do at work. Role conflict is the simultaneous occurrence of two or more opposing pressures such that a response to one makes compliance with the other impossible (for example, trying to be both consistent and fair). The most frequent role conflicts are (1) conflict between the individual's values and those of the organization; (2) conflict between the demands of the job and one's personal life; and (3) conflict between one's skills and abilities and the expectations of the administration and/or system. In numerous studies, role conflict has been identified as associated with low job satisfaction as well as high degrees of stress (Leiter & Maslach, 2000; Schaufeli & Buunk, 2003; Vandenberghe & Huberman, 1999). Role ambiguity is a lack of clarity about the job, or a discrepancy between the information available to employees and what is required for successful job performance.

Job control refers to the extent to which a person is capable of controlling their tasks and general work activity. With their capacity to control their teaching tasks dwindling, it is no wonder teachers are more stressed than ever. More specifically, job control is subdivided into two major aspects: skill discretion and decision authority. Skill discretion refers to a person's opportunity to use their specific job skills. In contrast, decision authority refers to the extent to which a person is autonomous in task-related decisions.

With mounting constraints imposed by the current high-stakes testing and accountability atmosphere, teachers have to grapple with how to support an increasingly diverse student population to realize their academic and social potentials. The ever-increasing reliance on tests to measure achievement along with curriculum mandates to meet imposed standards are making it more difficult for teachers to exercise much autonomy in their teaching. In addition, as their creative talents are stifled, the job becomes more mundane.

Job Demand-Control-Support (JDCS) Model

Some years later, social support was integrated into the model as a further fundamental characteristic of the work environment, thereafter named the Job Demand-Control-Support (JDCS) model (Johnson & Hall, 1988). The JDCS model identifies work situations characterized by high job demands, low possibility of controlling one's work, and little social support as most harmful to well-being. Conversely, when job demands are reasonable, one has task autonomy, and when social support is available, well-being prevails. This is clearly not the case for the teaching profession. Job demands are far from reasonable, teachers have little autonomy, and social support is lacking given the limited time available for interacting with peers.

Job Demands-Resources (JD-R) Model

The slightly different and more recent model, the Job Demands-Resources (JD-R) model, assumes that while every job has its own specific characteristics, these characteristics can be classified into two general categories: job demands and job resources. The basic premise of the model is that these two categories of work characteristics evoke two relatively independent processes that determine well-being in the work-place: a health impairment process and a motivational process.

Job demands are the physical, psychological, social, or organizational aspects of the job that require physical and/or psychological effort and are therefore related to physiological and/or psychological costs. High job demands exhaust mental and physical resources, which can lead to energy depletion. On the other hand, job resources are the physical, psychological, social, or organizational aspects of the job that function to achieve work goals, reduce job demands and the related physiological and psychological costs, and serve to stimulate personal growth and development.

While it is important to investigate what makes people feel exhausted, there is a growing interest in what makes people feel enthusiastic about their work. More recently, there has been increasing interest in determining what makes people stay motivated, enthusiastic, and engaged in their work rather than what depletes energy and engagement. A recent development in the conceptualization of burnout has been a focus on its positive antithesis—job engagement. It involves the opposite end of the three burnout dimensions—energy, involvement, and sense of efficacy.

The JD-R model specifies how health impairment, including burnout, as well as motivation, including work engagement, are related to work conditions (Bakker & Demerouti, 2007). Engagement could be thought of as the inverse of burnout. Work engagement is defined as a persistent, pervasive, and positive affective and motivational state of fulfillment in individuals who are reacting to challenging circumstances. Engagement is further conceptualized as consisting of three dimensions: vigor, dedication, and absorption (Schaufeli, Salanova, Gonzales-Roma, & Bakker, 2002). Dedication is the commitment to key life tasks, including dedication to family, work, students, society, and the preservation of the self. It involves a sense of significance, enthusiasm, inspiration, pride, as well as challenge. Absorption is characterized by being fully concentrated and happily engrossed in one's work, whereby time passes quickly and one may have difficulty detaching from work. It can also imply a process where one is so absorbed that one loses a sense of time. Vigor refers to high levels of energy and mental resilience while working, the willingness to invest effort in one's work, and persistence in meeting challenges.

Interestingly, results from in-depth interviews suggest that engaged employees work long hours but that they lack the obsession to work that is characteristic of workaholics (Schaufeli & Salanova, 2008). Engaged employees do not neglect their social life outside work; rather, they enjoy things in their lives other than work. They also spend time socializing, doing hobbies, and volunteering.

Unfortunately, our current educational climate offers the antithesis, diminishing resources extended toward teacher well-being as increasing teacher accountability makes the job more demanding, and stressful. The very taxing job of teaching needs to be offset with the availability of appropriate resources that can be the source of renewed energy and enthusiasm. The nature of the teaching profession places unrelenting demands on a teacher. Because the physiological and psychological costs are relatively fixed and predictable, the best opportunity to counteract teacher burnout is to provide the physical, psychological, social, and organizational resources that will support teacher well-being.

Conservation of Resources (COR) Model

Another theory of stress focusing on resources is the Conservation of Resources (COR) model. COR theory posits that people strive to obtain and maintain what they value—the resources (Hobfoll & Freedy, 1993). According to COR theory, psychological stress occurs under one of three conditions: (1) When resources (valued objectives that the individual strives to attain and maintain) are threatened, (2) when resources are diminished or lost, and (3) when the individual invests resources and fails to reap the anticipated level of return. When resources are lost, are inadequate to meet demands, or do not yield expected returns, burnout is likely to develop.

The two remaining theories or models are based on meeting individual needs.

Person-Environment Fit Model

Yet another theory for understanding and interpreting stress is the Person-Environment Fit model (French, Caplan, & Van Harrison, 1982). This model of job stress holds that two kinds of fit exist between the individual and the work environment. The first involves the extent to which a person's skills and abilities match the demands and requirements of the job. The second type of fit involves the extent to which the environment provides for an individual's needs. If a mismatch occurs involving either kind, the individual's well-being is threatened, and various health strains result, including stress and, potentially, burnout.

Self-Determination Theory (SDT)

Another way to understand the phenomenon of stress and burnout is in terms of three psychological needs that theorists such as Deci and colleagues posit as major intrinsic motivational determinants of behavior (e.g., Deci & Ryan, 1985, 2000, 2008). These are the need to feel competent, the need to feel self-determining, and the need to feel interpersonally connected. From this perspective, stress and burnout can be viewed as among the negative outcomes that result when these needs are threatened and thwarted. Clearly, such needs are regularly threatened and thwarted by the prevailing culture of schools that too often demand a great deal and give little.

RESEARCH ON THE IMPACT OF
JOB CHARACTERISTICS ON BURNOUT

Many studies, across many occupations and different countries, have identified the consistent impact of a range of job characteristics on burnout. Chronically difficult job demands, an imbalance between high demands and low resources, and the presence of conflict (whether between people, between role demands, or between important values) are consistently found in situations in which employees experience burnout.

Both the JDC and JDCS models are well supported in the research literature. Support for the additive effects of demands, control, and social support on general psychological well-being is consistently found in the research (see the review by Van der Doef & Maes, 1999). There is accumulated evidence that these now classic three variables not only *each* cause strain, but that their effect is cumulative (see the reviews by de Lange, Taris, Kompier, Houtman, & Bongers, 2003; Hausser, Mojzisch, Niesel, & Schulz-Hardt, 2010).

As mentioned earlier, research shows that burnout is expressed in three major dimensions, that is, emotional exhaustion, depersonalization, and lack of personal accomplishment. In general, research findings indicate that various job conditions are more strongly related to the emotional exhaustion dimension of burnout (Greenglass, 2007; Maslach et al., 2001). Some research indicates that while adverse job conditions better predict emotional exhaustion, an individual's personal characteristics better predict diminished personal accomplishment and depersonalization (Burisch, 2002; Dorz, Novara, Sica, & Sanavio, 2003; McCarthy et al., 2009). Whereas emotional exhaustion and depersonalization emerge from external factors of work overload and lack of social support, the decreased self-efficacy associated with lower personal accomplishment arises from insufficient personal resources.

Emotional exhaustion is predicted mainly by occupational stressors, such as work overload, inadequate skills, and interpersonal conflicts. Additionally, emotional exhaustion is considered the affective component that leads to depersonalization as well as reduced feelings of personal accomplishment in the teaching role. Through depersonalization, teachers attempt to limit the depletion of their emotional energy by treating their students as objects rather than individuals.

Gender Differences and Burnout

Research findings show that men have significantly greater levels of depersonalization than women (Greenglass, 1991). Greenglass (2007) offers one explanation for why men may be more prone to depersonalization. Accepted norms associated with the masculine gender role emphasize strength, independence, and invulnerability. Depersonalization may be viewed as a form of coping that allows men to continue their work with people yet remain untouched in any significant way by others' suffering. It is also possible that depersonalization is a result of an inability on the part of men to cope with work strain. Because it is socially unacceptable for men to openly express vulnerability, men have fewer options for emotional expression. Higher depersonalization in men is also associated with a lower quality of life.

Another explanation for women's lower depersonalization compared to men focuses on women's greater ability to cope with interpersonal stress. Yet, at the same time, women feel more stress. Women have an edge over men in dealing with the emotional strain of people because the feminine gender role emphasizes caring, nurturing, and concern for others. As a result, women may be less likely than men to respond to troubled individuals in an impersonal manner.

Some research indicates that women have higher scores than men on the emotional exhaustion aspect of burnout (Greenglass, 1991). Women may experience greater emotional exhaustion compared to men because their total workload, including both paid and unpaid work, is higher. Other research has shown that women's increased workload interferes with their ability to wind down from a stressful day, with resultant negative effects on their health (Greenglass, 2007).

Research on the Impact of Job Characteristics on Teacher Burnout

Researchers studying work-related variables with teacher samples have supported the general findings. In particular, Näring, Briët, and Brouwers (2006) found that more quantitative demands, less control, and less social support are significantly related to the two components of burnout, emotional exhaustion and depersonalization. Conversely, more control and more social support are related to both less depersonalization as well as a greater sense of personal accomplishment. McCarthy and colleagues found classroom demands significantly related to emotional exhaustion and to reduced feelings of personal accomplishment (McCarthy et al., 2009). This research also lends support to the transactional model of teacher stress discussed in chapter 1. The researchers found that individual differences among teachers within schools in perception of demands and resources predicted burnout symptoms, whereas actual differences in school context did not.

Research shows that the joint effect of high demand and low control, or decision authority, increases the risk of teacher burnout (Santavirta, Solovieva, & Theorell, 2007). In terms of gender differences, the results for teachers are similar to those in the general population. Male teachers show significantly more depersonalization than female teachers (Unterbrink et al., 2007; Yavuz, 2009). On the other hand, female teachers typically experience more emotional exhaustion.

RESEARCH ON THE IMPACT OF JOB CHARACTERISTICS ON WELL-BEING

While a great deal of research has concentrated on what makes teaching stressful, it is also important to consider what makes teaching enjoyable. Research also shows that teachers are engaged in their jobs and are satisfied with and enthusiastic about their work (e.g., Hakanen, Bakker, & Schaufeli, 2006; Roth, Assor, Kanat-Maymon, & Kaplan, 2007). Satisfied teachers emote happiness, confidence, and passion about their teaching (Winograd, 2003).

Tracking 300 teachers in 100 schools over a three-year period, Day, Sammons, and Gu (2008) found that 74% of teachers sustained a high level of commitment and self-efficacy, with 13% sustaining their level of commitment and self-efficacy despite challenging circumstances. The remaining 26% of teachers suffered a decline in sense of efficacy and commitment.

Work engagement has positive consequences for teachers. Studies indicate that work engagement predicts teachers' commitment (Hakanen et al., 2006; Schaufeli & Bakker, 2004). Another interesting finding is that the relationship between poor school climate and burnout can be mediated by teacher satisfaction levels for both the emotional exhaustion and depersonalization dimensions of burnout (Grayson & Alvarez, 2008).

Not surprisingly, organizations that have high levels of work resources also enjoy higher levels of both individual and team engagement (Bakker, Van Emmerik, & Euwema, 2006). Researchers have found that teachers working in schools with high resources stayed engaged whether or not they were coping with high levels of misbehavior in the classroom (Bakker, Hakanen, Demerouti, & Xanthopoulou, 2007). That is, teachers are able to stay engaged even when they are dealing with highly challenging behavior when they believe they have supportive resources.

Bakker and colleagues found that supervisor support, demonstrating appreciation, and positive school climate are important job resources for teachers as they can serve to offset the negative impact of student misbehavior on work engagement. Their research also showed that these job resources are particularly relevant under highly stressful teaching conditions because they can help teachers cope with demanding interactions with students. In contrast, those working in schools with low resources were engaged only if their students were well-behaved. In other words, when demand is high and resources low, engagement can be overwhelmed.

MAINTAINING WORK-LIFE BALANCE

Being able to create a healthy balance between your own needs and the demands put on you by others is an indispensable coping skill. Maintaining such a balance requires behavior that is both protective and responsive, which can be very tricky. For those teachers who live with a partner, the potential for tension is greater, especially if both work. The sheer overload of trying to cope with the teaching life and home life can be incredibly demanding, and interpersonal conflicts between the various members of the family unit often occur.

Every teacher has to take work home sometimes. If not literally in the form of grading papers and planning, it is in the form of mentally replaying scenes from the day, going over interactions with students, or rehashing unresolved conflicts. Teachers need to learn to erect an "emotional shield" to buffer them against feeling stress and to protect them from being overwhelmed.

Integration of work with other life aspects is an ongoing struggle for most of us. Because our resources of time and energy are necessarily limited, we have to constantly wrestle with incompatibility between work and family responsibilities. Success in balancing work with other roles is a strong contributor to our sense of well-being.

It is not surprising that work-family balance is predictive of well-being and overall quality of life (Fisher, 2002; Greenhaus, Collins, & Shaw, 2003). Conversely, failure to achieve such balance is associated with reduced job and life satisfaction (Allen, Herst, Bruck, & Sutton, 2000; Kossek & Ozeki, 1998), decreased well-being and quality of life (Grant-Vallone & Donaldson, 2001; Noor, 2004), as well as increased stress and impaired mental health (Grzywacz & Bass, 2003).

The results of numerous studies show that experiencing conflict between the work and family domains can have serious negative consequences on an individual's well-being, including burnout and depression (Allen et al., 2000). In the research literature, work/family conflict refers to the perception that joint role pressures from the work and family domains are incompatible in some respects, resulting in participation in one role becoming more difficult due to participation in another role.

Teachers generally have a poor work-life balance (Bubb & Earley, 2004). Often teachers are unable to effectively manage their professional and family roles. Teachers who are unable to effectively manage both their professional and family roles are more likely to be exhausted, which undoubtedly negatively affects their job satisfaction as well as their health.

Research shows that teachers spend on average 1 hour and 45 minutes each work day beyond the hours stipulated in their contract (Drago, 2007). That translates into about nine hours per week. Reporting on the findings from three studies based on teachers' diaries, Bubb and Earley found teachers work on average approximately 51 hours per week. But about one in six teachers work over 60 hours per week.

Although most teachers attribute importance to both their work role and their family role, female teachers in particular often have to work "triple-shifts," including teaching, housework, and childcare (Cinamon & Rich, 2005). Research shows that women experience greater role conflict between work and family roles than their male counterparts. Related findings indicate that there are different predictors of burnout in men and women. For women, role conflict between home and work roles is a significant predictor of burnout, whereas for men predictors of burnout tend to be confined to work. Employed women typically maintain major responsibility for the home and the family, and thus more often than men bear the burden of role conflict.

Preserving Self

Given that teachers must do some of their work at home, that time devoted to their work outside of school results in sacrificing time that could be devoted to family responsibilities. Not surprisingly, research has shown that work-related activities pursued at home have a negative impact on teachers' well-being (Sonnentag, 2001). This is particularly important in today's world in which the widespread use of technologies enable teachers to stay connected with work while at home, rendering the boundaries between work and nonwork time increasingly permeable.

Teachers need to be proactive to keep work-related stress from becoming a way of life. Especially for teachers who are highly engaged, the ability to detach from work to recharge their batteries during nonwork time is essential for well-being.

Anderson (2010) in his book *The Well-Balanced Teacher: How to Work Smarter and Stay Sane Inside the Classroom and Out*, advocates that teachers become positive stewards of their own wellness. Likewise, Holmes (2005) in her book *Teacher Well-Being: Looking After Yourself and Your Career in the Classroom*, tells teachers that they have to find a way to do the job while still preserving self. Both teachers themselves, they learned to take ownership of their own physical, mental, and emotional well-being. Their main message is that healthy teachers know that they have to set boundaries and first take care of their own needs.

Holmes suggests some ways teachers can set limits and boundaries.

   Set a cut-off time. Teachers need to create, and stick to, the habit of cutting off at some point at the end of the day and not return to work activities beyond this established cut-off time.

Have a no-bag day. Teachers can set a "no-bag day" at least once a week in which they do not take work home on this day.

Establish a transition zone. Teachers can establish a transition zone to separate their school life from their nonschool life. This could take many forms such as habitually making a journal entry to capture the highlights of the day, either positive or negative, or both. The act of closing the journal marks the transition from work.

Chapter Three

The Vital Role of Social
Support for Counteracting Burnout

As discussed in the previous chapter, there is considerable research to demonstrate the effectiveness of social support in lowering stress levels and burnout among teachers. This is not surprising given that research across many domains consistently finds that being positively involved with others ranks as one of the top stress buffers (e.g., Luskin & Pelletier, 2005; Seligman, 2011a).

THE IMPORTANCE OF PERCEIVED
SUPPORT FROM COLLEAGUES AND SUPERVISORS

Much research supports the beneficial effects of social support on individual well-being and job satisfaction, contrasting dimensions to burnout (Bakker & Demerouti, 2007; Matthiesen, Aasen, Holst, Wie, & Einarsen, 2003; Schaufeli & Bakker, 2004). Social support is considered an important job resource because it can mediate work engagement, job satisfaction, and mental health (Simbula, 2010; Xanthopoulou, Bakker, Demerouti, & Schaufeli, 2009).

Research indicates that support from colleagues and supervisors is negatively related to teacher burnout (Lee & Ashforth, 1996; Näring et al., 2006; Russell, Altmaier, & Van Velzen, 1987). Teachers who work in an environment that they perceive as being supportive are less likely to experience high levels of stress and burnout. Conversely, teachers with high burnout perceive less social support in their school environment than those with lower burnout levels (Greenglass, Burke, & Konarski, 1997). Some research indicates that support from a teacher's peers or co-workers is the most important buffer of burnout (Greenglass, Fiksenbaum, & Burke, 1996).

Social support may be effective in reducing burnout directly or as a buffering agent (Burke & Greenglass, 1995). When there is a direct effect, social support is positively related to physical and psychological health, regardless of the presence or absence of work stress.

Social support may moderate the impact of stress and burnout because it helps individuals experiencing stress to cope better. The buffering argument suggests that while stress may affect some teachers adversely, those with social support resources are relatively more resistant to the harmful effects of stressful events.

Regardless of general levels of work engagement, job satisfaction, and mental health, research shows that teachers receiving adequate support from their colleagues are more likely to be engaged in their work, and in turn, are also more satisfied and enjoy better health (Halbesleben, 2006). People working in highly engaged teams report higher levels of vigor, dedication, and absorption, the three dimensions that make up engagement, regardless of work conditions (Bakker et al., 2006). This finding lends support to the importance of working together with colleagues to offset challenging teaching conditions.

Relationships with colleagues are particularly important because there is evidence of a contagion effect of both the negative dimension of exhaustion as well as the positive dimension of work engagement (Kelchtermans & Strittmatter, 1999). Emotional contagion is defined as the transfer of negative, or positive, experiences from one person to another. That is, colleagues can influence each other with their emotional exhaustion and with its positive counterpart, work engagement. Although, research suggests that negative emotions are more easily transferred than positive emotions (Westman, 2001). This finding may in part account for the cynicism that can easily pervade teacher conversations in teacher gathering areas of the school.

Women are much more likely than men to seek social support under stress (Taylor et al., 2000). Yet studies show that men often have larger social networks than women and also seek social support in stressful situations, although to a somewhat lesser extent than women (Taylor, 2007). On another note, men as well as women feel protective of their families and friends under stress (Aldwin & Gilmer, 2004). This means that both men and women may change their stress responses to be more protective of others, especially young children.

Collegial support has also been linked to retention. Lack of support from supervisors and colleagues has a direct negative effect on intention to quit in that teachers may wish to change their career when they have conflicts with their supervisor or colleagues (Houkes, Janssen, de Jonje, & Nijhuis, 2001; Leung & Lee, 2006; Schaufeli & Enzmann, 1998).

First-year teachers' sense of isolation makes it all the more important for them to have support and guidance (Whitaker, 2000). Being able to share experiences with others is critical to first-year survival (Conderman & Stephens, 2000). Studying teachers during their student-teaching experience, researchers found that those experiencing high cooperating teacher support and guidance reported lower levels of burnout by the end of their practicum experience (Fives, Hamman, & Olivarez, 2007).

Reviewing studies conducted on the effects of support, guidance, and orientation programs for beginning teachers (collectively known as induction), Ingersoll and Strong (2011) found that support and assistance for beginning teachers have a positive impact on three sets of outcomes: teacher commitment and retention, teacher classroom instructional practices, and student achievement.

SYSTEM SUPPORT

Based on research conducted over the years, Greenglass (2007) suggests a number of ways that burnout in teachers can be reduced with interventions that actually change the work environment. Some specific recommendations include the following:

- Soliciting teacher involvement and participation in the decision making undertaken by the school
- Facilitating the development and provision of social support
- Improving supervision through the clarification of work goals so that there is less role ambiguity
- Establishing clear lines of authority and responsibility to help reduce role conflict

Preferably, all members of the school community would be involved in the establishment, evaluation, and ongoing improvement of the working conditions each member considers crucial for his or her optimal job performance. Soliciting teacher input in areas that affect their work life helps teachers gain greater involvement and commitment. The development of social support among teachers can be achieved by providing adequate time and location for interaction. Encouraging the development of mentoring relationships between older and younger teachers can also be useful in forging more committed relationships. It is important for beginning teachers to have helpful interactions and immediate functional advice before a problem takes on pathogenic proportions.

Writing about beginning teachers entering the profession, Intrator (2006) refers to the level of support from colleagues as a critical juncture, stating:

> They are ready to riff a solo in their own classroom, but "making music" with their life will hinge on whether they can find a "band or orchestra" of other adults in their school that can usher them into this great profession in ways that honor what it means to be a novice, can negotiate the emotional drama of teaching in ways that build self-awareness and authority, can attract the genuine attention of students, and can provide them with an appreciation of what it means to tend their own health and spirit. (p. 238)

Supportive school environments share resources that may be lacking and include teachers in shared opportunities for the success of the school. Often, in high-demand teaching environments, the school needs to provide support that is beyond individual or family capacity.

There is little doubt of the importance of a collegial and collaborative school culture in the prevention of burnout. Successful schools put in place a spectrum of collaboration structures. With such a teamwork mentality, each new teacher with limited resources does not have to "reinvent the wheel." They have support in tackling authentic issues in their daily work. Grappling with feeling insecure, beginning teachers often keep their doubts and concerns from colleagues. Seeking advice is considered an admission of failure, an indication of one's own inadequacy. Only in schools where there is a collaborative spirit will developing teachers feel secure enough to show their vulnerability. Ideally, these structures would be put in place by knowledgeable and caring administrators, but if they are not, teachers can be proactive in calling for and designing forums to support each other.

It is also important for administrators to institute systematic ways of celebrating their teachers' successes, such as establishing ceremonies and rituals to make sure teacher accomplishments are recognized on an ongoing basis. Effective principals not only provide visionary leadership, they also allocate the necessary resources to accomplish the goal of genuine support. At the system level, many districts now offer mentor programs for beginning teachers. Some districts also sponsor grade-level monthly meetings for sharing materials, strategies, and challenges particular to a given grade level.

Formats for Peer Support

Social support is enhanced when structures are instituted for teachers to work together on problems. When such supports are not in place, teachers can be the driving force for making collaborative opportunities available. Teacher work groups have been advocated for several decades now, where teachers get together on a regular basis to help each other better understand and solve the many problems they encounter. There are many vehicles for providing such support. Historically, these structures have been referred to as teaming or peer support groups, and more recently, as professional learning communities. Essentially, such peer support groups are composed of members who share a common condition, situation, symptom, or experience. They are largely self-governing and self-regulating.

Peer support groups can assume various forms, ranging from highly structured meeting formats to the more informal gatherings of friends and co-workers. The form of mutual support groups is limited only by the needs and ingenuity of their members. Benefits of peer support include developing mutual understanding and empathy, which helps build trust, openness, and a feeling of belonging, which, in turn, enhances coping, problem solving, and self-empowerment. Such support groups also provide the opportunity for optimistic peer comparisons, as members realize with relief that their problems really are not so extraordinary and that others with similar problems are working toward their resolution. Below are two examples of ways teachers can help each other.

Peer-Professional Help Group. This type of group is particularly tailored to helping teachers cope with professional problems and stressful situations (Friedman, 2000). In such groups, participants help one another in gathering information to overcome professional hurdles, trust each other with their capabilities and expertise, and share similar problems and experiences.

The basic assumption underlying these groups is that matters in task performance can be dealt with best by providing relevant know-how by peers, thus alleviating the sense of isolation and lowering stress levels. Peer-professional help groups usually deal with either specific professional matters of concern to the participants or with general stressful situations pertaining to the majority of the group. Participants raise issues, problems, and some possible solutions to current issues.

The common pattern of work in these groups is roughly as follows:

- A specific issue or problem is chosen for detailed elaboration and discussion.
- The participant who raised the specific issue or problem describes his or her way of dealing with it.
- Participants suggest and examine other different solutions.
- The "problem-raiser" picks up one or two suggested solutions to be tried out.
- The "problem-raiser" selects a member of the group with whom he or she shares obstacles and progress in solving the problem.
- The procedure is repeated for different problems shared by the participants.

Peer Collaboration Program. Another specific format for creating more regular opportunities for peer support is the Peer Collaboration Program, in which pairs of teachers learn to engage in supportive, constructive dialogue (Cooley & Yovanoff, 1996). This process consists of a four-step collegial dialogue to assist each other in identifying and solving student-related and other work-related problems.

Step 1: Clarifying
The initiating teacher brings a brief, written description of the problem and responds to clarifying questions asked by his or her peer. This step is designed to assist thinking of the problem in different or expanded ways. This step continues until the initiating teacher thinks all of the relevant issues have been covered.

Step 2: Summarizing
In this step, the initiating teacher summarizes three aspects of the problem:

1. Specific patterns of behavior that are problematic
2. The teacher's typical response to them
3. The particular aspects of the problem that fall under the teacher's control

Step 3: Intervention and Prediction
Together the teachers generate three possible action plans, and the initiator predicts possible positive and negative outcomes for each. Then the initiator chooses one for implementation.

Step 4: Evaluation
The initiator develops a two-part plan to evaluate the solution's effectiveness, consisting of a plan to answer the questions *Did I do it?* and *Did it work?*

CREATING A SPIRIT OF MUTUAL SUPPORT

In the absence of leadership from administrators, teachers can collectively allocate or reallocate their personal resources to create structures to support each other. Although teachers may not have the authority, they can be catalysts in requesting and organizing formal supportive peer structures.

Ways to Support Each Other

Teachers can be proactive and ingenious in creating a spirit of mutual support and encouragement. Below are some examples.

Appreciation Box. Teachers can encourage expressing appreciation by designing an "appreciation box" where students can drop brief notes about an act of kindness from a teacher that they either experienced themselves or witnessed. These appreciation boxes would be strategically located around the school where students and staff anonymously put notes reporting acts they want to acknowledge. Teachers can be creative in establishing a forum to showcase these notes.

Gratitude Reporter. Another strategy is to designate a "gratitude reporter" whose task is to watch for acts of kindness, briefly describe them in a notebook, and report weekly. This could be a rotating position until all faculty, administrators, and staff have held this position.

Secret Admirer Club. Teachers can initiate a "secret admirer" club. The way this club works is at the beginning of the school year, all faculty members draw a name and become that person's secret admirer (Froyen & Iverson, 1999). On some regular schedule, such as twice each month, thoughtful "gifts" are exchanged. The gift might be a solicited note from an appreciative parent, an invitation from a student to share a special box lunch, or a basket of fruit. Tailoring these gifts to the unique preferences and "soft spots" of an individual teacher can do much to boost morale. By providing these gifts on different schedules, some teacher is regularly expressing appreciation. The teacher's lounge is buzzing with talk about kind deeds, keeping everyone more attuned with the special gifts each person brings to teaching. The elements of mystery, excitement, anticipation, special attention, and personalized affection make this program especially rewarding.

Collaborative Study Group. In her book, *The Nurturing Teacher: Managing the Stress of Caring*, Vanslyke-Briggs (2010) suggests some ways teachers can support each other. One way is to form a collaborative study group in which members take turns providing a brief article from a professional journal on a designated topic of interest and/or concern. Participating teachers read the article and try the new strategies in their classrooms. Then the group meets to share their experiences and recommendations.

Collaborative Lunch. A twist on the collaborative group is a "salad day," on which a group of teachers agree to spend one day each week making a salad together. They email the assigned ingredients a week ahead or decide together at that week's meal what each one would bring the following week. Not only is this a healthy option, it also affords participants a sense of community. A lunchtime spent just sitting, eating, and enjoying each other's company rather than rushing through a meal on your own provides a vital opportunity to decompress.

Digital Support Groups

Obviously, there are opportunities for social networking via the multitude of options now available for the technically savvy, and even the not so savvy. While it may be a poor substitute for face-to-face interactions and "live" support and not be as gratifying, digital groups can be a viable option; although, even a video Skype meeting lacks the intimacy of human sharing. Yet, a digital world does provide other possibilities, such as the convenience of posting your concern at any time, even in the middle of the night when you find you can't sleep. Responders also have the option to respond at any time, which gives them an opportunity to reflect before responding.

Another advantage is that digital groups allow for the supportive community to be much larger than what one may typically find at a single school setting where an individual teacher may have only one or two others with whom to share. Some beginning teachers may feel too insecure to share with colleagues at their own school and may welcome the chance to have a support network outside of their school site.

One way to meet is to use a blog. However, this forum can become very stagnant. A preferable option is to use a Ning network. This social networking site for closed community members allows for many applications to stay connected. This format has many features similar to Facebook. Through a Ning network, teachers can stay connected in many ways, including posting pictures, notes, blogs, discussion forums, and a live chat. Ning also allows for individual conversations to emails and notes directly to an individual's page. The group will need to decide on specific guidelines, such as the frequency with which one commits to checking in.

Acknowledge Making a Difference

It is important to regularly acknowledge significant ways you and others are making a difference in the lives of students. Don't allow yourself to become paralyzed by the sheer magnitude of the task of teaching and fail to recognize ways teachers make a difference. It is easy to allow negative newscasts, periodic setbacks, and seemingly unappreciative students and adults to discolor your perceptions and rob you of the idealism that propelled you to be a teacher in the first place.

There are simple ways you can be proactive in acknowledging the contributions you and your fellow teachers make. When you see another teacher making a difference, take the opportunity to communicate in some way that you appreciate his or her efforts. One thing you might do for yourself is leave school on a positive note at the end of the day. Take a quiet moment alone in your classroom to knowledge one way you made a difference.

A SCHOOLWIDE CRISIS INTERVENTION
PLAN FOR TEACHERS UNDER STRESS

Teachers are educator's true "first-responders." They are the first to know when the school's administrative policies are failing, when a colleague is struggling, or when a student is in crisis. Unfortunately, when it comes to recognizing their own crisis, teachers are often ill-equipped.

According to Maxfield (2009), when teachers encounter problems, instead of facing them head on, four out of five teachers retreat. They clam up and do little to improve their situation or surroundings. Given today's stressful teaching environment, many teachers feel completely helpless and overwhelmed. When teachers retreat, they often cross the line between stress and burnout. As they withdraw, teachers feel increasingly powerless and begin a downward spiral of pessimism that can seem insurmountable.

Teachers today are coping with more needy and troubled students, often contending with ill-conceived administrative mandates and grappling with demanding and sometimes irate parents. Add to this time and scheduling constraints, looming accountability, and the imposing structure of school itself, it is no wonder that stress and burnout among teachers are rampant. As Vanslyke-Briggs (2010) expresses it, there are too many external mandates divorced from the heart of teaching.

Just as we are calling for schoolwide crisis intervention plans to be in place for students who may require it, it is just as imperative that we have such a plan in place to help a teacher cope with temporary, or more long-term, stressors. An individual teacher's burnout will have ramifications that affect the whole school climate, so it should be a concerted effort.

Because stress frequently emerges from areas beyond a teacher's immediate sphere of recognition, those individuals and structures within the school environment that can help to alleviate the stress need to be identified and readily activated when needed. While it is clear that teachers at risk for burnout need specific and individualized help, the more schools constitute a supportive, collegial, and collaborative work environment, the less individual teachers will run the risk of burnout. Addressing teacher burnout not only requires individual solutions, it also necessitates social and organizational measures.

Because burnout results from the complex interplay of individual, social, and contextual factors, it calls for a multilayered response. The relevant context extends beyond the level of the local school site to the level of educational policy in general, and to societal issues as well. Although the impact of personal and contextual factors is relative, the working conditions of teachers contribute significantly to the risk of burnout. To relieve those suffering from stress it is important to pinpoint the source(s) of the stress. Developing "antiburnout" interventions will be a well-made investment.

Actively tackling teacher stress and preventing burnout in teachers should be an integrated part of life and work in schools. Beginning teachers, especially, are often so overwhelmed they don't even know what to ask for in seeking out help. Teachers need to know that there is no stigma attached to asking for help when they have more on their plate than they can handle. When this mind-set is pervasive, burnout will then no longer be an albatross hanging around an individual teacher's neck, threatening his or her health and inducing feelings of failure and guilt.

Critical Incident Stress Debriefing

One intervention that could serve teachers well is having a debriefing process in place for a teacher after a stressful incident occurs. Creating a mechanism to debrief after a stressful incident is a strategy developed for crisis workers. As a stress reduction strategy, it attempts to mitigate the ill effects of stress. In this context, a debriefing is a professionally guided group discussion of a stressful or traumatic event. It could also be adapted for an individual teacher who has had a highly stressful encounter with a student, parent, colleague, or administrator. The school psychologist or counselor could serve in this role. It is intended to be a psychological as well as an educational process that both diminishes the impact of a stressful event and accelerates normal recovery in reactions to stressful events. The general recommendation is that such a session take place between 24 and 72 hours after the event.

Having a defined structure for debriefing would provide an opportunity to share information on stress and its effects, forewarn of predictable symptoms and reactions to stress, provide a forum to vent pent-up emotion, as well as offer reassurance and guidance. This would involve having a plan in place to cover a teacher's class so that he/she would have the opportunity to access this resource.

Chapter Four

Teaching Is Emotional Labor

As a frontline profession, teachers have to engage in emotional labor, or managing their emotions at work, to be successful in their multiple teaching roles.

EMOTIONAL LABOR: MANAGING EMOTIONS AT WORK

Hochschild (1983) was the first to note that, especially in service jobs, workers are often required to show certain emotions in order to please the customer or client, coining the term *emotional labor* to refer to the management of emotions for work purposes. Emotional labor is the effort required to express, repress, or manufacture emotions in order to do your job. Taken together, having to show emotions one is not actually feeling and having to suppress one's own emotions when their expression does not seem appropriate are the key aspects of emotional labor. Hochschild introduced the term *surface acting* to refer to the display of emotions that are regarded as appropriate, but not actually felt. He used the term *deep acting* to describe the activity undertaken to actually feel an emotion that is thought to be required.

Surface acting involves simulating unfelt emotions and/or suppressing felt emotions. Surface actors put on a mask, hiding actual emotions and faking the emotions that they do not actually feel or experience. Surface actors are fully aware that they are simply pretending to feel what they do not, so surface acting involves deceiving others, but not themselves. In surface acting, there is always *emotional dissonance*, a discrepancy between inner feelings and outer expressions. Emotional dissonance is the basis for the discomfort of emotional labor, which can cause cynicism, stress, and burnout.

Deep acting refers to attempts to invoke and actually feel the displayed emotions. In deep acting, you have to psych yourself into experiencing the emotions you wish to display. Deep actors change their emotions to reflect the desired emotion, actively inducing or summoning feelings.

Social Norms and Emotional Rules

People are classified in a myriad of social categories such as gender, ethnicity, political and religious affiliation, and organizational membership. As a result, social identities are constructed and defined through interactions with group members, which in turn affect individuals' beliefs, attitudes, and behaviors. Depending on the social situation, individuals display varying kinds of emotions. An individual's emotional responses are inseparable from the contexts in which they occur (Hochschild, 1983; Kemper, 2000).

Emotional labor involves managing feelings to comply with *display rules* (Hochschild, 1983, 2003). Workers, especially those in human service professions, such as teaching, are expected to display the appropriate emotions that fit with the organization's norms. Thus, emotional labor often involves the display of largely fake or inauthentic emotions given that there tends to be a schism between felt and displayed emotions (Ashforth & Humphrey, 1993).

Hochschild emphasized the appropriateness of emotions as functions of cultural expectations, noting that *feeling rules,* governed by social structures, guide our experiences and expressions of emotions. Teaching, like other professions, has its own unique set of social expectations. Zembylas (2003, 2007) noted that teachers learn to internalize and enact roles and norms *assigned* to them by the school culture through appropriate expressions and silences. If a teacher's felt emotions and "pedagogically desired emotions" are not congruent, then the teacher needs to put forth great effort to display the desired emotions. What a teacher perceives to be pedagogically desired emotions along with the teacher's decision to regulate emotions come about because of a need to maintain the social norm.

EMOTIONAL LABOR AND TEACHERS

The term *emotional labor* has subsequently been adopted within the field of education, most notably in the work of Hargreaves and his colleagues (Beatty, 2000; Hargreaves, 1998a, 1998b, 2000, 2001, 2004; Lasky, 2000). Hargreaves has applied emotional labor to the understanding of how emotions are involved and represented in teachers' work and professional development.

Hargreaves's theoretical framework for the "emotional politics of teaching" is based on seven underlying assumptions about individual experiences of emotions within the context of school (1998a, p. 319):

1. Teaching is an emotional practice.
2. Teaching and learning involve emotional understanding.
3. Teaching is a form of emotional labor.
4. Teachers' emotions are inseparable from their moral purposes and their ability to achieve those purposes.
5. Teachers' emotions are rooted in and affect their identities.
6. Teachers' emotions are shaped by experiences of power and powerlessness.
7. Teachers' emotions vary with culture and context.

Teaching is a profession that involves a high level of emotional labor. A teacher may attempt to show bubbling enthusiasm when praising a student for a good answer, or try to adopt an appearance of calm confidence when confronted with a highly challenging student behavior. In order to perform their daily tasks adequately, teachers have to show or exaggerate some emotions while minimizing or suppressing the expression of others.

Teachers supervise their own emotional labor by considering informal professional norms and expectations. This is particularly pertinent when considering teachers' work, which involves an ability and expectation to manage on an everyday basis a multitude of complex social interactions with others, including students, colleagues, administrators, parents, and community members.

Emotional labor has specific implications for women teachers. Traditional gender expectations in the home as well as in the workforce require women to perform a substantially larger proportion of emotional labor than men. Blackmore (1998) argued that women are often portrayed in our society as possessing innate caring and nurturing qualities that draw on assumptions of stereotyped characteristics of men and women. There is some research indicating there is no meaningful difference in the experience of emotional labor between men and women who perform the same job (Guy, Newman, & Mastracci, 2008).

Nurturing Suffering and Teachers

Drawing on the concept of emotional labor, Vanslyke-Briggs (2010) coined the phrase *nurturing suffering* to describe an invisible form of stress that results from the emotional ties teachers develop with their students. Although it might be assumed that nurturing suffering is exclusively within the domain of female teachers, men also fall prey to nurturing suffering. This nurturing role, while often considered a sign of teaching excellence, can also be a trait that leads to heightened levels of stress. Because nurturing suffering is directly linked to the well-being of students, it has long-lasting effects and keeps returning as the mind constantly rehashes the student's problem. Unresolvable issues keep tugging at a teacher's heartstrings.

As mentioned earlier, work-related stress is often experienced in the form of role conflict and role ambiguity, in addition to role overload. With nurturing suffering, each of these roles comes into play. Role conflict emerges when the distinction between teacher as deliverer of content and counselor, one concerned with students' emotional well-being, becomes blurred. Trying to be both teacher and nurturer leads to role ambiguity. As every teacher knows, the personal lives of students are not left at the door when the student enters the classroom. Role overload often occurs for teachers, manifesting in nurturing suffering, when the emotional needs of students are beyond the teacher's sphere of influence (Vanslyke-Briggs, 2010).

Palmer, in his book *The Courage to Teach*, eloquently expressed the emotional toll teaching can take.

> Small wonder, then, that teaching tugs at the heart, opens the heart, even breaks the heart—and the more one loves teaching, the more heartbreaking it can be. The courage

to teach is the courage to keep one's heart open in those very moments when the heart is asked to hold more than it is able. (1998, p. 11)

Emotional Labor and Stress and Burnout

It is not surprising that the requirement to express emotions that are incompatible with experienced emotions would cause stress. While both surface and deep acting require some degree of conscious effort, research indicates that surface acting is more harmful to individual well-being. Research supports the relationship between surface acting and emotional exhaustion, validating the notion that having to pretend certain emotions comes at a personal cost (Barber, Grawitch, Carson, & Tsouloupas, 2011; Bono & Vey, 2005; Brotheridge & Grandey, 2002; Carson, Plemmons, Templin, & Weiss, 2011; Grandey, 2003; Montgomery, Panagopolou, de Wildt, & Meenks, 2006; Pugliesi, 1999; Totterdell & Holman, 2003; Zammuner & Galli, 2005). Surface acting has also been found to be significantly related to depersonalization for teachers (Carson et al., 2011; Näring et al., 2006).

On the other hand, deep acting, or consciously trying to elicit an emotional state to align with an expected positive outlook, acts as a deterrent to burnout. Research reported with human service professionals has shown a negative relationship with burnout (Brotheridge & Grandey, 2002; Brotheridge & Lee, 2003). Likewise, research with teachers confirms the negative relationship between deep acting and burnout (Barber et al., 2011; Carson et al., 2011; Näring et al., 2006; Tsouloupas, Carson, Matthews, Grawitch, & Barber, 2010; Zhang & Zhu, 2008).

Emotional labor does not always entail emotional dissonance. Some argue that emotional labor should also include a third dimension, *authenticity* (Ashforth & Humphrey, 1993; Diefendorff, Croyle, & Gosserand, 2005). There are many cases in which employees genuinely experience and express the expected emotional display. Research indicates that the authentic expression of true feelings is associated with lower job alienation and burnout (Adelmann, 1995; Kruml & Geddes, 2000). Authenticity refers to the authentic expression of spontaneous and genuine emotion with little prompting. Diefendorff and colleagues found that the expression of naturally felt emotions was a third and distinctly different means of emotional labor.

The term *emotional consonance* has also been used in the literature to refer to effortlessly feeling the emotion that is required in a certain situation. While emotional labor is the effort to deal with the experience or the expression of emotions and contributes to stress, emotional consonance, or authenticity, is the absence of such effort. Research on teachers has also revealed a strong relationship between emotional consonance and a sense of personal accomplishment (Brotheridge & Lee, 2002; Näring et al., 2006).

CHALLENGING THE EMOTIONAL RULES TEACHERS LIVE BY

It is incumbent on teacher educators to develop a better understanding of what constitutes "professional" behavior as it relates to the expression of teacher emotions and how it should be developed and supported. Determining which levels of deep acting, faking, and suppression are adequate or healthy and which levels are harmful both to teachers and students alike will necessitate re-examining what has always been assumed to represent desired practice. Exposing students to strongly felt unpleasant emotions expressed respectfully and intentionally can provide valuable modeling for students. On the other side of the coin, learning to regulate constant emotional up-heaval can be an invaluable tool for reducing teacher stress.

Teacher educators need to help developing teachers not only acknowledge but also change the *emotional rules* that have become prescriptions for which emotions are ap-propriate to express and to what degree (e.g., showing too little affection or too much anger). Emotions can be powerful teaching tools, yet as Oakes and Lipton (2003) noted, a culture that denies emotions to teachers also denies them to students.

Appraisal Theory and Emotions

As mentioned earlier, the transactional model of stress posits that it is the *perception* of both resources and demands that determines whether stress will be experienced (Lazarus, 1991). An individual's perception of the environmental demand as a threat and the response capability of the individual to cope with the demand will determine the effects of a stressor.

According to this transactional model of coping and stress, individuals react to challenging situations by engaging in a process of appraisal to determine whether the event poses a challenge or a threat in relation to the individual's perceived competence to handle the situation (Aldwin, 2007). Next, an individual engages in cognitive and behavioral adaptation strategies to manage the event, or not.

Lazarus and Folkman (1984) identified four general types of stress appraisals. A situation may involve harm, loss, challenge, or the threat of future stressors. Ap-praisals are not necessarily a product of conscious, rational processes, but may occur at an unconscious, largely automatic level (Lazarus, 1991; Smith & Kirby, 2004). Subsequently, researchers found that these four original appraisals were not always sufficient to describe the range of stressful situations and added three more categories: hassle, at a loss for what to do next, and worry about others (Aldwin, Sutton, Chiara, & Spiro, 1996).

The emotional process is complex and consists of multiple components, including (Lazarus, 2001):

- subjective experience
- appraisal
- physiological change
- emotional expression
- action tendencies

The emotion process begins with making a judgment or appraisal of a situation (Roseman & Smith, 2001). Appraisal is often made instantaneously and uncon-sciously, even in complex circumstances. However, slower conscious appraisals also occur, including reappraisals that correct initial evaluations (Scherer, 2001). Emotions also involve action tendencies. The action tendencies typically associated with anger are lashing out, attacking, or retaliating (Lazarus, 1993). However, the action tendencies for frustration and anger often overlap, with individuals reporting they felt like hitting someone or yelling when they were frustrated as well (Roseman, Wiest, & Swartz, 1994).

Applying this model, teacher emotions are elicited by the appraisals they make about classroom behaviors, situations, and events. The judgments and assessments about the causes of events influence the types of emotions teachers have as well as the intensity of the emotions they may feel. Different emotions are elicited by a variety of appraisals. Appraisals are made with respect to goal compatibility, significance, accountability, controllability, perceived coping potential, and the future expectancy of the event.

Primary and Secondary Appraisals

According to Lazarus (1993, 2000), the intensity of aroused emotions depends on the way in which we evaluate the significance of events through both *primary* and *secondary* appraisals. The two components of primary appraisals are importance or what significance they have, and goal compatibility or whether or not the goal is congruent with set goals. Primary appraisal involves the assessment that the situation is important and congruent with one's goals for positive emotions, or incongruent for negative emotions. Emotions such as frustration and anger involve the primary appraisal that the situation is significant but incongruent with one's goals. During secondary appraisals, judgments about accountability and blame, coping potential, and future expectancy are made (Smith & Lazarus, 1990).

Anger, frustration, anxiety, and guilt have the common underlying appraisals of obstructing goals that are important to the teacher. This means the more relevant a teacher judges an incident or interaction to be, the more intense the emotional experience will be. The more a teacher cares about students, the higher the significance of an emotional encounter. Relationships may be perceived as more relevant to a teacher's goals when a teacher has a closer relationship with students. When a classroom incident occurs, the less a teacher cares about the student or the lesson, the less likely the incident is judged important and the less likely it is to elicit a negative emotion.

Folkman and Lazarus (1988) believe that emotion and coping have multidirectional relationships. For example, when teachers assess an incident as goal incongruent, then they are more likely to experience unpleasant emotions, such as anxiety or anger. These emotions may increase the desire to escape. Using such defensive coping, a teacher may in turn develop a depersonalized attitude toward students (a key component of burnout). While this change in attitude may produce a change in intensity or quality of emotions, a teacher may actually experience increased stress, eventually leading to burnout and ultimately to dropping out of the profession.

The teacher may set several goals, including maintaining order, managing student behavior, completing the lesson in a timely fashion, and helping students reach learning goals. Obviously, these goals often clash in the classroom, forcing the teacher to prioritize one over another. Students' disruptive behavior is a major source of emotional drain for teachers and such behavior also threatens the achievement of their goals, which increases the intensity of their emotional response (Schutz et al., 2004).

To assess accountability, the related major issues are degree of controllability, invested effort, and intent (Ben-Ze've, 2000). It is primarily the secondary appraisal that forms the kind of emotion and its intensity. In making this secondary appraisal teachers often ask themselves questions such as the following:

Who's responsible?
Was this an intentional act?
How much control do I have?
How much effort will it take?
What can I do? Am I capable of doing what needs to be done?
What might be the consequences of acting, or not acting?

Answers to such questions will impact the type of emotions elicited. For example, if a teacher determines a student is to blame, anger is likely, whereas if the blame falls on the teacher's shoulder, guilt is the likely emotion. Whether or not the teacher believes he or she has the potential to cope effectively, as well as what might be expected in the future, further determine the intensity of the teacher's emotions. If a teacher perceives his or her potential to cope as low, and/or the situation is likely to occur again, the intensity of emotions would be higher.

Appraisals are dependent on a teacher's past experiences, desired goals, and personal resources. This means that a teacher may make different appraisals at different times because a number of factors are always in play. One teacher may become angry with a student who often disrupts class, blaming that student for deliberately creating problems, whereas another teacher may become frustrated, believing that the student's behavior is caused by a system that requires students to sit for long periods of time. A third teacher may become sad at the same situation, perceiving the disruption as an indication of neglectful parenting affecting the child's learning and development. To complicate matters, an individual teacher may appraise the same interaction differently on various occasions and so may experience anger, frustration, or sadness. Given the scope of interactions that a teacher has and the personal resources brought to bear on a given day, it is no wonder emotions can be all-encompassing.

Table 4.1 summarizes how teachers' judgments systematically vary to produce different unpleasant emotions (Lazarus, 2001; Roseman & Smith, 2001).

Table 4.1. Underlying Appraisals for Difficult Emotions

	Difficult Emotions			
Appraisal	*Anger*	*Frustration*	*Anxiety*	*Guilt*
Significance	High	High	High	High
Incongruence	High	High	High	High
Accountability	Other	Self/circumstance	Circumstance	Self
Controllability	High	Low	Low	High

Teachers' Commonly Experienced Emotions

Given the nature of the job of teaching, three emotions teachers commonly experience are anger, frustration, and guilt. There are a number of types of appraisals related to feeling anger. In terms of accountability, anger is usually other-caused, guilt is self-caused, and frustration and anxiety are circumstance-caused emotions. Anger and guilt are aroused when events are perceived to have high control potential. That is, if a teacher believes a student could have controlled finishing the assignment, then the teacher is more likely to show anger toward the student. Similarly, if a teacher believes he/she should have been able to control an angry outburst, then the teacher deserves to be held accountable and will experience a feeling of guilt as opposed to anger. Frustration and anxiety are usually aroused when events are perceived to have low control potential; in other words, no one is to blame.

Anger typically involves the judgment or appraisal that someone is to blame for a blocked goal, an arrogant entitlement, or unfairness (Kuppens, Van Mechelen, Smits, & De Boeck, 2003; Roseman, 2001; Smith & Kirby, 2004). According to Lazarus anger often erupts when someone "commits a demeaning offense against me and mine" (1991, p. 222).

The appraisal that other people are responsible for our misfortune is central to the experience of anger. When we are angry, our students, colleagues, friends, and loved ones seem lazy, manipulative, and unyielding. Whereas, when we are sad we may see the same behaviors as signs of overload or real need (Keltner, Ellsworth, & Edwards, 1993). In addition, the judgments we make are based on the meanings we assign to events (Smith & Kirby, 2001). That is, the more important an event seems to us, the more likely it is to provoke an angry response.

Anger often erupts in response to a specific offense the teacher believes to be both unjustified and controllable (Ben-Ze've, 2000; Lazarus, 2001). For instance, teachers may feel anger toward disruptive students when they believe the behaviors are unjust and controllable by students. Teachers feel anger when they feel they are being undermined by others, their dignity is being hurt, or their authority is being threatened.

There is a characteristic set of physiological responses associated with each emotion. Research has shown that anger has the physical consequences of increased heart rate and cardiac output, elevated blood pressure, stimulation of acid secretion, and suppression of the body's immune response, increasing the vulnerability to stress. Additionally, chronic excess anger is linked to a higher risk of hypertension, diabetes, and heart disease (Cacioppo, Bernston, Larsen, Poehlmann, & Ito, 2000; Herrald & Tomake, 2002).

Research indicates that frustration is the most frequently experienced negative emotion reported by teachers (Chang, 2009a; Sutton, 2007). The core theme of frustration is the feeling of no control over a repeatedly undesirable situation. Frustration is usually the result of a circumstance, situation, or event rather than a specific person.

Teachers feel frustration when problems are caused not by a specific student but by circumstances over which they feel they have no control. However, Sutton (2007) found that the distinction between frustration and anger is often blurred. Because most teachers consider frustration to be more socially acceptable than anger, they tend to report or express frustration rather than anger (Liljestrom et al., 2007). Anger may turn into frustration when teachers feel there is nothing they can do about repeated misbehaviors or situations. Therefore, the main distinction between anger and frustration is the appraisal of accountability. A feeling of frustration is evoked when teachers appraise incidents as being caused by circumstances, whereas a feeling of anger is evoked when a situation is caused by a specific person, most often a student.

When you feel you have violated your own moral imperative or internalized social norm or value, the emotion aroused is guilt. Guilt is another unpleasant emotion teachers commonly feel due to caring and feeling responsible for their students (Hargreaves & Tucker, 1991; Prawat, Byers, & Anderson, 1983; Van Veen & Lasky, 2005; Zembylas, 2003). Guilt is common for teachers and involves the moral purposes embedded in a teacher's professional mission. Teacher guilt emanates from a sense of responsibility. Teachers feel guilty when students give up on learning (Prawat et al., 1983). Some teachers perceive it to be their responsibility, or moral duty, to help students and their family as part of their professional role, and they experience guilt when they feel they have not lived up to this responsibility (Liljestrom et al., 2007).

Analyzing the nature of guilt in teaching, Hargreaves and Tucker noted that teachers' guilt resulted from conflicts among several factors: teachers' commitment to nurture children, the ambiguity inherent in determining teachers' effects on their students, personal perfectionism, and increasing demands of accountability. These researchers discussed two kinds of guilt in teaching: *persecutory guilt* and *depressive guilt*. Persecutory guilt comes with accountability demands and bureaucratic controls. Depressive guilt originates from early childhood and is called out in later life in situations where individuals feel they have betrayed or failed to protect the people or values that symbolize good. For instance, persecutory guilt would lead a teacher to concentrate on covering the required content without compromise. Depressive guilt would appear when a teacher has failed to recognize a child who is being abused at home. The consequences of guilt can be resentment, cynicism, and eventually burnout.

EMOTION REGULATION AND COPING STRATEGIES

Emotion regulation refers to attempts to both modify aspects of an emotional experience as well as the expression of emotions in order to influence their intensity and duration (Ochsner & Gross, 2004). Research offers insights into individuals' attempts to influence the emotions they have, when they have them, and how they experience and express these emotions (Gross, 1998).

Research suggests that well-being may be most likely when:

- We regulate emotion antecedents so that we are emotionally engaged by those pursuits that have enduring value for us
- We attend to and experience our emotions in a richly differentiated fashion so that we notice subtle changes in our emotional responses
- We cultivate the capacity to modulate our emotional responses in a variety of ways

The emotion-generating process begins when something signals an individual that something important may be at stake. When attended to and evaluated in certain ways, these emotional cues trigger a coordinated set of response tendencies (Gross, Richards, & John, 2006). Once these emotional response tendencies arise, they may be modulated in various ways to shape an individual's actual responses.

Gross refers to "five families" of specific strategies that are located along the timeline of the emotional process. Strategies for controlling emotions can be grouped according to whether they are antecedent-focused or response-focused (Gross, 1999). Antecedent-focused emotion regulation strategies are used early in, or before if possible, the occurrence of the emotional response, whereas response-focused strategies are used following an emotion-invoking episode. Antecedent-focused strategies are anticipatory strategies that are aimed at managing or even preventing an upcoming emotional state.

Five Emotion Regulation Strategies

Emotion regulation can occur at several points between the initiation of an emotion and its expression (Gross, 2009). Four of these points are preventive (antecedent-focused); that is, it is what individuals do before the emerging emotion becomes fully activated. The fifth point is reactive (response-focused) and involves the modulation of experiential, behavioral, and/or physiological emotional responses.

The four basic antecedent strategies are:

- *Situation selection*, which involves selecting aspects of the environment, such as people or situations best suited to obtaining a desired emotional state.
- *Situation modification*, which refers to actions aimed at altering the environment to modify an emotional response.
- *Attentional deployment*, which involves directing, or redirecting, attention and efforts toward aspects of the environment that help achieve a desired emotional state.
- *Cognitive change*, also called *cognitive reappraisal*, which involves reinterpreting the situation to modify its emotional effects.

Response-focused strategies are things you do once emotion is already under way, after the response tendencies have been generated. These strategies attempt to manage existing emotions. For example, an individual might try to appear unfazed by a hurtful comment despite underlying feelings of anger. Attempts to control an emotional response after it has occurred fall mainly in the category of response modulation. Response modulation involves actively changing an existing emotional response, such as concealing a laugh with a look of concern after another's clumsy fall or restraining from an angry counterattack.

Once arousal begins, you can use situation selection to approach or avoid certain people, places, or activities to regulate emotion. In situation modification, you try to change the situation to modify its emotional impact. Next, because situations have many different aspects, you use attentional deployment to pick which aspects to focus on. With cognitive change, you construct one of the many possible meanings that might be attached. Finally, in response modulation you attempt to influence emotional response tendencies once they have already been elicited. This is actively attempting to decrease a negative emotional impact.

Antecedent-focused strategies are things you can do before the emotional response tendencies have become fully activated and have changed your behavior as well as your accompanying physiological response. For example, when receiving a critical comment from a colleague, you might use cognitive change to reappraise the comment, attributing it as a sign of the person's insecurity, thereby altering the entire emotion trajectory, feeling pity or even empathy for your colleague rather than getting angry.

Cognitive Reappraisal versus Suppression

Cognitive reappraisal is a strategy for modifying emotions in which you try to change the way you think about a situation very early in the generation stage of an emotion. It involves construing a potentially emotional situation in a way that will lessen its emotional impact. On the other hand, *suppression* is a form of emotion regulation typically occurring late in the generation of an emotional response. It involves inhibiting ongoing emotion-expressive behavior such as trying to control facial expressions and verbal responses (Gross & Levenson, 1993).

As a general coping strategy, cognitive reappraisal refers to recasting a stressful event as in some way positive, beneficial, or meaningful. In the coping literature, it is sometimes labeled simply *reappraisal, positive reappraisal*, or *benefit finding*. Regardless of the term used, the concept implies a conscious effort to "look for the silver lining," and there is ample evidence for its effectiveness. This strategy is covered in more detail in several later chapters.

Because reappraisal occurs early in the emotional process, it has the potential to modify the entire emotional sequence before emotion response tendencies are fully generated, and so it requires relatively few additional cognitive resources to implement. In contrast, suppression primarily modifies the behavioral aspect of your emotional response tendencies without reducing the experience of negative emotion. Because it comes late in the emotion generation process, it requires you to effortfully manage emotional response tendencies as they continually arise. These repeated efforts consume cognitive resources that could otherwise be used for attending to the task at hand.

In a series of studies, Gross and colleagues found that cognitive reappraisal effectively decreased both the emotional experience and expressive behavior in a negative emotion-eliciting situation, doing so without appreciable cognitive, physiological, or interpersonal cost (Gross & John, 2002, 2003, 2004). In contrast, suppression, while it is effective in lessening expressive behavior, fails to provide relief from negative emotions. Suppression also has substantial physiological and cognitive costs. Specifically, suppression leads to increased activation of the cardiovascular system (Richards & Gross, 2000) as well as to less satisfying social interactions (Butler et al., 2003). Over the longer term, individuals who make more frequent use of suppression show worse functioning in emotional, interpersonal, and well-being domains (Gross et al., 2006).

Research findings substantiate the positive impact of using cognitive reappraisal. Greater use of cognitive reappraisal is related to:

• Greater experience of positive emotion
• Lesser experience of negative emotion
• Closer relationships with others
• Being better liked
• Fewer symptoms of depression
• Being more satisfied with life
• Being more optimistic

The opposite is true for using suppression. Use of suppression is related to lesser experience of positive emotion, greater experience of negative emotion, lesser social support, elevated levels of depressive symptoms, low levels of satisfaction and well-being, and a less optimistic attitude about the future. Those using suppression frequently show low levels of well-being across the board, with the greatest effect on positive relations with others. Overall, this pattern of findings shows that the use of cognitive reappraisal is associated with multiple indicators of healthy functioning, while the use of suppression is associated with multiple indicators of unhealthy functioning.

Surprisingly, given our stereotypic beliefs about men and emotions, Gross and colleagues also found in their research that there were no significant gender differences in the use of emotion regulation, with 82% of men and 85% of women reporting controlling negative emotions to a greater extent than positive emotions (Gross et al., 2006). Similar to other researchers, they also found that the three most common types of emotions experienced were anger (23%), sadness (22%), and anxiety (10%).

According to research by Gross and John (2002, 2003) described earlier, suppression of emotions requires continuous self-monitoring and self-corrective actions for as long as the emotional experience lasts, and therefore reduces cognitive resources for other activities. In contrast, reappraisal does not require continuous self-monitoring, freeing cognitive resources for other activities. This means that teachers using reappraisal compared to suppression have more cognitive resources to monitor classroom activities.

Coping Strategies

In the psychological literature, there is considerable overlap between the terms *coping* and *emotion regulation*, with coping being the broader term for strategies used to manage stressful events. To the extent that coping is directed toward amending negative emotions, it falls within the category of emotion regulation. Similar to Gross's consideration of emotion regulation strategies as preventive or reactive, general coping strategies can be conceived in a corresponding way. In the model Schwarzer and Knoll (2003) present, coping can occur not only as a response to an adverse situation or in anticipation of upcoming stressful demands, it can also involve a more proactive approach. Their perspective distinguishes among four types of coping to grapple with events of the past, present, and future.

- *Reactive coping* is used to deal with stress experienced in the past or present.
- *Anticipatory coping* is used to deal with a pending threat that is certain or likely to occur in the near future.
- *Preventive coping* refers to efforts to prepare for uncertain threat potential in the long run.
- *Proactive coping* reflects efforts to build up resources to face any upcoming challenges.

Proactive and preventive coping represent more long-term efforts to be prepared for uncertain events by building up general resistance resources that will result in less strain in the future (Aspinwall & Taylor, 1997; Folkman & Lazarus, 1985; Greenglass, 2002). Most potential stressors allow for preparatory thoughts and actions that may either prevent anticipated negative consequences or serve to reduce their severity and impact.

Coping Skills and Burnout

In terms of general coping skills, research has shown the emotional exhaustion and depersonalization dimensions of burnout are associated with the defensive coping mechanism of escape (Leiter, 1993). Similarly, denying the problem is associated with emotional exhaustion and depersonalization, whereas more proactive planning strategies for problem-solving predict a sense of personal accomplishment (Dorz, Novara, Sica, & Sanavio, 2003). Lee and Ashforth (1990, 1996) also found using more proactive coping strategies is associated with a sense of personal accomplishment.

Other researchers have also found a negative relationship between teachers' use of proactive coping and burnout (Chang, 2009b; Greenglass, 2002). Schwarzer and Taubert (2002) categorized teachers as low, medium, and high proactive teachers. They found a significant pattern of decreasing burnout with increasing levels of proactive coping. Highly proactive teachers reported less emotional exhaustion, less depersonalization, and more personal accomplishment than low proactive-coping teachers.

McCarthy and colleagues (2009) reported similar findings. They found that teachers reporting higher levels of preventive coping resources had lower levels of all three dimensions of burnout. They also concluded that while emotional exhaustion and depersonalization emerge from external factors of work overload and lack of social support, the decreased self-efficacy associated with diminished personal accomplishment arises from insufficient personal resources; that is, not having strategies to both prevent and effectively react to stress.

STRATEGIES TEACHERS USE TO REGULATE THEIR EMOTIONS

Although there are a variety of theoretical perspectives on emotion regulation, the model proposed by Gross is especially relevant to teacher emotions. This model focuses on the timing of emotion regulation strategies based on the assumption that emotions unfold over time. Early career teachers especially need to learn strategies for emotional regulation, including strategies that help teachers prevent a situation, keep their cool in the heat of the moment, and cope with a full-blown emotional episode.

In Sutton's research on emotions, teachers reported using a myriad of strategies to help them regulate their emotions (Sutton, 2007; Sutton, Mudrey-Camino, & Knight, 2009). Examples of the preventive categories identified by Gross discussed in the previous section were evident. For example, when their day got off to a bad start, teachers used *modifying the situation* strategies to make sure they were well prepared before school started, to let students know when they were not up to par by actively soliciting students' cooperation, and to modify their lesson plans to have students doing activities that they found easier to manage.

Teachers frequently used *attention deployment* strategies, including talking to peers or reading positive thoughts each morning. More experienced teachers also reported learning to ignore students' minor behavioral infractions as a way to help them regulate their emotions in the immediate situation to keep emotions from surfacing. To prevent negative emotions from fully developing, teachers also reported talking to themselves about staying calm, or reminding themselves not to take their students' comments personally, as examples of *cognitive reappraisal*. These are also examples of Meichenbaum's (1985) *stress inoculation* strategy involving calming self-talk as anger symptoms begin to arise. This strategy is discussed in chapter 8.

Teachers also reported using a variety of response modulation strategies to modify the emotions they experienced in the classroom, including physically moving away, taking deep breaths, controlling facial expressions, and thinking of a serene place. The most common strategy used after the fact by teachers was talking to colleagues and friends, generally after school. Other strategies included reducing physical activity such as sitting quietly, or expending physical energy. More experienced teachers indicated that they had to learn to manage their emotions on their own because they received little or no help in their teacher education preparation program (Sutton & Knight, 2006).

Research conducted by Sutton and Knight showed a positive relationship between cognitive reappraisal and teacher self-efficacy beliefs regarding student engagement and classroom management. This relationship was supported for early childhood and middle school teachers, but not for high school teachers.

Unlike many other professions, teachers are constantly exposed to emotionally provocative situations with a limited range of options available for self-regulation. When strong emotions arise, teachers don't have the luxury of excusing themselves in order to calm down. In addition, given the emotional immaturity of students, especially younger students, one student's behavior can easily set off a chain reaction.

Teachers have little opportunity to exercise the *situation selection* strategy, or approaching or avoiding certain people, places, or activities as a means of regulating their emotions. Because they have no say over the students assigned to them, they don't get to choose who they spend their time with in the classroom. But they do have choices about which colleagues they befriend and spend their limited time with at school. They also can choose to use their precious time without students in school to rejuvenate themselves. Strategies for doing this are discussed in later chapters.

Chapter Five

Why Teacher Emotions Are Important

Teachers' understanding and expression of their own emotions are integral for navigating life in the classroom. Many teacher educators argue that teachers' emotions are crucial for bonding with students and parents, and must, therefore, be taken more seriously by those involved in teacher development (e.g., Tickle, 1991; Golby, 1996; Nias, 1996; Noddings, 2005). Nonetheless, addressing emotions has largely been ignored in most educational research, professional practice, and especially teacher education (e.g., Hargreaves, 2001; Linston & Garrison, 2003; Ria, Sève, Saury, Theureau, & Durand, 2003; Rosiek, 2003).

While emotions have always been essential for understanding classroom dynamics and student-teacher interactions, studying emotions has been relegated to low priority among competing agendas. More recently, the fact that teachers often report dropping out of the profession due to emotional stress has led educators to seek a better understanding of both the role emotion plays in teaching as well as emotional management.

Coping with their own negative emotional responses is a major stressor for teachers (Carson, Templin, & Weiss, 2006; Sutton, 2004). Emotional stress and poor emotional management consistently rank as the primary reasons teachers become dissatisfied and leave teaching (Montgomery & Rupp, 2005). Research has identified difficult emotions, such as anger and anxiety, as core factors influencing teachers' decisions to dropout of teaching (Gaziel, 1995; Wilhelm, Dewhurst-Savellis, & Parker, 2000; Wisniewski & Gargiulo, 1997).

Addressing emotions is critical because emotions have far-reaching impact affecting both students' and teachers' interest, engagement, and performance, as well as their development, health, and general well-being. Now more than ever, with tensions running high in the heat of the standards movement, it is important to further develop current understandings of teachers' emotions.

Despite this increasing recognition of the importance of emotions, the emotional terrain in teaching is still relatively unexplored. Recently though, some literature is starting to emerge. The past decade has seen a steady increase in interest and research about the nature of emotions experienced by teachers and students alike (Efklides & Volet, 2005; Jennings & Greenberg, 2009; Linnenbrink, 2007; Schutz & Lanehart, 2002).

Emotions are believed to have evolved in humans to enhance adaptation to environmental challenges. Research suggests that emotions are patterned in complex ways within individuals, across individuals, as well as over time. Emotions are influenced by such factors as gender, race, culture, and individual propensities (Pekrun & Schutz, 2007; Turner & Waugh, 2007).

Some basic emotions such as joy and anger are universal across cultures. Research has identified six facial expressions that are universal: anger, fear, sadness, disgust, surprise, and happiness (Ekman, 1992). A possible seventh may be embarrassment (Bocchino, 1999). Even though there is a core set of emotions across cultures, there are wide cultural and individual variations in emotional experiences. Specific expressions, intensity, and duration of emotions can vary widely between cultures and contexts.

Emotion is also perceived differently in different cultures. In the Western culture especially, emotion is conceived as volatile, and therefore needing to be regulated. Traditionally, emotion and reason have been considered competing processes with emotion interfering with rationality. However, recent brain research confirms that emotion and reason should be conceived of as a continuous process with emotional processes and cognitive processes inextricably intertwined.

Studying emotions requires integrating perspectives from a number of disciplines, some of them far removed from educational research as traditionally conceived. Fully understanding emotions calls for integrating a broad variety of disciplines, including not only education and psychology but also the neurosciences, sociology, and cultural anthropology.

EMOTIONAL TRIGGERS AND THE BRAIN

Emotions may originate in the brain, but they don't confine themselves there. They express themselves in the body as well. While strong emotions usually come and go and normal physiological equilibrium is restored, when emotional stressors endure for prolonged periods of time they tip the balance of chemicals in the brain and body, negatively affecting health. Given the physiological consequences of emotions, teachers need to work to find ways to establish emotional balance in their lives. Such balance will help them avoid many health problems that may result from the way they react to their world, both inside and outside of the classroom.

The brain is constantly sensing the needs of our body via specialized "thermostats" that monitor our internal and external worlds. When they sense something is wrong (for example, that the body is stressed), they activate the brain's alarm systems. The stress-response systems then act to help the body get what it needs. Much of this regulation takes place automatically without our awareness. When the external world is overwhelming or threatening, our body signals us to prepare to fight, freeze, or flee.

Recent knowledge of how the brain processes, stores, and retrieves information radically changes our conception of both teaching and learning. The core mission of the brain is to sense, perceive, process, store, and act on information from our external and internal worlds to promote survival. To do this, the human brain has evolved an efficient and logical organizational structure.

In the very distant past, survival depended on a quick reaction in response to threat. To this day, our brain is literally programmed to protect us from perceived danger, whether real or not. According to Goleman (1995), as we move through our daily lives, our emotional responses are shaped by three things:

- Rational judgment (perceiving and assessing facts)
- Personal history (what has happened to shape us)
- Our ancestral past (our neurobiology)

These three factors operate simultaneously, and often do so without relying on the current facts. In other words, if you have experienced an emotional trauma, you will react with both emotional and physical responses when experiencing a trigger for the memory, even though your current situation may be safe. This happens because your brain signals the presence of danger. This can occur for any emotional memory for which you have a strong "emotional tag." In a paradoxical way, the brain's response is very rational, because the trigger for the physical response is perceived as real, sending the brain into survival mode (Thomsen, 2002).

The brain has a hierarchical organization, from the lower, more simple areas to the higher, more complex cortical areas. The bottom regions control the most simple functions such as respiration, heart rate, and blood pressure, whereas the top regions control more complex functions such as language, abstract thinking, and emotion regulation (Perry, 2006).

The brain develops and modifies itself in response to experience. The brain's ability to change as a result of experience, called *plasticity*, is well documented (Diamond, 1988; Huttenlocher, 2002; LeDoux, 2002; Schwartz & Begley, 2002). Because of this plasticity, the brain is capable of changing in response to experiences, especially repetitive and patterned experiences. Although the "sensitive" brain of an infant or young child is most malleable to experience, the functioning of the mature brain continues to be altered and changed through experience throughout our lives.

How the Brain Responds to Emotional Triggers

Scientists believe the brain's ability to record and recall emotionally significant experiences likely results from the release throughout the body of emotion-arousing substances putting a vivid memory tag on emotionally charged events (Cahill & McGaugh, 1998; Gazzaniga, Ivry, & Mangun, 2002). In a very real way, emotion actually enhances memory by causing the release of hormones signaling brain regions to strengthen memory.

Extensive brain research overwhelmingly leads to the conclusion that emotion and cognition cannot be separated, as once believed (Calkins & Bell, 2010; Damasio, 1999, 2003; Pert, 1997). Emotional states have a profound influence, with emotions actually facilitating the storage and recall of information in memory. Emotions interact with reason to support or inhibit learning and behavior (Detweiler, Rothman, Salovey, & Steward, 2000). It could be said that emotions are part of every thought, decision, and action.

Emotional data take high priority. When you respond emotionally to a situation, the brain's emotional system takes a major role, suspending more cerebral processes (Sousa, 2006). Anger, fear of the unknown, or even joyous elation can quickly overcome your rational thoughts. This reflexive override of conscious thought can be so powerful it can cause temporary inability to talk or move. This is evident in the statements people often make when experiencing an extreme emotional reaction, such as *I was speechless* or *I froze*.

When a teacher feels positive in the classroom, endorphins are released, stimulating a pleasurable feeling. Conversely, if a teacher has a negative feeling about a student or a class or is stressed, cortisol is released and travels throughout the brain and body, activating defense behaviors. This reduces brain activity to focusing on the cause of the stress and how to deal with it, leaving little attention left for the teaching task (Kagan, 1989; Kuhlmann, Kirschbaum, & Wolf, 2005). Strong emotions can shut down conscious processing during the event while enhancing our memory of it. According to Sylwester (2003), attention is both hooked and sustained by emotion. Before a teacher can turn his or her attention to the task at hand he or she must feel emotionally secure. Of course, this is also true for students.

Emotional Memory

We all have automatic emotional responses. Although it may appear that we are acting impulsively without thinking, we are actually drawing on defensive responses set in habitual memory. The brain can detect hostility or rejection in less than a quarter of a second, before conscious awareness of these cues, triggering emotions and behavior. For example, someone who grew up with highly critical parents may lash out at the slightest hint of criticism. To an unaware observer, what appears to be an impulsive act may well be a "fast draw" to perceived threat. Research has shown that everything we see, hear, touch, or smell triggers automatic and unconscious associations within 200 milliseconds. In that instant, the brain has already evaluated this input to decide whether the situation is safe or threatening (Azar, 1998).

Emotional memory is the place where our feelings and emotions about our experiences, thoughts, and ideas are stored. Previous experiences are filed away with attached "emotional notes" in an individual's personal warehouse (Wood, Quirk, & Swindle, 2007). When we are upset we do things on impulse that we would not do in a calmer, more rational state of mind. In order to avoid always being in a reactive state, a teacher needs to understand how emotions work and develop the skills to intercept emotions before they lead to stress-producing behavior.

Classroom events trigger highly personalized associations in memory that have attached feelings and thoughts. The same event will evoke different associations for individual teachers. Although these associations are not consciously recalled, through the filter of stored past experiences they tap both cognitive and emotional memory.

When emotional memories are triggered by a troubling event (for example, here he goes again), they can dominate a teacher's actions, diverting mental functioning to cope with these aroused feelings and leaving diminished capacity to attend to other things. When intense emotional memories are activated, a teacher may either shut

Table 5.1. **Behavior Progression Along the Arousal Continuum**

Mind State	Behavior
Arousal	Vigilance, defensiveness
⇩	⇩
Alarm	Resistance
⇩	⇩
Fear	Defiance
⇩	⇩
Terror	Aggression

down or lash out. Unless there is a reduction in the intensity of aroused emotions, a teacher's behavioral responses will be defensive and usually counterproductive. This compounds the problem by reinforcing the strength of the association and expanding the negative associations in stored emotional memory to create a vicious cycle (Parrott & Spackman, 2000).

When under threat, our minds and bodies respond in an adaptive fashion, making changes in our mental state and in our body's physiology. According to Perry's (2006) research, in responding to threat we move along the arousal continuum—from calm to arousal, to alarm, to fear, and to terror (see Table 5.1), and different areas of our brain control and orchestrate our mental and physical functioning. The more threatened we become, the more primitive (or regressed) our style of thinking and behaving becomes, moving from defensiveness to aggression.

NEGATIVE EMOTIONS AND FLOODING

One of the worst consequences of negative emotions is that it can lead to *flooding.* Flooding is a term used in the psychological literature to describe an extreme emotional override that hijacks attention, literally shutting down our brain's capacity to think (Gottman, 1994). When flooding occurs, you feel so overwhelmed by what's going on and your own reaction that you experience "systems overload," swamped by distress and upset. Once you are feeling this out of control, you may become extremely defensive, hostile, or withdrawn.

Research in the neurosciences has shown that negative emotions focus attention by causing a mobilization and synchronization of the brain's activities, frequently intruding and flooding consciousness (Derryberry & Tucker, 1994; LeDoux, 1996; Phelps & LeDoux, 2005). Teachers' negative emotions are central because they focus attention so powerfully. Students' behavior that elicits negative emotions in teachers diverts attention from instructional goals. Teachers often report getting distracted and losing their concentration because they can't divide their attention between a student's challenging behavior and the task at hand.

High anxiety can reduce the limited resources of working memory because of intrusive thoughts and worry. This loss of memory resources impairs "task-relevant processing," rendering less brainpower available to the anxious person (Eysenck, 1997). This means that a beginning teacher who is highly anxious about lesson plans and disruptive student behavior is less likely to be able to access creative options to solve the myriad of classroom problems that arise on a moment-to-moment basis.

In contrast to the negative impact of anxiety, certain positive emotions such as joy, interest, or pride expand "momentary thought-action repertoires"; that is, more thoughts and actions come to mind (Fredrickson & Branigan, 2005). Thus, teachers who experience more positive emotions may be more capable of generating different ways to solve problems. This is a classic catch-22 for early career teachers—just when their ability to generate creative solutions to classroom and behavior problems they face is most needed, in a state of high anxiety, their brain's cognitive capacity shuts down.

In any intense exchange, it's normal for some negative feelings and thoughts to arise. As long as they don't get too extreme, most individuals can handle them. We all have a built-in meter that measures our level of arousal. When the level gets too high, the needle starts going haywire and flooding begins. Just how readily one becomes flooded is an individual matter. A rare few of us have a very high threshold, while others may feel flooded at the mere suggestion of a criticism or complaint. Not surprisingly, flooding is also affected by how much stress you have going on outside of the current situation. The more pressure you're under, the more easily flooded you will be.

It is certainly not unusual to feel flooded in the heat of an argument or when responding to a student's hurtful behavior. However, if this happens often enough, a catastrophic shift may occur in how you think about your students. You start to react to everything with dread—"What now?" You become hypervigilant, continually on guard against an attack, and become immersed in your own stress-maintaining thoughts. Distorting and distressing thoughts become the rule, not the exception. In effect, your negative thoughts and your aroused body conspire to throw your personal thermometer into the negative range for good.

Over time, you pay more attention to your students' actions that confirm your negative assumptions, rather than those that might refute them. For example, if you have concluded that your students are untrustworthy and selfish, then you may overlook examples of them being trustworthy and considerate. Negative expectations and assumptions become the norm, and any evidence of a positive nature is ignored.

If your self-talk is dominated by thoughts that exacerbate your negative emotions rather than soothe them, you are likely to become flooded in response to your students' defensiveness, aggression, or anger. Symptoms of flooding include increased heart rate and flow of adrenaline. When your body feels these symptoms of flooding, the less able you are to soothe yourself and respond to the situation calmly. Instead, your thoughts and emotions co-conspire to contribute even more to your sense of being overwhelmed. Over time, you become conditioned to look for and react to the negatives in your students and your work. This becomes a self-fulfilling prophecy— the more you expect and look for negatives, the more likely you are to find them, and to highlight their significance in your mind.

When flooding goes on unabated, the results can be devastating. Teachers experiencing emotional exhaustion, the major component of burnout, are likely to be encountering flooding on a regular basis.

Beginning Teachers Have Stronger Emotional Responses

Due to their insecurity, fear, and perceived incompetence, the intensity of beginning teachers' emotional responses is stronger than that of more experienced teachers (Sutton & Wheatley, 2003). Beginning teachers' emotions are especially intense and erratic. Erb (2002) likened beginning teachers' emotions to a whirlpool, stating:

> From one experience to another, the world of the beginning teacher is never still. Although the direction of the whirlpool may be predictable, the degree of activity is less predictable. Opposing currents may create small or large whirlpools. Objects may stay afloat in gentle currents, or get sucked underneath the waters' surface by the overwhelming intensity of the force. (p. 1)

Researchers conducting life span research have found that negative emotions decline during adulthood, continuing to decrease with age (Carstensen, Pasupathi, Mayr, & Nesselroade, 2000; Mroczek & Almeida, 2004). This means that the ratio of subjectively experienced negative to positive emotions is likely to be higher for novice teachers in their 20s than for older, more experienced teachers.

ADDRESSING TEACHER ANGER

Literature concerning difficult emotions such as anger in the school context is typically not research based. Instead, much of the available literature offers recommendations for teachers to deal with angry students or parents as well as ways to prevent violence and aggression in classrooms and schools. Some empirical studies have focused on teachers' emotional lives, especially on anger. Anger is the emotion most studied with teachers, perhaps because of the potential deleterious impact on both students and teachers.

Not surprisingly, researchers studying teacher anger have found it to be a pervasive classroom experience. In fact, in Sutton's (2004) research conducted with middle school teachers, over 90% of the teachers talked about holding in their anger, reducing their anger, stepping back from their anger, or trying to keep themselves in check. In examining female teachers' expressions of anger in stories they told, Dorney (2000) found anger to be a theme identified as being very present in their work.

Golby's (1996) study included teachers' descriptions of how they managed negative emotions in their work, in particular annoyance, irritation, and anger. In this research, teachers reported that they learned to control their anger because they viewed professionalism as controlling one's emotions to effectively work within the constraints of the system. Golby suggested that the strong need to be in control might result in a restricted set of emotional responses in the school setting.

Tickle (1991), in a study of beginning teachers, found that teachers' emotions were often the focus of their discussions as they met for their weekly debriefings. With findings similar to Golby, he found that these new teachers perceived emotional management to be a pertinent aspect of growing into their professional role. These research findings lend support to the notion that teachers internalize "feeling rules" accepted by the profession discussed in the previous chapter.

Also focusing on the topic of anger, deMarrais and Tisdale (2002) asked teachers to describe specific school-related and classroom-related situations in which they experienced anger. Analysis of these teachers' narratives revealed that teachers' descriptions of their anger experiences were intimately connected to their expressed beliefs and assumptions about teaching, schooling, education, and students' welfare. These researchers found that teachers' "moral purposes," or what they believe is important to achieve in their work as teachers, are inextricably intertwined with their descriptions of anger experiences. They were very clear in what they proposed to achieve in their work, and they often expressed anger when they perceived that they were impeded from attaining their purposes. In other words, anger resulted when teachers felt that they were impeded in carrying out their moral purposes.

The experience of anger itself often caused further moral qualms. Teachers explicitly stated beliefs about not expressing anger at their students or in their presence. Even though teachers frequently described a reluctance to express any anger in front of or at students, they did expect students to be team players and to show respect for their teachers. These researchers concluded that anger was a complex and problematic topic for many teachers.

Studying a sample of female teachers, researchers found that these teachers experienced discomfort and qualms when their anger was triggered, expending considerable energy to avoid expressing or even feeling anger (Liljestrom et al., 2007). Anger was, in these teachers' view, incompatible with being a good teacher, and the teachers often reported assuming full responsibility for handling their own emotions and the emotions of others as part of their role as teacher.

These teachers believed that being professional involves both emotional management and avoidance of the experience of anger. In cases where it was not possible to avoid expressions of anger, anger was nevertheless perceived to be incompatible with the professional role of teacher. These women teachers spoke of adopting particular pedagogical practices to avoid classroom situations that might anger them, for example, by being well prepared and also by deepening their understanding of students' backgrounds and their circumstances.

Liljestrom and colleagues saw a clustering of emotions—disappointment, frustration, fury, rage, surprise, shock, anger, guilt, sadness, shame, and fear—in these teachers' descriptions of anger experiences. Teachers appeared to be unable to separate these difficult emotions, which often occurred at the same time. Their fear was often of the very expression of anger itself, since these teachers often talked of the fear of being out of control. The authors concluded that teaching and learning are intensely emotional experiences, encompassing the full gamut from joy to rage.

In Sutton's (2004) research, teachers reported experiencing a wide range of positive and negative emotions, but they were more likely to describe experiences of their negative emotions as frustration rather than anger. Two-thirds of the teachers talked about their frustration, whereas only one-third talked about their anger in response to an interview question asking about what emotions come to mind relative to their classroom teaching. Some teachers were uncomfortable with anger and were much more likely to spontaneously talk about their frustrations than their anger. Teachers in Sutton's research reported that they most commonly got angry and frustrated when their academic goals were blocked by the misbehavior, inattention, or lack of motivation of students.

In a follow-up diary study, Sutton and colleagues found that the majority of teachers reported that most experiences of anger and frustration were not minor, momentary feelings; rather, they were intense, lasting more than an hour. The teachers reported that intrusive thoughts made it difficult for them to concentrate on what they were doing before the emotion episode (Sutton, Genovese, & Conway, 2005). As in the research described previously, episodes of anger and frustration were blurred in the teachers' minds, and they reported similar reactions to both emotions. This is consistent with the finding that everyday meanings of anger and frustration vary widely (Clore & Centerbar, 2004). The teachers were most likely to attribute the cause of their anger and frustration to others (83%).

WHAT TEACHERS NEED TO KNOW ABOUT EMOTIONS

These research findings have important implications for teachers. Some of those implications include the following:

- Teachers must understand that their own and their students' emotions will permeate the classroom and exert an enormous influence on how they feel about teaching.
- Experiencing intense emotions is inherent in teaching.
- Teaching brings out the full range of emotions—from joy to rage.
- Emotional swings are particularly powerful for beginning teachers.
- Difficult emotions arouse around deeply held beliefs, especially when these are challenged.

Teachers need to learn strategies that will help them negotiate the moment-to-moment fluctuations in their emotions. Prospective and developing teachers need to better understand the important role emotions play in their lives as teachers. To help reduce teacher stress and prevent burnout, teachers have to build resilience to their unpleasant emotional experiences and have strategies for moderating their emotional reactions. Arming teachers with the knowledge of the emotional nature of teaching is the first step in helping equip them with the tools to handle their own emotional experiences and emotional events within the classroom as well as scaffolding student emotions (Schutz, Cross, Hong, & Osbon, 2007).

It is vital that teachers have realistic beliefs about the nature of teaching and the classroom environment. They need to know teaching is essentially an emotional practice. They also need to become more aware of the "emotional rules" they are expected to play by, and more importantly, challenge these emotional rules.

With educational reform running rampant, this constant change has a direct impact on teachers and is another cause of teacher stress. Schools are constantly undergoing change. Such changes range from national policy mandates for teacher accountability, statewide standards, and district initiatives for curriculum reform. For teachers, such initiatives often involve transforming current perceptions or beliefs about curriculum and pedagogy, challenging their identities and goals. As such, implementing new curriculum mandates can be an effort in belief change, which is not only a long and slow process, but more importantly can be an emotionally laborious process as well. School reform efforts in themselves are stressful, but even more nerve-racking is confronting dearly held beliefs about effective curricula, desired pedagogy, and quality instructional practices.

Dealing with Difficult Emotions

It is easy to fall into your automatic patterns without realizing that you actually have a choice. With the cumulative pressure of the teaching day, it can be difficult to acknowledge that the feelings of stress or of being overwhelmed are totally logical and make sense. At times, given the complexity of what goes on in the classroom, feelings of anger, desperation, and distress are to be expected. The aim is not specifically to try to make the feeling go away; rather, the important point is to raise your awareness and understanding about what is happening, to acknowledge your feelings, and to explore alternative ways of thinking, and ultimately, feeling.

Being together with students in close contact, in a small space for hours daily, it is unrealistic to think that a teacher will not sometimes feel anger. In such intimate living quarters, it would indeed be highly unusual for any teacher to experience a total lack of angry feelings. It is a normal reaction for a teacher to feel anger at times—it is the expression of this anger that a teacher needs to be able to manage.

It is also important to acknowledge that difficult feelings have the potential to serve you in many ways. Such feelings can:

- Give you valuable information about your own needs
- Assist you in identifying and healing old wounds
- Create deeper connections in your relationships
- Signal you to make better choices

At the heart of many theories of psychological change is the principle that only when you completely accept yourself are you free to change. Handling difficult emotions first requires awareness and then acceptance before you can exercise choice.

Learning to Read Your Body's Signals

Learning to read your body's signals is central to the process of healthy development of stress-response capability. Many of the sensations you feel when you are out of balance are clear, like thirst. But the body uses a common set of alarm sensations for many different kinds of potential threats. The alarm response and the resulting feelings caused by frustration are very similar to those caused by fear. This means you may act angry in response to feeling anxious, insecure, or overwhelmed. The internal distress a person feels when hungry may also lead to an angry response. You have probably found yourself responding angrily to a student, friend, or family member when you have missed a meal. Mislabeling a feeling (for example, anxiety as anger) often leads to an exaggerated emotional response. This is why it is important to learn to label your feelings.

The mere act of labeling your emotions when they arise can have important psychological implications because it can help gain a degree of distance, cultivating the awareness that you are the creator of your emotions—you are not your emotions. According to Gottman, Katz, and Hooven (1997), the act of naming your emotions produces a soothing effect on the nervous system, which serves the function of helping you to recover more quickly from a distressing event. By talking about an emotion to yourself or to others as you are experiencing it, you engage the part of the brain where language and logic are housed. In so doing, you take the focus away from the area of the brain where emotion resides.

Paying Attention to Physical Cues

It is important to learn to recognize your disempowering patterns of behavior so you have the opportunity to make a different choice. The key is to be proactive and not wait until your thoughts are negative and blaming because then they are much harder to redirect. The goal is to learn to intercept sooner and sooner. By paying attention to physical cues you can become more attuned to your early warnings. Ask yourself such questions as the following:

Ask yourself . . .
Am I feeling hot?
Am I starting to talk fast?
Are my palms sweaty?
Is my stomach feeling queasy?
Is my heart pounding?
Am I short of breath?
Are my muscles tensing up?
Am I clenching my teeth?
Have I raised my voice?

The idea is to make the shift to paying attention to your physical sensations as a way to pause and acknowledge the emotions you are experiencing to help curtail a reactive response. The many strategies offered in the rest of this book will help you manage your emotions, cope more effectively with your stress, and make better choices to sustain yourself.

Part II

BECOMING STRESS HARDY: GUARDING AGAINST BURNOUT

Chapter Six

Approaches to Student and Classroom Behavior Management That Reduce Stress

As mentioned in the beginning chapter, the stress inflicted by trying to manage students' challenging behavior frequently triggers burnout. Managing students' behavior is an essential element of a teacher's job and is a central ingredient of professional identity. Teachers who have continuing discipline problems are at a higher risk for stress and burnout.

CLASSROOM MANAGEMENT AND TEACHER STRESS AND BURNOUT

The relationship between classroom management and teacher stress is well documented in the research literature. A preponderance of research validates the relationship of teacher perceptions of student behavior problems to stress levels (Boyle, Borg, Falzon, & Baglioni, 1995; Brock, 1999; Brouwers & Tomic, 2000; Center & Callaway, 1999; Friedman, 1995; Giallo & Little, 2003; Hastings & Bham, 2003; Kijai & Totten, 1995; Kinnunen & Salo, 1994; Kokkinos, 2007; Little, 2003; Miller, 1995).

Some of the research findings related to managing student behavior and stress and burnout include the following:

- Teachers become emotionally exhausted and develop negative attitudes toward students when the classroom environment deteriorates (Burisch, 2002; Evers, Tomic, & Brouwers, 2004; Näring et al., 2006; Schlichte, Yssel, & Merbler, 2005).
- Teachers who feel overwhelmed and emotionally exhausted have fewer personal resources available and may not have the emotional reserve to deal with students who pose behavior problems (Abel & Sewell, 1999; Egyed & Short, 2006; Hakanen et al., 2006; Quinn, 2003).
- Teachers who become emotionally exhausted develop feelings of detachment from their students, and as feelings of depersonalization increase their sense of personal accomplishment decreases (Byrne, 1999; Durr, 2008; Maslach, Jackson, & Leiter, 1996).

- Teachers who experience stress tend to have less access to effective ways to respond to students who misbehave (Maag, 2008).
- Teachers who hold authoritarian-demanding attitudes toward students and student discipline experience excessive stress in the face of disruptive student behavior (Bernard, 1988).
- Teachers who use reactive intervention strategies, characterized by reprimands, threats, and negative consequences, rather than proactive strategies, experience greater amounts of teacher stress (Clunies-Ross et al., 2008).
- Teachers' use of verbal aggression is significantly related to all three dimensions of teacher burnout, emotional exhaustion, depersonalization, and lack of personal accomplishment (Avtgis & Rancer, 2008).
- Teachers' use of punitive actions is correlated with the lack of personal achievement dimension of burnout (Bibou-Nakou et al., 1999).
- Teachers with a punitive, moralistic attitude toward student control experience higher levels of burnout (Bas, 2011; Friedman, 1995).
- The most burnt-out teachers attribute less value to personal relationships with students, whereas the least burnt-out teachers value personal relationships with students (Cano-García et al., 2005).

When emotional exhaustion sets in, it becomes more difficult to find the emotional reserve to deal with students who are challenging. As the classroom environment goes sour, teachers develop a negative attitude toward students, treating them harshly, doling out reprimands and punishment. When teachers constantly take punitive action against students, the student-teacher relationship necessarily deteriorates and teachers are often left feeling a lack of personal accomplishment.

It is not surprising that when teachers lack the resources to effectively manage the social and emotional challenges they face in the classroom, their students have low levels of on-task behavior (Marzano, Marzano, & Pickering, 2003). Disruptive behaviors erode teachers' self-efficacy beliefs that they can find effective solutions to the problems they face, destroying their belief in their own capacity to bring about change. Teachers with lower levels of self-efficacy are more likely to report high levels of behavior problems (Mashburn, Hamre, Downer, & Pianta, 2006).

When teachers see students' actions as threatening their need for control, and as intentional inappropriate behavior, they become pessimistic about their likelihood of producing any improvement (Brophy, 1996; Brophy & McCaslin, 1992). Teachers' lack of success with students exhibiting challenging behavior perpetuates a sense of powerlessness that, in turn, leads to a continuing pattern of ineffective, often increasingly more hostile, teacher responses.

Doubts regarding teaching efficacy can head teachers on a downward spiral. Less effort or easily giving up leads to poor outcomes, which then produces decreased teacher efficacy (Tschannen-Moran, Woolfolk Hoy, & Hoy, 1998). When beginning teachers encounter a problem of classroom control they tend to see it as a direct reflection of their own inabilities, both personal and professional, rather than seeing it more realistically as one of the unavoidable challenges of managing a classroom full of students.

Over time it is easy to see how teachers can end up dispirited and discouraged. With eroded self-efficacy about their teaching tasks, teachers experiencing burnout withdraw from student-teacher relationships (Burke, Greenglass, & Schwarzer, 1996). As a result, it becomes a vicious cycle—the more they detach the more they face problems managing their own as well as their students' behavior.

TEACHER BURNOUT AND TEACHER RENEWAL CYCLES

As the classroom climate deteriorates, it triggers what Jennings and Greenberg (2009) refer to as a "burnout cascade." The deteriorating climate is marked by increases in troublesome student behaviors, and teachers become emotionally exhausted as they try to manage them. Under such conditions, teachers often resort to reactive and excessively punitive responses that only contribute to a self-sustaining cycle of classroom disruption (Osher et al., 2007; Osterman, 2000). Using reactive, punitive interventions leads to greater amounts of stress (Clunies-Ross et al., 2008).

Curwin and Mendler (1988) labeled a similar cycle the "discipline-burnout cycle." When teachers respond ineffectively to student misbehavior, typically using either denial or attacking tactics, their response leads to the continuation or worsening of students' behavior, causing anxiety and stress. Faced with not knowing what to do, the teacher either holds in the tension or yields to explosive outbursts. If the tension accumulates with no relief in sight, the teacher responds with either withdrawal or aggression. When the cycle becomes repetitive, burnout sets in. Figure 6.1 depicts the typical sequence in the burnout cycle.

On the other hand, as shown in Figure 6.2 when the teacher's interventions result in appropriate student responses, it leads to enhanced self-efficacy. Believing that they are capable of finding reasonable solutions to the day-to-day problems they face helps teachers stay actively engaged and enthusiastic about their work, maintaining a renewal cycle. Research shows that as classroom management efficacy increases, levels of teacher burnout decrease (Brouwers & Tomic, 2000; Durr, 2008; Ozdemir, 2007). Research also shows that teacher efficacy beliefs about handling student misbehavior mediates the relationship between perceived student misbehavior and emotional exhaustion (Tsouloupas et al., 2010).

One of the best buffers against undue stress and potential burnout is for teachers to learn intervention strategies and communication patterns that result in the student responses they want. Some effective strategies shown in Figure 6.2 can be categorized as preventive or responsive. Such strategies serve not only to deescalate student behavior, when used proactively they limit misbehavior in the first place.

As teachers respond more effectively, students have less need for confrontation, their behavior improves, and teachers in turn become more confident of their own resources for solving problems. Having effective strategies for addressing challenging behavior keeps teachers in a continuous renewal cycle (Larrivee, 2009). Conversely, when teachers use ineffective strategies it can head them down the path to burnout.

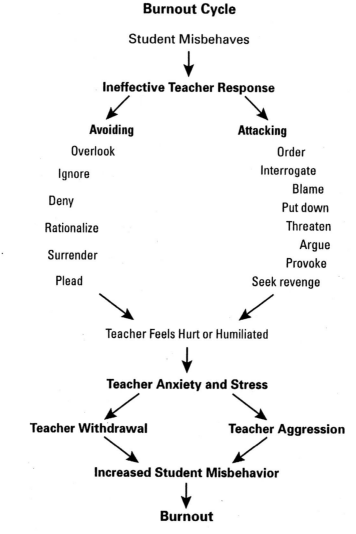

Figure 6.1.   Burnout Cycle

Renewal Cycle

Student Misbehaves

Effective Teacher Response

Preventive

Express feeling
Clarify teacher expectations
Accept ownership
Provide rationale
Invite participation
Solicit information
Enlist cooperation
Request help

Responsive

Validate student feelings
Acknowledge student feelings
Respect student perspective
Assert teacher needs
Provide options
Offer assistance
Mutually explore resolution
Negotiate a plan

Teacher Feels Valued and Respected

Teacher Self-efficacy

Teacher Remains Engaged and Enthusiastic

Increased Student Appropriate Behavior

Renewal

Figure 6.2.   Renewal Cycle

THE IMPORTANCE OF FORGING RELATIONSHIPS WITH STUDENTS

Research has consistently shown that when students perceive their teachers as caring and supportive they are more likely to be both academically engaged and regulate their own behavior to act responsibly (McNeely & Falci, 2004; Murdock & Miller, 2003; Patrick, Anderman, Ryan, Edelin, & Midgley, 2001; Wentzel, 1997, 1998; Whitlock, 2006; Woolfolk Hoy & Weinstein, 2006). Students' perceptions of being in a class in which the teacher encourages the development of personal mastery and self-improvement contribute significantly to students' confidence and use of self-regulatory strategies (Wang & Holcombe, 2010; Middleton & Midgley, 1997; Pintrich, 2000; Wolters, Yu, & Pintrich, 1996). When students feel their efforts and abilities are recognized and when they do not fear being embarrassed or compared to peers, they are more likely to use cognitive strategies that contribute to academic success as well as feel confident in their ability to learn (Ryan & Patrick, 2001).

Students are more likely to participate in school and bond with school when teachers create a caring and socially supportive environment because such a climate meets students' needs for connectedness. Although the need to connect and belong is pervasive throughout the school years, during adolescence the need to connect with others through mutually supportive relationships is at its peak (Midgley, Feldlaufer, & Eccles, 1989).

Research substantiates that students' perceptions of the school and classroom environment influence their behavioral, affective, and cognitive engagement in school, which in turn effects academic achievement. A recent meta-analysis based on 99 studies including preschool to high school students found significant associations between affective qualities of teacher-student relationships and both students' school engagement and achievement (Roorda, Koomen, Spilt, & Oort, 2011). While overall, stronger effects were found in the higher grades, the adverse effects of negative teacher-student relationships were more pronounced in primary than in secondary school. This finding supports the current advocacy for early intervention as a preventative measure.

There is substantial research validating the importance of the quality of student-teacher relationships in minimizing behavior problems. A meta-analysis of more than 100 studies showed that teachers who had high-quality relationships with their students had 31% fewer behavior problems than teachers who did not (Marzano et al., 2003).

Research examining a large-scale national database from birth through adolescence found the teacher-student relationship was the only factor in the school environment related to problem behavior (O'Connor, Dearing, & Collins, 2011). This research showed that high-quality teacher-student relationships predicted low levels of externalizing behaviors, or behaviors that manifest as overactive, impulsive, or aggressive behaviors. Silver and colleagues similarly found that high levels of conflict and low levels of closeness in kindergarten teacher-child relationships were associated with rapid increases in externalizing behaviors from kindergarten to third grade (Silver, Measelle, Armstrong, & Essex, 2005).

There is substantial evidence that the teacher-child relationship is an important contributor to, and can play a vital role in, a child's socioemotional and behavioral development, and children with socioemotional and behavioral challenges are the most vulnerable to classroom influences (Buyse, Verschueren, Doumen, Van Damme, & Maes, 2008; Entwisle & Alexander, 1988; Morrison & McDonald Connor, 2002; Rimm-Kaufman, La Paro, Downer, & Pianta, 2005; Rutter & Maughan, 2002).

High-quality relationships act as protective factors, helping to prevent children with high levels of internalizing behaviors (those that manifest in depressive symptoms and social withdrawal) in early childhood from developing trajectories of long-term internalizing behavior problems (O'Connor et al., 2011). Children with early internalizing behaviors that developed high-quality relationships with their teachers evidenced levels of internalizing behavior by the fifth grade comparable to those of their peers who had low levels of internalizing behavior in early childhood. In other words, positive teacher-student relationships help to prevent behavior problems in middle childhood.

Having the benefit of a supportive relationship with teachers can help prevent the development of behavior problems while, conversely, low-quality relationships hinder the development of more proactive behavior (Baker, Grant, & Morlock, 2008; O'Connor et al., 2011; Silver et al., 2005). Within supportive teacher-child relationships, young children learn to use adaptive inter- and intrapersonal strategies. According to Baker (2006), high-quality relationships scaffold children's formation of important social and behavioral skills.

The Detrimental Effects of Authoritarian Management Practices

Research findings have coalesced in the educational, neuroscience, and mental health domains to substantiate the detrimental effects of disciplinary and management practices based on an authoritarian style characterized by dictums, coercion, and systems of punishments and rewards. Ironically, teachers who focus more on negative behaviors than positive behaviors may maintain and even increase aggressive behaviors in their students.

Research at both the individual teacher level and the school level indicates the importance of the dual processes of support and structure that appear to act in concert to counteract student disengagement. Studying schools labeled *authoritative* (as distinguished from *authoritarian*) characterized as both highly supportive and highly structured with academic and behavioral expectations, Gregory and colleagues found that such schools had significantly lower schoolwide suspension rates (Gregory, Cornell, & Fan, 2011). On the other hand, schools low on both support and structure had the highest schoolwide suspension rates as well as the largest racial discipline gaps.

In the same vein, Pellerin (2005) found that authoritative schools, compared to permissive and indifferent schools, had students with the highest engagement. Based on a nationally representative sample of 10th and 12th grade students, schools high on both responsiveness and standards for academic and behavioral performance had the least amount of cutting classes, tardiness, absenteeism, and lack of preparation for class.

Recent brain research has far-reaching implications for educational practice, including classroom management. Brain research indicates that optimum learning takes place when students are actively engaged and operating in a state of low threat and high challenge (Caine & Caine, 1997; Caine, Caine, McClintic, & Klimek, 2009). A classroom emotional climate that is supportive and respectful activates a state of "relaxed alertness" in students. In contrast, a classroom environment of looming threat and coercion causes the brain to "downshift," and students literally lose access to portions of the brain (Hart, 1983). Feeling threatened, helpless, or fearful activates the brain's threat response, setting defensive behaviors in motion (Kuhlmann, Kirschbaum, & Wolf, 2005; Wallenstein, 2003).

Brain research has also made important contributions in explaining the intricate connections between emotions and learning, which point to the essential role of developing social-emotional competencies. The term *social-emotional learning* (SEL) refers to educational efforts to promote students' social and emotional competencies (Elias & Schwab, 2006; Devine & Cohen, 2007). In a review of more than 700 SEL programs for students preschool to high school, participating schools had a 44% decrease in suspensions and a 27% decrease in other disciplinary actions.

SEL programs also significantly improve students' attachment and attitudes toward school, while decreasing rates of violence and aggression, disciplinary referrals, and substance abuse (Weissberg, Dymnicki, Taylor, & Shellinger, 2008). Findings from a more recent meta-analysis of 213 SEL programs found that participating students demonstrated significantly improved social and emotional skills, attitudes, behavior, and academic performance, reflecting an 11 percentile point gain in achievement compared to students in control groups (Durlak, Weissberg, Dymnicki, Taylor, & Shellinger, 2011).

Research in these varied domains has led to changing views of the nature of students' learning, and correspondingly it has prompted a move toward less authoritarian and more cooperative and proactive approaches for managing student behavior (Caine & Caine, 2011; Jennings & Greenberg, 2009). These approaches advocate establishing supportive and nurturing relationships, providing guidance and assertive limit setting, and using preventive strategies rather than controlling negative behaviors through coercive measures such as punishment (e.g., Brophy, 2006; Larrivee, 2009; Marzano et al., 2003; Noddings, 2005; Osher et al., 2007; Watson & Battistich, 2006).

Supportive Teacher-Student Relationships

Research also dispels common myths related to developing a supportive teacher-student relationship. One myth is that developing caring connections requires that the teacher show overt affection, yet the research indicates that teachers can also be firm and professionally detached and still be nurturing (Deiro, 1996; Ladson-Billings, 1995). Another misconception is that nurturing is associated with leniency and indulgence, even weakness, but those studying teachers who are able to make connections often describe teachers as strict disciplinarians.

Research findings substantiate a profile of effective classroom managers that includes developing caring personal relationships with students while simultaneously communicating clear and high expectations (Bondy, Ross, Gallingane, & Hambacher, 2007; Brown, 2003, 2004; Deiro, 1996; Delpit, 1995, 2003; Irvine, 2003; Ladson-Billings, 1995; Thompson, 2004; Ware, 2006). Such successful managers are assertive, yet compassionate disciplinarians. The strategies they use include the following:

- Setting definite boundaries while at the same time preserving respectful and caring connections
- Making their expectations explicit
- Using proactive strategies
- Providing the rationale for their rules and procedures
- Modeling desired behavior
- Redirecting students who fail to participate appropriately
- Avoiding power struggles
- Refraining from humiliating students

A number of these strategies are represented in Figure 6.2, including clarifying teacher expectations, providing rationales, asserting teacher needs by setting boundaries, inviting participation by redirecting students, and enlisting student cooperation by maintaining respectful and caring connections with their students.

What emerges as the critical variable is treating students with respect. Teachers do this by engaging in "respectful dialogue" with students, listening to students, showing interest in their students, soliciting their opinions, valuing their ideas, and demonstrating a belief that they are capable. It is crucial that students perceive the teacher as caring and that perception is created by a communication style that emanates respect.

Effective intervention strategies are nonpunitive, solution-oriented, and focused on problem solving, not fault finding. Such strategies include soliciting information, requesting help, providing options, negotiating plans, offering assistance, and mutually exploring solutions to students' problems. This perspective relies on much forethought and reflection on the part of teachers coupled with their own ability to self-regulate so they can provide the guidance and example students will need to also become self-regulating.

Developing students' capacity for self-regulation means that teachers will also need to become comfortable with a certain level of ambiguity and disorder that comes with allowing students more freedom to figure things out for themselves and learn from their mistakes. As is often the case with novice teachers, their first line of defense against feeling anxiety or discomfort is to reel in students with tighter control. Michie (2011) aptly captured his urge to control as a beginning teacher, remarking that "If my plans started to unravel, I resorted to demanding silence, surrendering to a misguided quest for control (p. 61)."

TEACHER REFLECTION AND CLASSROOM MANAGEMENT

A teacher's capacity for reflection is a key element for effective classroom management. Reflection involves questioning the goals, values, and assumptions that guide your work. With reflection comes a deeper understanding and insight, forming the basis for not only considering alternatives but also taking continuous action to improve your practice throughout your teaching career.

Reflective practitioners operate in a perpetual learning spiral in which dilemmas surface, constantly initiating a new cycle of planning, acting, observing, reflecting, and adapting (Larrivee, 2006a). Being a reflective practitioner means perpetually growing and expanding, opening up to a greater range of possible choices and responses to classroom situations.

A teacher needs to strike a balance between regulating student behavior to maintain an environment conducive to teaching and learning and potentially stifling student creativity, choice-making power, and problem-solving autonomy. Successfully managing today's classroom requires a teacher to remain fluid and able to move in many directions, rather than being stuck in automatic responses to situations. The reflective mindset for managing student behavior that poses a problem is one of recognizing that there are many ways to view a particular circumstance, situation, or event. When considering an intervention, teachers who reflect on their practice remain open to multiple pathways for solving behavior problems.

Being reflective frees you from routine and impulsive acts, enabling you to act in a more deliberative and intentional manner. When teaching becomes so habitual that it is tantamount to a mechanical act it can be the path to teacher burnout. Routine action is dictated by tradition and external authority. On the other hand, reflective practice entails willingly taking responsibility for considering personal actions.

Being a reflective practitioner allows you to move out of focusing on your dissatisfaction with what is happening now to concentrate on closing the gap between your current situation and what you would like to see. By focusing on your vision for the preferred future you can put your energy into narrowing the discrepancy between what *is* and what *could be*. In *Burned In* (Friedman & Reynolds, 2011), teachers tell their stories of how they fought past their despair to stay passionate and committed about their work. One teacher eloquently told how holding onto the vision that he could somehow close the gap between the sort of classroom he envisioned in his mind and the one he actually stepped into each morning eventually led him to become *burned-in* rather than *burned-out* (Michie, 2011).

Becoming a reflective practitioner involves coming to grips with feelings of frustration, anger, guilt, and disillusionment. It requires a journey into the deepest recesses, where both fears and hopes reside (Larrivee, 2010). Untangling and re-evaluating taken-for-granted, even cherished, practices requires breaking down well-entrenched myths that are not easily dislodged (Smyth, 1992). Working through difficult emotions is essential to becoming a reflective practitioner.

Two distinguishing characteristics of reflective practitioners are their capacity to discover the potential in a situation and their capacity for authenticity.

Repositioning Events, Situations, and Circumstances

When faced with a problem, teachers basically have two choices—change the situation or change their reaction to the situation. Teachers often can't change the situations they encounter, but they can change how they emotionally respond to cope more effectively. Teachers can learn to "reposition" classroom events and individual student behaviors by shifting their perspective to view the situation from a different angle or to include parts of the picture that weren't visible from their initial vantage point.

The term *reposition* connotes the idea of changing your perception by moving out of your old position and creating a new position from which to view a situation (Larrivee, 1996). It involves developing the ability to look at what's happening, withholding judgment, while simultaneously recognizing that the meaning you attribute to it is no more than your interpretation filtered through your cumulative experience. Repositioning is similar to the psychological term *reframing*, which signifies the notion of putting a situation in a new frame. While both reinterpret the situation, repositioning is somewhat different in that with repositioning you actually create a wider lens through which to "see" the situation. It is also similar to *cognitive reappraisal*, an emotion regulation strategy discussed in other chapters that is another way to "take a second look" to reassess your initial reaction.

It's your personal "positioning" that shapes how you attribute meaning to your experiences. Seeing new ways of interpreting a situation moves you beyond a limited perspective. By challenging yourself to create a new vantage point you can assign new meaning to the classroom situations you encounter. Breaking through familiar cycles necessitates a shift in ways of thinking, perceiving, and interpreting events. For example, if you reflect on your own past you can most likely find an event such as a job loss or the ending of a relationship that seemed truly horrible when you experienced it. However, as you look back now, you realize that it was a valuable turning point. In losing the job, it may have prompted you to reassess your interests and to move into a more satisfying job. Or, you might now realize that ending a relationship allowed you to develop another relationship that has been far more rewarding.

By repositioning a seemingly negative event, you seize the opportunity to discover the potential in a situation. When a student acts out, one teacher may see a personal attack, while another sees a cry for help. It is your interpretation of a student's behavior, or the meaning attached to the behavior, that determines how you will respond. In repositioning, you look for openings to extend and learn in any situation. When you reposition, you grasp the learning opportunity by attuning yourself to the more constructive potential in the situation.

Some helpful ways of repositioning in the classroom include the following (Larrivee, 2006b):

- Repositioning conflict as an opportunity for relationship building
- Repositioning confrontation as energy to be rechanneled
- Repositioning an attack as a cry for help
- Repositioning defiance as a request for communication
- Repositioning attention seeking as a plea for recognition

When dealing with challenging student behavior, repositioning calls for a change in your perception of the behavior, by making the shift in thinking from "This kid is a problem" to "This kid poses a problem for me to solve." Rather than trying to teach the kid a lesson for misbehaving, you actually do teach a lesson by using the problem situation as an opportunity to teach a new coping strategy. By using a problem-solving approach instead of just trying to stop the behavior, you work *with* rather than *against*

Personal Exercise: Repositioning

Activity Directions:

Step 1:   Think of a student who pushes you to your edge.

Step 2:   List all the things that student does that are a problem for you in the first column.

Step 3:   Select a word that describes your judgment of each behavior and put it in the second column.

Step 4:   Next, try to find something positive or more accepting about each behavior (this may be challenging for some behaviors). Place the word in the third column. Two examples are provided.

Behavior	Judgmental Label	Constructive Label
talks to peers	off-task	friendly
bullies others	hurtful	hurt
_____	_____	_____
_____	_____	_____
_____	_____	_____
_____	_____	_____
_____	_____	_____
_____	_____	_____
_____	_____	_____

Step 5:   Now, looking at just the words in your third column, what would you think about this student?

Reflective Question: What effect did deliberately repositioning have for you?

the student by seizing a teachable moment to show the student how to get what he or she wants in a more appropriate way.

Authenticity

Authenticity is an essential trait of reflective practitioners. First and foremost, authenticity comes from aligning with your integrity, both morally and emotionally. As discussed earlier, the term *authenticity* is used within the emotional labor literature to refer to the authentic expression of spontaneous and genuine emotions, and research has shown it is negatively related to burnout.

Interestingly, research indicates that authentic alignment between ethical conviction and action are at the core of professional fulfillment and efficacy (Gardner, Csikszentmihalyi, & Damon, 2001). In their book, *The Mindful Teacher*, MacDonald and Shirley (2009) identified authentic alignment when teachers' inner convictions and outer practices are in harmony, as an essential quality for teachers to act mindfully.

When you are authentic, you act with self-assurance, trusting your own capabilities so you don't need to use threats, gimmicks, or tricks to manage students. In effect, you manage yourself and the rest follows. As you become more aware of your beliefs and the assumptions that drive them, you become aware of the dissonance between what you say and what you do. With that awareness comes the capacity to become more authentic. Authenticity begins with being honest with yourself. This journey through your own fears, limitations, and assumptions is the gateway to becoming more authentic. Being authentic means not having to appear in control, or "look good."

Authentic teachers exude self-acceptance and self-confidence and likewise inspire these qualities in their students. Being authentic means being real. Teachers who are authentic do not act out assumed roles or roles others expect them to play. They know who they are and are clear about what they stand for. They have let down their masks and disguises. To use the colloquial expression, authentic teachers "walk their talk."

Authentic teachers share what's really going on with them. At the same time, they speak their truth without blame or judgment. They validate their right to the feelings they experience and respond honestly to students. They aren't afraid to be wrong, and they communicate to their students that it's okay for them also to make mistakes. When teachers are authentic they create a climate in which their students feel safe enough to be authentic as well.

Being authentic is acting without pretense. Brookfield (1995) describes authenticity as being alert to the voices inside your head that are not your own, the voices that have been deliberately implanted by outside interests rather than springing from your own experiences. Similarly, Palmer in *The Courage to Teach* described being authentic as learning to listen to one's *inner teacher* and develop the authority granted to people who author "their own words, their own actions, their own lives rather than playing a scripted role at great remove from their own hearts (1998, p. 33)."

Defensiveness is the opposite of authenticity. Authentic teachers do not deny their fears and have little to hide. In essence, they believe they have nothing to lose that is worth keeping. Authentic teachers exude a powerful sense of inner authority, or *natural* authority, and do not need to depend on others for their sense of well-being. They don't try to prove themselves. Authentic teachers affirm their right to choice and are not affected by the judgment of others, neither criticism nor praise.

Making Time for Reflection

Engaging in systematic reflection means making it an integral part of your daily practice. Making time for thoughtful consideration of your actions and critical inquiry into the impact of your own behavior keeps you alert to the consequences of your actions on students. Given the uncertainty every day brings, teachers need reflective time. Any effort to become a reflective practitioner involves negotiating feelings of insecurity, and even rejection. Taking solitary time helps you come to accept that such feelings are a natural part of the task of teaching. As you develop the capacity to be reflective, you see problems as natural occurrences and use them as opportunities to create better solutions. Keeping a reflective journal is one vehicle for ensuring time is set aside for daily reflection.

Journal Writing as a Reflective Process

Journal writing is a useful tool for systematic reflection. It allows you to become more aware of your contribution to the experiences you encounter. Journaling can provide the clarification necessary for you to gain, or regain, a sense of meaning and purposefulness in your teaching. Finding personal meaning is an important ingredient for preventing burnout.

Journals can be instrumental in helping you reduce daily stress. Making regular journal entries helps you remain clear and more aware of what is going on in both your inner and outer worlds. Most of all, a journal is a place where you can talk to yourself. The act of reviewing a journal over time can be a therapeutic tool.

Having a record of your thoughts, feelings, concerns, crises, and successes provides a window of the past and a gateway to the future. By making journal entries you can look more objectively at your behaviors in the classroom. When maintained over time, it can serve as a database offering both a historical perspective and information about patterns of thought and behavior (Moon, 2006).

Journals can serve several important purposes for teachers. They can provide a safe haven for:

- Dumping your daily frustrations
- Storing your private thoughts and feelings
- Working through internal conflicts
- Recording critical incidents
- Posing questions for deliberation
- Identifying cause-and-effect relationships to help solve problems
- Discovering patterns of unsuccessful strategies
- Acknowledging successes
- Tracing themes

ESTABLISHING THE CLASSROOM AS AN ARENA FOR RESPECTFUL DIALOGUE AND AUTHENTIC COMMUNICATION

To lead the kind of supportive, cooperative classroom called for by more proactive approaches to managing classrooms and solving discipline problems, teachers may need to develop new communication skills that significantly transform student-teacher interaction patterns. Such approaches rely on styles of teacher talk that encourage respectful and reciprocal dialogue. For some teachers, this may mean a fundamental

Personal Exercise: Daily Reflection

Activity Directions:

One way to build reflection into practice is to take some time at the end of the school day and before you go home to reflect on the day. Based on what is important to you and the values you want to uphold in your classroom, write a few personal daily reflection questions. For example, if you value respect, a question you may want to ask yourself is *Did I speak respectfully to all of my students?*

My daily reflection questions:

1. _____

2. _____

3. _____

Reflective Question: What can I do to build reflection time into my daily practice?

shift that replaces destructive words about the student with constructive words about what needs to happen. Carrying on "respectful dialogue" with students means talking *to* students rather than talking *at* students. The attributes of respectful dialogue are (1) reflection, (2) respect, (3) nonjudgment, (4) acceptance, (5) willingness to listen, and (6) vulnerability.

Traditional communication channels are one-way, involving the teacher giving praise or criticism, evaluating student work and behavior, and making value judgments. Such styles of teacher talk often invoke student defenses and create negative interchanges. When teacher responses are reactive, rather than proactive, they typically take the form of commanding, threatening, criticizing, blaming, labeling, or degrading. Or they may take more subtle forms of disrespect, such as moralizing, lecturing, diagnosing, or interrogating. These kinds of messages serve to block further productive communication, moving the interaction to confrontation, a battle of attack and counterattack. These styles of teacher talk inhibit, and often halt, the two-way process of communication that is essential for building and sustaining relationships with students.

Expressing dissatisfaction for either work performance or behavior can be done in a way that is punitive and disrespectful or in a way that is facilitative and respectful. As Arrien (1993) reminds us, the derivation of the word *respect* merges *spect*, meaning "look," and *re*, meaning "again," or "look again." In other words, as you take a second look, you see beyond what you saw at first glance to see "more of" the person. In essence, respect is acknowledging the whole person.

Developing the Art of Questioning

When teachers embrace respectful dialogue they invite two-way communication. One of the primary shifts to engage in respectful dialogue is from giving directives to soliciting student responses. This fundamentally translates into changing the communication dynamics from the teacher *telling* to the teacher *asking*. By posing strategic questions, teachers foster student self-reflection. When teachers try to help students extend their thinking about the issues, take into account others' perspectives, and consider alternatives with open-ended questions, they encourage student self-assessment.

Questions are important tools for helping students understand and change their behavior. Asking students what they were doing or how their behavior helped or hindered them is an important step in problem solving. It is preferable to ask questions to enlist student cooperation rather than make statements telling students what to do.

When students behave inappropriately, teachers frequently bombard them with questions, leaving them feeling intimidated and defensive. When the question creates a need for students to defend themselves, it redirects students away from taking responsibility for their own behavior.

Effective questioning is a particularly difficult skill to master. Much questioning is typically of a fact-finding nature, where the major purpose is to get the answers you're looking for. Because so many questions are of this type, a twinge of defensiveness is often experienced when hearing a question, even when it is innocent or a genuine request for information or action. Questioning can be either productive or it can be counterproductive to both problem solving and two-way communication.

Most questions aren't really questions at all. In fact, some linguists suggest that up to 90% of those sentences that end with a question mark are either requests for action, judgments, or statements of opinion disguised as questions (Bocchino, 1999). These are referred to as pseudo-questions. In our socialization process, we learn that questions are a more palatable way of stating a preference or making a request. Some examples of pseudo-questions are

- *Wouldn't it be better if you took that to your seat?* (request for action)
- *Do you really think you should be doing that now?* (judgment)
- *Don't you think you would improve your paper by making your argument stronger?* (opinion)

Other types of pseudo-questions include the following:

Appearing to give choices when there is really no choice: *Jason, could you do this for me?* (means do it)

Disguised solicitation of others' opinion where the real intent is to tell others what they should be doing: *Don't you think it would be better if you . . .?*

Sarcastic questions: *Are you done yet? Could we now get back to work?*

Cross-examining questions for the purpose of shooting holes in others' arguments, making them wrong, persuading them that you are right, or getting them to admit wrongdoing: *Didn't you realize what a problem you would cause? Don't you know what you did was wrong?*

One type of question to avoid is asking "why" questions. The word *why* establishes a mindset of disapproval—*Why didn't you . . .?, Why can't you . . .?, Why are you . . .?, Why do you have to . . .?* Consequently, "why" questions evoke the need to rationalize or defend. They are often character assassinations in disguise, just another form of blame and criticism. "Why" questions don't prompt self-reflection. Such hostile inquiries as the following don't really call for answers and are used primarily to make students feel guilty.

Why aren't you in your seat?
Why are you always the last one finished?

Questioning as an Inviting Communication

Consider the difference in the following two messages to students.

Why can't you ever find your work? versus *What could you do to keep better track of your work?*

An alternative line of questioning is not for the purpose of finding out who is wrong to dole out a fitting punishment; rather, it is an inviting communication based on the assumption that both or all parties are active participants in the problem-solving process. When questioning is used as an inviting communication, it is not a fault-finding mission. Here the questioning is not to incriminate; it is to explore and clarify.

When teachers skillfully ask questions it helps them get information they may need for clarification while also helping students gain a better understanding of the problems they face. Some examples are given below, followed by the response category in parentheses from the effective teacher response categories listed in Figure 6.2.

Do you think you would get what you want if you did that? (acknowledging student needs)
Would you like to leave the room for a few minutes? (providing options)

As an alternative to judgmental responses, calling on students to make their own judgments about their work and behavior allows new alternatives to surface and helps students become more autonomous (Glasser, 1986, 1998). Questions such as the following encourage students to take responsibility for their behavior.

What should you be doing now? versus *You should be paying attention, not talking.*
What could you do that would be more helpful to the group? versus *That isn't helping your group.*

Asking *what, when, where,* and *how* questions are more likely to help students gain insights that will help them clarify for themselves those factors that might be contributing to the problem situation.

How would you like this to turn out? (respecting student perspective)

How do you think Jack is feeling now? How would you feel if it were you? (soliciting information)
   What would make things better? (mutually exploring resolution)

An inviting question might also be structured to engage consideration of positive potential, such as:

What might be the best result you could hope for?

Thoughtful questions demonstrate a willingness to listen for the answer. The most effective questions empower students to think more clearly about the situation and discover new alternatives. Penetrating questions can actually help students learn to contemplate their own thinking process.

Communicating Authentically

Authentic communication is a thoughtful, purposeful, and deliberate way of relating to students. It requires that a teacher be willing to be vulnerable. Communicating authentically means there is congruence between your words and your feelings.

Constantly concealing your feelings and trying to act as if nothing bothers you can be as much a problem as expressing your feelings in inappropriate ways. As discussed in previous chapters, research shows that suppression, or inhibiting emotional expression, doesn't provide any real relief from negative emotions—it actually heightens the experience of negative emotions. Over time, suppression comes with the added cost of diminished positive relationships with others.

Personal Exercise: Analyzing Your Responses to Students

Activity Directions:

Step 1:   Use a tape recorder to record a class period or lesson about an hour long, or enlist an observer (e.g., peer, aide, student, parent, volunteer) to record every personal response you make to students.

Step 2:   Transfer the data to the worksheet below. You will probably need to make several copies of this worksheet to fit all of your data. First list every statement and question.

Step 3:   Classify each comment as either a statement (S) or a question (Q).

Step 4:   Now, classify each statement and question as either inviting or inhibiting to respectful dialogue and authentic communication. Some examples are provided.

Behavior	Statement or Question	Inviting or Inhibiting	
You should know better than to do that.	S		✓
It's time to put that away.	S	✓	
Why aren't you in your seat?	Q		✓
Where should you be now?	Q	✓	
_____	___	___	___
_____	___	___	___
_____	___	___	___
_____	___	___	___
_____	___	___	___
_____	___	___	___
_____	___	___	___
_____	___	___	___
_____	___	___	___
_____	___	___	___
_____	___	___	___
_____	___	___	___
_____	___	___	___
_____	___	___	___
_____	___	___	___
_____	___	___	___
_____	___	___	___

Step 5: Select one response you are especially pleased with. What was the effect of that response on the student?

Step 6: Select the response you are least satisfied with. What was the effect of that response on the student?

Step 7: Answer the following questions to analyze your data.

> In which category did most of your responses fall?
> What was your ratio of statements to questions?

Step 8: Based on your analysis of this data, what would you like to change about your responses?

Step 9: Set a specific goal to modify your response pattern.

Step 10: List the action steps you will need to take to change your responses to students. As with any exercise where you collect data on your own classroom behavior, significant changes will occur only with a long-term commitment. Continuous analyses over time, drawing comparisons and noting trends, are necessary if you are serious about changing any aspect of your behavior.

Trying to deny or suppress your feelings can also lead to "lingering resentment." Dealing with emotions as they emerge keeps lingering resentment from settling in to erode your relationship with students. On days when a nasty blowup is lurking just behind the surface, you are most likely harboring resentment charged by a harsh judgment of a student. When resentment is left to fester, eventually it can lead to rejection of a student—a far worse option than dealing with your anger when it happens. The goal is to authentically express an emotion, then let it go so that you can quickly move on.

In interviewing teachers who were at the most extreme low end of the emotional exhaustion dimension of burnout, researchers found that these teachers were able to genuinely express their true feelings (Carson et al., 2011). As an example, they quote one teacher as saying:

> I just address situations and then we move on. And I think the kids know that. If they cross the line they know I'm going to call them on it, but I'm not going to hold it over their heads and it's not going to be poison for me. It's done, we're past it, let's move on.

Teachers are human, and they have strong feelings about what is important to them. The way you interact with students tells them what you value. Expressing anger and disappointment about a cheating incident shows students the value you place on honesty and integrity. Expressing a deep concern when a student is picking on another student communicates that you value kindness and respect.

On the other hand, when you also call students unkind names or use sarcasm, they see the incongruence between what you expect from them and how you act. Responding to students "in kind" only serves to reinforce the very behaviors you are trying to eliminate in your students. Raising your voice to stop loud talking or being rude to students who are showing disrespect are examples.

Given the demands placed on both teachers and students, it is natural to get frustrated and angry at times. It is important not to deny either your own or your students' feelings. You need to express your anger directly with comments that address the problem situation without attacking students personally. Such messages address the situation that is creating the problem, acknowledge students' feelings, and express the teacher's anger appropriately.

When teachers experience negative emotions, they tend to communicate with students in ways that blame students for whatever is going on with them. Their comments focus on students' shortcomings, rather than a genuine expression of the feeling they are experiencing, such as,

> *I'm so angry I need to take some time to calm down before I talk to you*
> *Authentic communication also entails being proactive and confronting students' behavior by respectfully challenging them and calling on them to be accountable. The following are examples:*
> *I'm not comfortable with your tone of voice. I'd like you to start over and speak respectfully to me.*
> *I'm very upset because there was a fight on the playground at recess and I think you can handle conflicts without trying to hurt each other.*

Balancing Your Expression of Emotions

Although teachers may be aware of and sympathetic to students' feelings, they may not communicate that to students. It is also important to validate students' rights to express their feelings. Explicitly validating students' feelings can help build bridges to students whose behavior teachers find difficult and can be the starting point for changing ways of responding to students.

Some teachers find it easier to share their positive feelings with students but not their sadness, hurt, or frustration. Other teachers have no difficulty communicating such feelings, but seldom communicate their positive emotions and reactions to students. As a teacher, and as a human being, you tend to have a predisposition either to openly express more negative or positive emotions with your students. It is important to become aware of your predisposition for expressing either type of emotion more exclusively so that you can create more balance in your expression of emotions.

Proactively Confronting Students

Teachers are faced with many situations in which they need to be proactive and confront students. Responding assertively is an effective way to manage students' unproductive and inappropriate behavior. Assertion is standing up for your rights in ways that help ensure that others won't ignore or circumvent them. Responding assertively means stating your needs and wants without deriding, attacking, or making another person responsible for your reaction or feelings (Duckworth & Mercer, 2006). Being assertive means letting others know what you want, need, like, don't like, and how their behavior affects you (Bower & Bower, 2004).

Asserting your rights does not interfere with respecting the rights and needs of your students. Assertion is an honest expression of your thoughts and feelings without attributing blame. An assertive response expresses your needs and desires directly and nonjudgmentally. Assertive responses could take any of the forms in Table 6.1.

Table 6.1. 10 Ways to Respond Assertively

Assertive Response Category	Assertive Language
1. Express a need	*I need everyone in their seats now.*
2. Request a behavior change	*I'd like you to start your work now.*
3. State an intention	*I will give the directions as soon as everyone is quiet.*
4. Describe the impact	*When you call out the answer, it doesn't give everyone a chance to think.*
5. Take a stand	*You're not allowed to do that here.*
6. Refuse to do something	*I'm not willing to do that.*
7. Make your position clear	*I want you to know this is important to me.*
8. Express a feeling	*I get upset when I see that.*
9. Respect student perspective	*I can appreciate why you think that. I see it differently because I'm concerned about what could happen.*
10. Acknowledge student needs	*I see you need more time to finish, but I need to review for the test now.*

Below are three situations when student behavior typically causes a problem for a teacher and an assertive response is warranted.

When telling a student you don't like his or her behavior:

I don't want to see that again.
This is not the time for that.

When being interrupted:

I'd like to finish what I was saying.
Please wait until I'm done giving the directions.

Personal Exercise: Examining Your Language
When Confronting Students

Activity Directions:

Step 1:   For one week, collect a sample of your typical comments when you confront a student's behavior. Take time several times a day to record comments you made when confronting students.

Step 2:   At the end of the week, review your list of recorded comments and ask yourself these four questions.

Did my comment send a direct or implied message of blame?
Did I use sarcasm?
Did I merely describe the behavior, or did I use a label?
Did I clarify the impact the behavior had on me or others?

Step 3:   From your analysis, identify a response pattern you want to change.

Step 4:   Choose two or three of the assertive response categories you want to begin using, or use more often. List those categories.

Step 5:   During the next week try to be more mindful of your responses when confronting students by taking a short pause before responding to remind yourself of the preferred responses you want to use.

Step 6:   Response patterns are often so ingrained that it will take a more deliberate plan in order to change your responses. Develop a specific action plan for increasing your use of nonblameful, assertive language when you need to confront students.

When a student reads a magazine during a lesson:

I know that's really interesting, but it's time for math.
I need you to put that away now.

Reflective Questions to Ask Yourself

The following questions are helpful to consider when confronting students.

Did I avoid a direct or implied message of blame?
Did I refrain from using sarcasm?
Did I describe rather than label the behavior?
Did I clarify the impact the behavior had on me or others?

Choosing to Respond Rather Than React

When teachers recognize that managing student behavior begins with self-control, they can learn to avoid mere knee-jerk reactions to provoking student behavior. Teachers can't control how students act and react, but they can exercise control over their own actions and choose to *respond* rather than *react*.

No teacher enters the classroom with a symptom-free personal history, nor a perfect psychological fit that works equally well with all students whom he or she happens to be assigned. Each teacher's psychological makeup is better suited for dealing with some students, and necessarily not others (Long, 1996).

Teachers, like everyone else, are sensitive to, or self-conscious about, some aspect of their background, status, or image. Physical appearance, lack of content knowledge, computer illiteracy, and the need for acceptance are a few of the areas that may be a source of insecurity or concern for a teacher. Students are astute observers of teachers' reactions. Teachers often reveal much about themselves in how they react when their students find the right button to push.

Some students become very skillful at detecting what will "set you off," so you need to be aware of how students push your emotional buttons. Such students can provide the opportunity to put you to the test of examining your reasons for the way you respond. Awareness of your primary emotional triggers improves your chances of making rational decisions based on conscious choice, rather than unconscious emotional conditioning.

Long advocates that a teacher must be a *thermostat* (setting the temperature) instead of a *thermometer* (responding to the temperature), learning to cool down personal emotional reactions to keep conflict from escalating. As you become more aware of how students push your emotional buttons, you can do significant *damage control* when you respond in a calm, yet decisive, manner.

When your buttons are pushed, it is difficult to avert being sucked into mirroring a student's attacking behavior with your own counterattack. If you respond in kind, it gives momentum to the conflict cycle, making it very hard to interrupt. Once a conflict escalates into a power struggle, there are no winners. Even if the student loses the battle by the teacher dispensing punishment, the student wins the psychological battle.

The best hope for de-escalating an emotionally charged exchange lies in the teacher's ability to respond in a way that breaks the cycle. By pausing and choosing how they want to respond, teachers can refrain from sending blaming you-messages, such as the following.

Can't you ever use your head? What's wrong with you?

Receiving such a blaming message only serves to support the student's negative view of himself or herself and fuels the fire by creating more stress, leading to even more inappropriate behavior. When under stress, a plethora of emotions may be going on for the student—fear, feeling misunderstood, helplessness, anger. The teacher's response needs to avoid adding unnecessary stress to a student's already emotional vulnerability.

One alternative is to send an *authentic* message. When a teacher is upset about aggressive, hostile, or defiant student behavior, the message the teacher sends should be about the impact the student's behavior has on the teacher or others, not about the student's shortcomings, as in the following message:

I really get upset when you come into my room, kick stuff around, and yell in my face. I can see you're angry, but that kind of behavior doesn't help me understand why you're angry or make me want to help you.

From the student's perspective, he hears a statement about how bad he is in the first case and a statement about the teacher in the second case. When there is no character assassination and self-worth is not at stake, there is no need to become defensive.

Such an authentic response has the following benefits:

- Helps limit the teacher's impulse to retaliate
- Models exercising control over angry feelings while simultaneously acknowledging the teacher's right to express those feelings
- Keeps the communication channel open
- Substitutes destructive words about the student with constructive words about what needs to happen
- Puts the focus on what the student needs to do to regain control

When you consciously choose to express your anger by replacing destructive words about the student with honest words about why you are upset, it communicates respect for students' capacity to make appropriate adjustments on their own. By providing students with feedback about the impact of their behavior on you or others, you model a constructive outlet for expressing negative emotions. Long asserts that by taking ownership of negative feelings such as anger, frustration, and disdain, teachers are more likely to recognize the difference between *having feelings* and *being had* by their feelings.

In later chapters more strategies are provided to develop greater self-awareness for managing your emotions more effectively. Strategies are offered that will help you challenge and change destructive thought patterns and self-talk that fuel negative emotions.

Personal Exercise: What Pushes Your Buttons?

Activity Directions:

Step 1: Indicate which of the following behaviors frustrate you or make you angry by checking the appropriate box in the first column.

Step 2: Put those you identified in priority order in the second column of boxes.

Challenging you	☐ ☐	Not beginning work on time ☐ ☐
Talking back	☐ ☐	Sulking ☐ ☐
Disrupting the group	☐ ☐	Constantly asking questions ☐ ☐
Not following directions	☐ ☐	Taking others' things ☐ ☐
Bullying other students	☐ ☐	Always moving around ☐ ☐
Showing anger	☐ ☐	Demanding attention ☐ ☐

Step 3: For your top priority, consider why this behavior might be difficult for you. List reasons that come to mind for why this behavior causes you to react rather than respond.

In daily classroom life, a student's behavior can sometimes make a teacher uncomfortable, angry, or even furious. Such feelings are inevitable, so you have to learn to balance your own feelings and reactions with your responsibility to serve as a role model for your students. The challenge is to respond appropriately in spite of such feelings—not to deny or invalidate your feelings. Effectively communicating negative emotions can be an important teaching moment. Keep in mind that you are a coping model, not necessarily a mastery model. Mistakes are valuable learning tools, and these too can be openly shared with your students.

One of the greatest potential gifts you can bring to your students is to present yourself as a human being. A teacher does not forfeit respect in the eyes of students simply because he or she may have trouble managing a student's behavior in the classroom from time to time. On the contrary, loss of respect comes from ill-considered threats, futile commands, and shattered composure. Teachers who remain calm and objective, and obviously in full control of themselves, communicate resilience that their students can admire, even envy.

Using the intervention strategies discussed in this chapter will keep you from becoming emotionally exhausted, the core component of burnout. Having a repertoire of successful strategies sustains engagement with your students buffering against feelings of detachment, another key dimension of burnout. Feeling competent that you can respond effectively to the daily student challenges you face will help preserve your sense of self-efficacy, shielding you from the third component of burnout, a diminished sense of personal accomplishment. When you feel enthusiastic, engaged, and capable it limits your stress exposure and insulates you from the onset of burnout.

Being reflective, mindful, and authentic are important defenses against burnout. Challenging yourself to reposition seemingly negative events, perfecting the art of questioning, striving to make respectful and authentic communication the norm in your classroom, and when faced with challenging student behavior, consciously choosing to respond deliberately and purposefully rather than reacting automatically, pave the path to continual teacher renewal.

Chapter Seven

Modifying Destructive Ways of Thinking

Many believe it is your mental appraisal of events that determines your emotional tone, and hence your stress level. Beginning in the 1960s, cultivating the ability to monitor and regulate harmful thought patterns has been a predominant theme for managing distress (e.g., Beck, 1976, 2005; Ellis & Bernard, 1984; Ellis & Harper, 1961, 1975/1997; Harvey, 1988; Lazarus & Folkman, 1984; Meichenbaum, 1977). This position is represented in a broad range of interventions that fall within the realm of cognitive-behavioral therapy (CBT), which has a long history and a proven record of effectiveness.

A meta-analyses of studies on the effectiveness of CBT confirms its status as a valuable intervention (Butler, Chapman, Forman, & Beck, 2005). This analysis supported the effectiveness of CBT for treating depression, anxiety, social phobia, and post-traumatic stress, as well as for dealing with the stress created by chronic pain, marital discord, and anger. As a workplace intervention, a meta-analysis of effective interventions found cognitive-behavioral interventions had the most significant effects on work-related stress (Van der Klink, Blonk, Schene, & Van Dijk, 2001). Additionally, research on the brain reported in other chapters substantiates the intricate dance between thought patterns and emotional states.

CHALLENGING IRRATIONAL BELIEFS

Albert Ellis, a forefather of the self-help movement, and some consider the grandfather of CBT, developed a therapeutic approach based on the premise that it is not what others do to us, or what happens to us, that causes upset and stress. Rather, it is how we choose to interpret our life experiences, so in effect we cause our own distress. He first proposed what he labeled *rational emotive therapy* (RET) with coauthor Harper in *A Guide to Rational Living* published initially in 1961. Later in the second revised edition of 1997, he renamed the approach *rational emotive behavior therapy* (REBT) to emphasize that both our actions and our emotions are influenced by our irrational beliefs. As with CBT, there is a comprehensive body of literature spanning more than

50 years that supports the usefulness and value of REBT (David, Szentagotai, Eva, & Macavei, 2005).

Irrational Beliefs

According to REBT, many of our basic beliefs learned in childhood are actually irrational beliefs (Ellis, 1973). Irrational beliefs have no factual basis, are illogical, and are harmful to those holding them. The five defining attributes that distinguish rational beliefs from their irrational counterparts are shown in Table 7.1.

Much of our behavior is influenced by the way we feel, and our feelings are a product of our beliefs. When we hold an irrational belief, we are likely to behave in stress-producing ways because the irrational thinking leads to a negative emotional state (for example, anger, anxiety). An event triggers a counterproductive belief, often at an unconscious level, and strong emotions surface. Hence, our thoughts, feelings, and behaviors are interrelated, interactional, and codependent.

Our irrational beliefs develop early in life from a variety of sources (Ellis & Harper, 1975/1997). These include:

1. Our inability early in life to accurately distinguish real from imagined dangers
2. Our dependence as a child on the thinking of others
3. Biases and prejudices inculcated by our parents
4. Indoctrinations by the mass media of our culture

As a child grows, the child begins to incorporate a sublanguage that serves to attribute meaning to the events occurring in the child's life. This sublanguage eventually becomes the child's belief system, which develops as does language, primarily through modeling. The belief system of the significant person(s) in the child's life will largely determine whether the child thinks rationally or irrationally about the events in his or her life. If, for example, the child misbehaves and the parent(s) says, "You know better than to do that!" the child will most likely come to believe "It's bad to make a mistake, I am bad because I make mistakes and because I'm bad I should be punished." The more rational belief is that mistakes are a normal part of learning and life and that making a mistake doesn't make me bad. If I didn't learn this as a child, I am likely to continue to interpret my mistakes as intolerable. If I hold onto this belief,

Table 7.1. Rational and Irrational Beliefs

Rational Beliefs	Irrational Beliefs
Are reality based	Do not follow from reality
Can be supported by evidence	Are not supported by evidence
Lead to more constructive feelings (irritation, regret, concern, sadness)	Lead to stress-producing feelings (anger, guilt, anxiety, depression)
Are realistic assessments of a situation (inconvenient, frustrating)	Are extreme exaggerations of a situation (awful, terrible)
Are preferences, wants, or desires	Are demands placed on oneself, others, or life (*shoulds, musts, oughts*)

I will set unrealistic expectations for myself and others throughout my life unless I am able to reconstruct my belief.

These irrational beliefs typically continue to plague us throughout our adult lives. One of the most common irrational beliefs that can cause much stress is that people who harm us or commit misdeeds are bad individuals, and we should blame and punish them. We not only turn this severely critical thinking on others but also turn it on ourselves. A more rational alternative is that we can tell people directly what they are doing that has negative consequences for us, but we don't have to berate them or go as far as to try to punish them.

Although individuals express their irrational beliefs in personally distinctive ways, these beliefs tend to be some variation of three sets of demands (Bernard, 1988; Ellis & Harper, 1975/1997).

Demands about self: "I must do well and win approval or else I am an inadequate, horrible person." Putting these rigid demands on yourself results in feelings of insecurity. The more rational belief is "I will do my best. I don't want to make mistakes, but if I do I can stand it. It might be unfortunate, but it will not be awful."

Demands about others: "Others must treat me kindly and considerately and if they don't they should be blamed and punished." This belief results in feelings of anger and resentment. The more adaptive counterpart is "It's nice to have the approval of others. However, if I don't it will still be okay."

Demands about the world/life conditions: "Life must be easy for me, give me what I want without too much trouble or annoyance." This belief results in feelings of frustration leading to avoidance, self-pity, and inertia. The adaptive, more rational counterpart is "People are the way they are. I cannot change them, but I can change the way I react to them."

Most of us have a tendency to take our preferences for achievement, approval, comfort, and fairness and convert them into *musts*, *shoulds*, and *oughts*. For example, a teacher who prefers students to speak respectfully is likely to experience irritation or disappointment when confronted with swearing, but a teacher who demands that students *must* speak respectfully is likely to experience rage or low self-esteem, or both.

While there are literally hundreds of irrational beliefs that produce stress and cause emotional distress, there are 10 major and powerful irrational beliefs that prohibit people from dealing effectively with their lives. These irrational beliefs are included in Table 7.2.

When we hold more rational beliefs we tend to be more optimistic and hopeful. The life-enhancing beliefs that serve to reduce stress are included in Table 7.3. These are especially important for teachers whose work is inherently stressful.

CHANGING SELF-DEFEATING THOUGHTS

Although we often escalate our desires or wants into absolute *musts*, Ellis makes the important point that human beings also have the power of choice and the capacity to identify, challenge, and change irrational thinking. Learning to exercise control over your thoughts does not refer to some automatic process like switching a light on or

Table 7.2. Stress-Producing Irrational Beliefs

1. I must be loved and approved by all the people I find significant.
2. I must be thoroughly competent, adequate, and achieving.
3. When people act badly, I should blame them, and see them as bad, wicked, or rotten individuals.
4. I have to view things as awful, terrible, and catastrophic when things don't go my way.
5. My emotional misery is caused by events or people, and I have little ability to control my feelings.
6. If something seems unpleasant, dangerous, or fearsome, I must be preoccupied and continually upset over it.
7. It is easier to avoid facing many problems and responsibilities than undertake more rewarding forms of self-discipline.
8. Things that have happened in the past are all important and will continue to limit my possibilities for the future.
9. People and things should be different from what they are, and it is awful if I do not find good solutions to life's realities.
10. I can achieve maximum happiness by inaction or by passively enjoying myself.

off as if you can turn distressful thought patterns on and off. Rather, it is a process of redirecting the activity of the mind. Control in this sense means that you are aware of and then can exercise choices that affect your thinking. You learn to direct the mind away from patterns that create anxiety and stress toward patterns that lead to composure and coping.

Table 7.3. Stress-Reducing Rational Beliefs

1. Everybody doesn't have to love or like me. I don't need approval all the time. If people like me, that's great. If some people don't, I will still be a worthwhile person.
2. Making mistakes is something everyone does. I will accept mistakes I make and those others make.
3. I can accept things and people the way they are. Things will not always be the way I want them to be. I cannot control or change other people. I can only control and change my reactions to situations and to others.
4. I can't always get what I want. I can handle it even if things go wrong. Worrying is a drain on my energy and causes me stress.
5. Unhappiness and stress are caused by my reactions to circumstances, not the circumstances themselves. I am responsible for how I feel and for what I do. Nobody can make me feel a certain way. My reactions are mine.
6. There are many possible ways to solve a problem. There is no one way. Some ways may seem more sensible to me, but others have worthwhile, workable solutions, too.
7. In most cases, I don't need someone else to take care of my problems. I am capable. I can make good decisions for myself.
8. My past does not have to force me to be a certain way. Every day is a new beginning, and I can change.
9. I don't need to change other people or fix them. I can show concern and care, but I don't have to own others' problems or take away their responsibility to solve their own problems.
10. Avoiding a task that seems difficult does not provide me with an opportunity for success and satisfaction. It is important to try.

Because our actions are a manifestation of the feelings produced by what we think, the way to change a self-defeating behavior is to modify the irrational thinking that led to the behavior. The goal of REBT is not to eliminate all negative feelings; rather, it is to behave in ways that are more constructive and productive. If teachers can learn to accept reality and eliminate extreme, absolute evaluations, they can take a major step toward that goal.

According to Ellis, the irrational ideas we acquired in our early lives still continue to cause us distress largely because we both consciously and unconsciously perpetuate them. He believes most conditioning is self-conditioning. Acknowledging this self-creation and continued reinforcement is critical in the process of working to change your beliefs. For example, you have a choice whether to hold onto the belief that your parents were the source of all your troubles and still are, or alternatively, to acknowledge that your parents kept criticizing you during childhood and you still keep taking them too seriously and thereby continually keep upsetting yourself. Choosing the latter interpretation allows you to acknowledge that you still think poorly of yourself when they criticize you and consequently feel worthless. When you are able to acknowledge your self-reinforcement you can begin to move away from blaming your parents for something they did to you to cause your current behavior to taking responsibility, and you can begin to look within for change. Applying this kind of *cognitive mediation* allows you to restructure your thinking about your parents' behavior so that you are able to acknowledge that the problem was how you interpreted the behavior and what you did to yourself that caused and continues to cause a problem.

What Ellis has to say is just as useful in dealing with mentally sound individuals as it is for those with diagnosed psychological conditions because healthy individuals often *catastrophize* and talk to themselves irrationally. It is more a matter of degree or severity. This explains why a person becomes totally incapacitated (psychotic/mentally ill), or partially incapacitated (neurotic/emotionally disturbed), or occasionally incapacitated (bouts with tension headaches, occasional depression, stress, tension, anxiety).

Replacing destructive thought patterns with more constructive ones involves developing an awareness of those events and thoughts associated with negative feelings and resulting stress-producing behaviors. You first need to be in touch with your feelings, then reflect on the event or action that led to the feeling, before you can identify the thinking that mediated between the event and the feeling. Once you recognize your thinking patterns, the process of mental appraisal takes your automatic responses and brings them to awareness. By paying attention to your internal dialogue, you can identify your self-defeating thoughts.

Forman and colleagues have demonstrated that REBT can be effective in reducing teacher stress and anxiety (Forman, 1981, 1982; Sharp & Forman, 1985; Cecil & Forman, 1988). Gaining greater emotional and behavioral control first requires teachers to take a close look at how they experience classroom events. REBT is not an easy process because the irrational beliefs teachers apply for interpreting situations may have become unconscious after years of repeated activation.

Fundamentally, REBT attempts to show how we behave in self-defeating ways and how to change these ways. The ABC framework is a cornerstone of REBT (Ellis,

2001). At point A (Activating experience) an event happens accompanied by thoughts and feelings. At point B (Belief system), you process that information based on your belief system. Your self-talk at point B mediates between situation A and response C. The nature of your response (for example, rational, irrational, sane, crazy) is directly related to the self-talk you engage in about the situation. Point C (emotional and behavioral Consequence) is your emotional reaction and the action you take.

Below is an example of an activating event with three different sets of teacher beliefs and thoughts about the event, and the resulting emotional consequences.

Activating Event: It's the second week of school, and James just threw a book across the room. He has been out of his seat, running around the room, and he hasn't completed any of his work.

Teacher A: Self-defeating, internalizing beliefs and thoughts

1. This is terrible.
2. I'll never be able to control this kid.
3. He's going to destroy the entire class.
4. The other teachers are going to hear about this and think I'm incompetent.
5. They'll all be talking about me in the teachers' room.
6. I can't do anything right.

Emotional Consequence: Depressed, anxious

Teacher B: Stress-producing, externalizing beliefs and thoughts

1. This is awful.
2. What a little monster.
3. I shouldn't have to deal with this.
4. His parents should do something about his behavior.
5. By this time he should know how to act.
6. He's a hopeless case.

Emotional Consequence: Angry

Teacher C: Stress-reducing, problem-focused beliefs and thoughts

1. Looks like I have a problem here.
2. He doesn't seem to respond the way most other kids do.
3. Oh well, I know I'm not the only one with this type of classroom situation.
4. Since I don't like it I'll have to do something about it. Getting upset at myself or him isn't going to help.
5. He hasn't learned how to behave appropriately so I'm going to try to teach him.
6. I don't like this. If I want him to act differently I'll have to try a different approach.

Emotional consequence: Concerned, calm

As these examples clearly illustrate, turning the blame on yourself or the student triggers negative emotions that are stress producing, whereas taking a solution-oriented focus leads to a more productive emotional state. Using stress-reducing self-talk in challenging situations will take a lot of practice, especially if you have had years of practice distorting and magnifying situations, thinking irrationally, and blowing things way out of proportion; in short, making yourself crazy.

An expanded framework adds disputing thoughts (D) and the more effective result (E) shown in Table 7.4 (Ellis, Gordon, Neenan, & Palmer, 2003).

In this example, the teacher's self-talk is initially demanding that things be other than they are. This self-talk is stress producing and leads to a negative response. When the teacher recognizes the demanding thoughts and disputes them, more rational self-talk comes into play to mediate the teacher's reaction. The new response flows from a more constructive pattern of self-talk and reflects a more realistic and supportive appraisal.

The specific irrational beliefs commonly held by teachers that contribute to school-related stress are listed in Table 7.5 (Bernard & Joyce, 1984).

Irrational Teacher Beliefs Intensify Stress

When stress reactions begin, particularly anxiety or anger, it is likely that irrational beliefs with their corresponding self-defeating statements are playing a role. Irrational teacher beliefs operate proactively to exacerbate potential stressors in the teaching environment. Teachers with high needs for achievement and approval are more likely to experience emotional stress than teachers who hold fewer irrational beliefs (Bernard, 1988). Bernard's research indicates that teachers high in irrational beliefs experience more stress than those who are less irrational. Teachers who bring irrational beliefs to their teaching are likely to experience teaching demands as more emotionally stressful than those teachers who confront the same teaching stressors from a more rational perspective. This can become a vicious cycle—the more teachers experience strong, negative emotional arousal the more they will tend to think irrationally.

Personal Exercise: Replacing Irrational Self-Talk

Activity Directions:

Step 1:   In a few words or sentences, describe a stressful teaching situation you have recently experienced.

Step 2:   List your typical accompanying irrational self-talk statements.

Step 3:   Convert your irrational self-talk to rational self-talk statements you can try using the next time you face a similar situation.

Table 7.4. ABCDE Framework for REBT

A Activating Experience	B Belief System	C Emotional/Behavioral Consequence	D Disputing Thought	E The New Effect
What happens or takes place	Beliefs and interpretation of the experience	Feelings and actions	Detecting and disputing irrational beliefs	Revitalized thoughts, emotions, and behaviors based on rational coping statements to counter old irrational beliefs
		EXAMPLE OF A—> B —> C —> D —> E		
Student refuses to take seat.	Students have to do what I tell them. I must be in control at all times.	Get upset and make sarcastic comment, "Just take your time."	Students don't have to always do what I say. Maybe there's a reason he needs more time.	I'm going to take a deep breath and pause.
			I can't control what every student does all of the time.	

Table 7.5. Stress-Producing Irrational Beliefs Commonly Held by Teachers

1. I must have constant approval from students, other teachers, administrators, and parents.
2. Events in my classroom should always go exactly the way I want them to.
3. Schools should be fair.
4. Students should not be frustrated.
5. Students who misbehave deserve punishment.
6. There should be no discomfort or frustration at school.
7. Teachers always need a great deal of help from others to solve school-related problems.
8. Those who don't do well at school are worthless.
9. Students with a history of academic or behavioral problems will always have problems.
10. Students or other teachers can make me feel bad.
11. I can't stand to see children who have unhappy home lives.
12. I must be in total control of my class at all times.
13. I must find the perfect solution to all problems.
14. When children have problems, it's their parents' fault.
15. I must be a perfect teacher and never make mistakes.
16. It's easier to avoid problems at school than to face them.

Guarding Against Setting Unattainable Expectations

Using the ideas of REBT can provide a useful framework for anxiety-prone beginning teachers. Those just learning to teach are often operating from three of Ellis's major irrational beliefs (Manning & Payne, 1996):

- I have to be a perfect teacher.
- Everyone must think I'm doing a great job.
- My students have to change and behave exactly the way I want.

Clearly, such teachers' beliefs can cause serious problems. Teachers are much more likely to find teaching a more pleasant and successful experience if their belief systems become more rational. A more rational belief system would be supported by self-talk such as:

- No perfect teachers exist, and that includes me!
- Everyone will not approve of everything I do. I'm learning, so I'm supposed to receive some constructive criticism.
- These students are the way they are. They will only change when they see the need to do so.

Beginning teachers often set themselves up for failure by having irrational beliefs about their own performance in the classroom. For example, if a teacher thinks a classroom should run smoothly all the time without conflicts and snags, this kind of thinking can lead her to make unrealistic demands, both on herself and her students.

In addition to the anxiety created by the often unreasonable demands of today's classroom, a teacher's own dissatisfaction with self can add to feelings of helplessness. Sometimes teachers can't discriminate between the actual demands of teaching and their own self-imposed demands. As Ellis reminds us, making unrealistic demands couched in the language of *shoulds* and *musts* are the cause of much of our distress. Idealism and perfectionism can result in unreasonable and virtually unattainable expectations.

The pressure to conform to a picture of the perfect teacher lies at the root of much self-induced stress. A teacher's own limiting assumptions about a problem, or a student perceived as a problem, can undermine more productive behavior. For example, if a teacher believes "If I don't get this student to behave, it will be awful. I can't stand it when I can't get everyone to behave the way I want them to." This belief causes the teacher to magnify the importance of never making a mistake. The feelings that occur as a result of such *awfulizing*, as Ellis calls it, are most likely feelings of inadequacy and anxiety. The more rational and stress-reducing belief is "I am a human being, which means I will make mistakes. I'll do the best I can and if I make a mistake, I'll handle it and try to make amends." This is putting "mistake making" in its proper perspective. Behaviors following such self-talk are much more likely to be both productive and emotionally healthy.

Combating Commonly Held Limiting Teacher Beliefs

Some beliefs can be especially devastating for teachers to try to measure up to. When teachers set unattainable standards for themselves they are headed for disillusionment at the very least.

The following *I should* statements represent some commonly held limiting teaching beliefs.

I should like and care for all students equally.
I should have no biases or prejudices.

Personal Exercise: Confronting Limiting Beliefs

Activity Directions: For each of the eight limiting beliefs, write a corresponding belief that is more realistic and accepting of being human.

Limiting Belief   **Accepting Belief**

I should like and care for all students equally.
I should have no biases or prejudices.
I should be consistent in all my actions with
    students.
I should remain calm and collected at all times.
I should hide my true feelings and place students'
    feelings above mine.
I should be able to readily solve all problems.
I should cope with all situations without anxiety,
    stress, or conflict.
I should run my classroom so that there is no
    confusion, uncertainty, or chaos.

I should be consistent in all my actions with students.
I should remain calm and collected at all times.
I should hide my true feelings and place students' feelings above mine.
I should be able to readily solve all problems.
I should cope with all situations without anxiety, stress, or conflict.
I should run my classroom so that there is no confusion, uncertainty, or chaos.

STRATEGIES FOR DISPUTING AND REPLACING DESTRUCTIVE THOUGHT PATTERNS

Your irrational thinking spurs some negative emotions that cause a great deal of pain and discomfort and lead to self-defeating behavior that can immobilize you. In contrast, other negative emotions can motivate you to engage in self-enhancing behavior that mobilizes you to action. Table 7.6 shows some examples of emotions that tend to immobilize and their corresponding more constructive counterparts that can serve as catalysts for taking action.

For example, when you do something that goes against your own moral code, if your emotional response is one of guilt, you may just wallow in self-condemnation and become immobilized. However, if your emotional reaction is one of feeling remorse, you are more likely to be mobilized to take some action to compensate for your behavior, perhaps even try to seek restitution for what you may have done to another.

Cognitive Restructuring: A Strategy for Disputing Irrational Beliefs

Strategies earmarked for modifying beliefs are labeled *cognitive restructuring* based on the premise that our beliefs (cognitive structures) strongly influence both the way we think about something (cognitive processes) and our self-talk (inner language). Our thinking processes take form in our self-talk, which drives how we behave, and consequently, is the target for intervention.

Cognitive restructuring incorporates principles of REBT through four phases to help individuals:

1. Recognize that beliefs and ways of thinking mediate emotions
2. Recognize the irrationality of certain beliefs
3. Recognize that their own irrational thoughts mediate their own stressful emotions
4. Change their irrational thinking

Table 7.6. A Comparison of Immobilizing Emotions with Mobilizing Emotions

Situation	Immobilizing Emotion	Mobilizing Emotion
Faced with threat or danger	Anxiety	Concern
Faced with loss or failure	Depression	Sadness
Breaking of own moral code	Guilt	Remorse
Betrayal from other	Hurt	Disappointment

The path to rechannel your thoughts involves examining the filters through which you perceive your experiences, and disputing, altering, and acting against your familiar inner dialogue. Below is an example of using the process of disputing irrational beliefs.

Event: My friend didn't call to tell me he had gotten a job after months of being out of work. We had been in regular contact and had spent hours discussing options.
   My thinking: I was thinking he was inconsiderate.
   My self-talk: "How inconsiderate. He knows how concerned I am."
   My feeling: I was initially annoyed and then became angry about how *he* was treating *me*.

Personal Exercise: Challenging Irrational Thinking

Activity Directions: As a way of challenging your irrational thinking, go through the following steps to talk yourself through a situation.

Step 1:   Think of a recent situation in which you were upset. Briefly describe the situation.

Step 2:   Identify the thinking triggered by the event that caused you to be upset by reflecting on what you were thinking and saying to yourself when the event occurred.

   I was thinking:
   I was saying to myself:

Step 3:   Be aware of the feeling associated with your thinking at the time and ask yourself how your thoughts made you feel.

   I was feeling:
   My thoughts made me feel:

Step 4:   Explicitly dispute the irrational thinking by providing evidence that what you were thinking is not true by questioning whether your thinking was based on reality.

   Evidence to dispute irrational thinking:

Step 5:   Identify more productive thoughts to take the place of your irrational thoughts.

   More productive thoughts:

How my thoughts made me feel: My thoughts moved me from annoyance to anger.

Evidence to dispute irrational thinking: He's probably just totally self-absorbed right now and his sense of self-worth has been so eroded that he's doubting whether this new job is going to work out. He doesn't want to face the prospect of having to tell people he lost another job.

More productive thoughts: I'm happy that he found a job. I realize he was probably feeling so vulnerable that he couldn't think about anyone else.

One way to use cognitive restructuring for disputing irrational beliefs is to go through a series of self-questions. The following set of self-questions can be helpful to use in your classroom to determine if your thinking is rational or irrational. These questions can be especially beneficial for assessing your thinking when dealing with a student who poses a challenge for you. It might be useful to keep these questions on an index card in your desk drawer for easy reference.

You can discover what types of self-talk are creating and maintaining your emotional response by pausing to reflect on these questions.

Ask yourself . . .
Am I making rigid and inflexible demands of myself? of others? of life?
What *shoulds* am I telling myself?
Am I accepting what has happened, or am I denying reality?
Am I trying to understand some of the possible causes for the situation?
Am I telling myself that what happened is interesting, or am I engaging in *awfulizing* about it?
Am I projecting that this awful state will go on forever?
Am I believing that I, another person, or the situation itself can *never* change?
Am I describing myself or others as without value, totally unworthy of affection, empathy, or respect?

Then ask yourself . . .
Is my self-talk helping me to creatively solve this problem?
Is my self-talk being a good friend to me?
Is my self-talk helping me feel the way I would like to feel?

In translating Ellis's irrational beliefs for use with children, Roush (1984) identified categories of irrational thinking that can be just as useful for adults.

1. Robot thinking ("It's not my fault.")
2. "I Stink!" thinking ("It's all my fault.")
3. "You Stink!" thinking ("It's all your fault.")
4. Fairy Tale thinking ("That's not fair!")
5. Namby-Pamby thinking ("I can't stand it!")
6. Doomsday thinking ("Woe is me!")

Fairy Tale thinking of the vintage of "Oh what a wonderful place this would be if only I didn't have to deal with Marly" keeps a teacher in a fantasy land where "everyone is supposed to live happily ever after." This kind of thinking often plagues

Personal Exercise: Self-Questions for Disputing Irrational Beliefs

Activity Directions:

Step 1: Recall a recent situation when you felt a strong negative emotional response.

Step 2: With this situation in mind, go through the following set of questions to assess your irrational thinking and self-talk.

> Did you use any of the words—should, ought to, or have to?
> Did you project that this bad feeling would go on and on?
> Did you think of yourself, or someone else, as worthless?
> Did you try to look at your own actions or accept any responsibility?
> Did your thinking help you to take action to try to solve the problem, or did it immobilize you?

Step 3: Now answer the following reflective questions.

> Was your self-talk a friend or foe?
> What did you discover?
> What was your most important learning from this exercise?

teachers, leading to comments like "It's not fair that they put him in my class" or "I shouldn't have to deal with so many students with problems." This kind of thinking can immobilize teachers. If teachers keep bemoaning their plight, they may never take any action to improve the situation because they believe they *shouldn't* have to deal with it because *it's not fair*. Teachers who engage in Fairy Tale thinking often experience self-righteous anger, manifested in interaction patterns with students such as verbal abuse, getting in power struggles, and seeking retaliation.

"You Stink!" thinking is the kind of thinking that keeps teachers in a defense mode—always on guard to ward off impending attacks by others, especially students. Robot thinking leads to the faulty logic that if it's not my fault, then I don't have to look at my own actions or accept any responsibility.

Logical, Empirical, and Functional Self-Questioning for Challenging Irrational Thinking

Another cognitive restructuring process involves three forms of self-questioning for challenging irrational thinking. The first is to consider whether it is logical, second is to do a reality check, and third is to think about its usefulness. The idea is to talk yourself through the situation by moving progressively through the three types of arguments: logical, empirical, and functional.

To illustrate the process, consider Doomsday or "Woe is me!" thinking, the kind of irrational thinking in which you believe you deserve better than what life is giving you. Suppose you were about to go on a trip and got sick and had to cancel. So you're thinking, "Bad things *always* happen to me."

Logical Questioning: Is it logical?

Why should I think bad things only happen to me? Disappointments are part of life. They happen to everyone. Bad things happen to good people. It doesn't get me anywhere to wallow in self-pity about things over which I have little control.

Empirical Questioning: Is it consistent with reality?

Do only bad things happen to me? What are some of the good or positive things that have also happened to me over the last week?

Personal Exercise: Disputing Your Negative Thoughts

Activity Directions:

Step 1:   For this exercise you need a package of index cards. Begin with five index cards and use each one to write one of your typical negative thoughts. The idea is to capture your inner critic, that voice in your head that is skeptical of you, your students, and sometimes just about everything.

Step 2:   Shuffle your cards and pick one at random. Read it out loud.

Step 3:   Now, as fast as you can dispute it—out loud and with conviction. Bombard your negative thought with as many facts as you can muster.

Is it logical?
Does it represent reality?
What does this thinking do for me?

Step 4:   When you are satisfied that you have shot down your stress-producing negative thought, move on to the next card and repeat Steps 2 and 3 until you have gone through all five negative thoughts.

Step 5:   During the next week, whenever you catch a negative thought lurking in your mind, externalize it by adding it to your deck of cards.

Step 6:   Repeat this activity with each new negative thought you added to your deck.

Step 7:   If you find this activity useful, continue to add to your deck as you notice a negative thought. Each time you practice, randomly select five cards from your deck.

Functional Questioning: What results will it bring me?

What does expecting bad things to happen do for me? Does this kind of thinking make me feel better? Do I like feeling bad? Wouldn't I like to feel better? If I'm expecting something bad to happen all the time, I'll cut myself off from experiencing any joy in my life. If I change my thinking I might start to feel better.

Try disputing your negative thinking by doing the personal exercise. This strategy uses "rapid-fire facts" to help you become just as quick at disarming your negative thoughts as you are at generating your automatic negative thoughts. It is a cognitive-behavioral intervention adapted from *The Resilience Factor: Seven Essential Skills for Overcoming Life's Inevitable Obstacles* (Reivich & Shatte, 2003).

Many more strategies specifically targeting the way you talk to yourself are offered in the next chapter.

Chapter Eight

Changing the Way You Communicate with Yourself

The constant running commentary going on inside your head has the potential to either positively or negatively impact your mood, self-esteem, interpersonal relationships, stress level, and your health. Nearly every minute of your conscious life you are engaging in self-talk. As discussed in the previous chapter, at the heart of cognitive-behavioral interventions for modifying behavior is the belief that the kinds of things you say to yourself act as powerful mediators for your behavior.

If your self-talk is accurate and in touch with reality, you function well. If, on the other hand, your self-talk is exaggerated and out of touch with reality, you experience emotional upheaval and stress. Your emotional state depends on what you believe and tell yourself. When what you tell yourself is pessimistic, irrational, and hopeless you feel sad, miserable, and depressed.

CURBING STRESS-PRODUCING SELF-TALK

About 77% of our self-talk is negative (Helmstetter, 1990). This highly negatively skewed ratio of negative to positive self-talk means you have to be proactive in taking steps to "feed" yourself a higher quality of self-talk. If a majority of your self-talk is destructive, it certainly will have a disproportionately negative influence on you. You learn to accept a less than positive image of yourself. On the other hand, if your self-talk is rational, uncritical, and supportive, it promotes a healthier stance. When teachers have a positive, realistic, and accepting view of themselves, they are far more likely to respond to students and classroom situations in similar supportive and accepting ways, viewing their students as capable and responsible.

On average, teachers have 1,000 face-to-face interactions per day (Jackson, 1968). They are called on to make critical decisions approximately every two minutes (Clark & Peterson, 1986). Butler's (1991) clinical research indicates that individuals make approximately 50,000 self-talk utterances per day. Becoming aware of what you are telling yourself that leads to anxiety, stress, worry, or panic is the first step to making a conscious choice to talk to yourself in more helpful ways.

If you have a long history of flagellating yourself, it will take a determined effort, patience, and persistence to become aware of, and then to moderate, your self-talk. The quality of this inner language directly affects the quality of your life as well as the quality of your students' lives.

People tell themselves various sane and insane things. Beliefs and attitudes emerge in the form of self-talk—the realm of conscious interpretation. You talk to yourself around the clock, as you're driving, as you're doing the dishes, and as you're interacting with students. Often with a student who poses a problem, your self-talk is a negative running commentary about the student.

The repetitive stories you tell yourself about how things should be serve to perpetuate automatic ways of interpreting your experiences. Your mind is a realm of myths and movies, weaving your own tall tales. Although these stories are self-invented, nonetheless they serve the function of putting your immediate experiences into your past experience framework, continuously replaying the past. These stories in the background of your mind keep you locked in your judgments, assumptions, and interpretations.

Your self-created storylines can wreak havoc in the classroom, creating a mental picture of how things ought to be—stories such as "It's impossible to teach this class the way they behave" or "These kids just don't want to learn" or "I should be able to control all the students in my class." These stories provide the backdrop for the expectations you have for your classroom and can set you up for disillusionment, loss of vision, and ultimately, burnout.

Self-talk is learned from family imprinting and cultural conditioning. If self-talk is learned, then you can learn to use different self-talk. Your patterns of responding create a groove in your mind, making it difficult to take a different route. If you fail to break out of your groove, you stay trapped behaving automatically. If you change the way you communicate with yourself, you can change the stress level in your life.

Assumptions About Self-Talk

Embracing the following four guiding assumptions provides the foundation for addressing your specific patterns of self-talk and beginning to replace destructive and stress-producing thoughts with more constructive and health-enhancing thoughts (Harvey, 1988).

Four Guiding Assumptions About Self-Talk:

1. Only I can upset myself, and I do that with my self-talk.
2. My self-talk is learned, and I can learn to use different self-talk.
3. Although it may be difficult to change old patterns, with effort and persistence I can change these patterns.
4. Ultimately, I can learn to regulate the nature, intensity, and duration of my emotional responses.

If you change the way you communicate with yourself, you can change the stress level in your life. Your self-talk serves as a mediator between any situation and your response to that situation. Situations are actually neutral, and it is what you say to yourself about a situation that causes a positive or negative reaction (see Ellis & Harper, 1975/1997; Harvey, 1988; Witte, 1985). In other words, your inner language creates your reality. By learning to modify your self-talk you can regulate the amount of stress in your life.

TYPES OF STRESS-PRODUCING SELF-TALK
AND STRATEGIES FOR TRANSFORMING STRESS

Many have categorized types of self-talk that initiate, maintain, and intensify the negative emotions of stress (Beck, 1976; Butler, 1991; McKay, Davis, & Fanning, 2012; Ellis & Harper, 1975/1997; Witte, 1985). Of the many, there are six major categories: (1) making demands, (2) denial, (3) overreacting, (4) always/never thinking, (5) all-or-nothing thinking, and (6) mind-reading. The following sections describe these categories, the reasoning that supports them, and specific coping strategies to dispute each type of stress-producing self-talk.

Making Rigid Demands

One especially dysfunctional pattern of self-talk that leads to anxiety-producing thoughts typically takes the form of making unrealistic demands. These demands can be made of yourself, of others, or of life in general. When you apply these rigid demands to yourself by telling yourself you *must* succeed or you *shouldn't* make mistakes, this belief causes you to magnify the importance of never making a mistake. Putting these rigid demands on yourself leads to feelings of inadequacy, worthlessness, and insecurity, causing anxiety, tension, depression, migraine headaches, nervous stomach, and other such unhealthy manifestations.

Unrealistic demands are frequently couched in self-talk characterized by the words *should, must,* and *have to.* Phrasing your expectations in these terms creates rigid demands, and when these demands are not met, you experience upset. When you frame your expectations of others in terms of rigid demands, then you tell yourself that your colleagues *have to* respect you, your boss *must* treat you fairly, or your lover *should* understand you. When your demands are not met, you feel frustrated, hurt, resentful, and angry.

Desires and their ensuing attachments, embodied in the language of *shoulds, musts,* and *have-tos,* are at the root of emotional imbalance. The reality is, people behave the way they want to and not necessarily the way you want them to. When you make demands for how the world should treat you, you believe that bad things shouldn't happen to you. This belief leads to feelings of self-pity, often accompanied by low frustration tolerance, avoidance, and inertia. These dogmatic beliefs inevitably lead to emotional distress and to self-defeating behavior. They all result in forms of acute and chronic whining about your own or others' failings.

Holding unconditional expectations for yourself, others, or situations will keep you unfulfilled. Viewing life as awful when things do not go the way you would like them to go keeps you acting and feeling victimized. Having unreasonable expectations leads you to condemn yourself and others and to feel and act helpless.

Strategies for Dealing with Making Rigid Demands

1. *Recast your expectations as preferences.* Making rigid demands is probably the most difficult thinking style to overcome. If you can recast your expectations as preferences, you can become more accepting when you don't fulfill your own expectations. You can use this perspective to better cope with upsetting life events by having no expectations, only preferences. There's no guarantee that any of us will be spared life's trials. Accepting the possibility that such things can happen to you allows you to glean whatever value might come from life's difficulties and to more fully embrace life.

   The healthier alternative is to learn to temper your inner language to a language of preference rather than demand. When things go wrong, you can be unhappy, frustrated, or angry, but there is no need to make yourself miserable. Instead, ask yourself, "What can I do to change the situation?" and accept that sometimes the answer will be nothing. Then you need to ask yourself "What do I need to do to make things better?"

2. *Rephrase should statements.* Replace *shoulds, musts,* and *oughts* with wants, desires, and preferences. You engage in "demandingness" when you use demanding words when you do in fact have a choice. Such words as *must, have to, ought to, should,* and *shouldn't* connote that you have no choice. If the behavior is a must then you are accepting that you are compelled by forces beyond your control.

   Start paying attention to how often you use the word *should* in your self-talk. Most likely you will find it is quite often. Another strategy is when you can catch yourself saying *should* or *have to,* rephrase your statement beginning with *I will, I won't,* or *I'm choosing to* as appropriate for your message. For example, rather than telling yourself "I'm really pressed for time, but I have to visit my mom today," instead say, "I'm choosing not to visit my mom today. I'll bring her favorite dessert tomorrow when we can enjoy ourselves together because I won't feel so stressed."

3. *Refrain from rating yourself.* The idea here is to strive to eliminate all kinds of self-ratings (Ellis & Harper, 1975/1997). When you refrain from rating, evaluating, or judging yourself you develop a protective shield to keep others' evaluations of you from penetrating. Instead rate only your acts, deeds, and performances. Rate acts as "good" when they are self-enhancing and "bad" when they are self-defeating. Becoming detached from your evaluation of your level of performance is the essence of self-acceptance. While you might prefer to be more capable, have more, or achieve more, acknowledge and accept your imperfections, mistakes, and vulnerabilities. Don't try to prove yourself; instead strive to accept and appreciate yourself.

Denial

The second major category of stress-producing self-talk is denial, and it typically follows making rigid demands and compounds its effect. There are actually two aspects of denial: denying that something happened, and denying insight into the event. In the first case, your self-talk involves statements such as "I can't believe this is happening." Denying insight is more complex and is characterized by self-talk like "I can't understand why she would do that."

Strategies for Conquering Denial

1. *Accept what has happened.* Learning to cope more effectively involves asking yourself if the event happened and then trying to accept what has happened. The reasons why things happen or people react the way they do are often not readily apparent. It will take both time and persistence to unravel someone else's or even your own behavior. You can help yourself by accepting the fact that both you and others often behave in an impulsive or unconscious manner. Acknowledging this impulsiveness and automaticity can dramatically reduce excessive negative emotions.
2. *Do a reality check.* It is important to acknowledge the reality of the situation. Any attempt to change reality to the way you want it to be is futile. Trying to turn the clock back is a waste of time and emotional energy and prevents you from responding effectively.

   When the situation has already happened, it cannot be changed. Now, the challenge is to substitute honest preferences or desires by using phrases such as *I would prefer* or *I would like.* Saying "I would like you to lower your voice" is a request for a behavior change, whereas saying "You can't talk to me like that" is denial. So, for example, to say to a student "You know better than to do that" is futile because she has already done it, so it only serves to rile you up and create defensiveness in the student.
3. *Shift your mindset.* When you find yourself stuck perseverating with comments such as "I can't understand how anyone could act like that," you need to shift your fixed mindset to an open mindset. One way to do this is to intentionally pose the question, "What might make a reasonable person act this way?" This question creates the possibility of gaining insight, and moving forward.

Overreacting

Overreacting involves the way you evaluate things when your expectations are not met. Ellis refers to this tendency as *awfulizing* or *catastrophizing* (Ellis, 2001). Harvey uses a similar term, *horribilizing.* Another term used is *magnifying* (Davis, Eshelman, & McKay, 2008). When something contrary to your expectations occurs, you tell yourself, "It's horrible; I can't stand it." The event might be something relatively minor, such as a traffic jam, waiting in line, or criticism from a friend. Nevertheless, Harvey's research shows that if you continually flash the message in the cerebral cortex, "It's horrible," your autonomic nervous system and endocrine glands begin to respond as though the event is a true emergency. This happens because our inner physiology does not have direct sensory input; it relies on the decision making of our conscious mind. Therefore, whenever you overreact you also produce an excessive physical response with a resultant state of internal imbalance and stress.

Harvey offers the following analogy to illustrate this physiology.

> Imagine the body as a great fortress. On the top of the fortress is a watchtower and control room which represent the senses and the brain. Deep within the fort is an engine room, where all the heating, air-conditioning, and electrical generation equipment is housed. These systems are analogous to the body's regulation systems. The functioning of these systems depends on the information received and the decisions made in the control room. The engine room itself has no direct contact with the outside world and depends on the watchtower and control room in order to know when regulation is required.
>
> Now imagine a scenario where the person on duty in the watchtower continuously activates an emergency response for rather minor problems. If there is a slight draft, the heating system is brought up to a maximum level, and if the sun shines through one window the air-conditioning is turned up to its maximum. And anytime there is the least little threat, a general alarm is sounded. The resources of the fortress are being squandered by the tendency to overreact in the watchtower and control room.

An analogous situation occurs when you continually overreact to the ups and downs in your life. Your body's regulating systems depend on the decisions and cognitive evaluations made in the brain. These, in turn, are based on the words you use to interpret and appraise events. Words mobilize the systems of your body. Over time, through your life experiences and the modeling of others, words come to take on emotional meaning. You develop conditioned emotional responses. Words in the "watchtower of your mind" act to set off, maintain, and heighten negative emotions. These involve words such as *awful*, *terrible*, or *miserable*, and such phrases as, *I can't stand it*, *It tears me up*, *It kills me*, and *It breaks my heart*. These words and statements have a powerful emotional effect.

Strategies for Combating Overreacting

1. *Use time distancing: the "six-by-six" test.* Time has a great "dehorribilizing" effect. Something that was terribly upsetting years ago can often be viewed with greater equanimity now. Because you have more distance and a wider perspective on the issue you no longer label it as horrible. You can use the perspective of time to cope better with upsetting life events by using Harvey's "six-by-six" test. While in the throes of overreacting to some event, ask yourself how you might feel about it six years from now. Then, ask how you will feel in six months. You will likely realize that the event won't bother you much at all. Then continue to move the time frame closer to the present, asking the same question for six weeks, six days, six hours, and six minutes. Invariably the six-by-six procedure helps reduce negative emotions and stress as you find yourself using such coping self-talk as, "I may not like what has happened but I certainly can deal with it and know I'll get over it" or, "Even though I may be uncomfortable about my situation, I can be open to the potential for learning, positive change, and personal growth that it may bring."

2. *Use the bodily damage scale.* It is important to acknowledge that nothing is inherently good or bad—you assign a value to it. Another tool for combating overreacting or awfulizing is the bodily damage scale shown in Table 8.1 (Miller, 1986).

Table 8.1. The Bodily Damage Scale

Percentage Bad	Type of Injury
100	Death
90	Quadriplegic
80	Paraplegic
70	Broken jaw
60	Dislocated shoulder
50	Broken finger
40	Gash requiring stitches
30	Black eye
20	Contusion with swelling
10	Mosquito bite
0	Nothing

The idea here is that by comparing a negative event to physical injury you can assess your degree of upset proportionately to the bodily damage scale.

For example, when a student tells you to shut up, you can assess the degree of "badness" on the bodily damage scale by asking yourself "How bad is it?" You ask yourself, "How much physical pain would I be willing to trade to have prevented the student from saying shut up to me?" Few teachers would likely go any higher than about 10%. An individual teacher can create his/her own bodily damage scale aligned with any hierarchy of pain that makes personal sense (Maag, 2008).

3. *Put it in perspective.* Seligman (2011b) offers another way to minimize catastrophic thinking by considering worst-case, best-case, and most likely outcomes. Moving from the worst-case scenario to the best-case scenario, and finally to the most-likely scenario, you are able to take a more objective look at what has happened.

Always/Never Thinking

Self-talk in this category concerns your perspective on the future. You often project your emotional upset into the future and then reinforce this projection with the use of always-never self-talk. Because some negative event occurs now, you tell yourself it will always happen in the future. Because you have been rejected, made an error at work, or feel sad, you tell yourself that in the future you will always be rejected, make errors, or feel sad. When you feel alone and dissatisfied with yourself or when you fail to achieve your goals, you tell yourself that you will never feel fulfilled and that you will never achieve your goals. Such self-talk gives your nervous system a powerful yet contradictory message. On the one hand, you activate the nervous system because things aren't the way you demand they should be, but on the other hand, you shut down because you are convinced that there is nothing you can do. This is comparable to trying to drive away from danger by pushing the accelerator and brakes of a car simultaneously.

Strategies for Ridding Yourself of Always/Never Thinking

1. *Acknowledge the nature of emotions to change.* First, you need to understand the nature of emotions: unless reinforced by destructive self-talk, feelings tend to come and go rather quickly. In Eastern psychology, the changeable nature of emotions is well understood. Emotions are often compared to a river. If you stand calmly on the bank, you will notice that the river constantly changes. Even the mightiest of floods is followed by a return to a more moderate water level in time. It is the nature of emotions to change. If you can train yourself to observe your feelings rather than being obsessed with them, you can reestablish emotional balance sooner. Arrien (1993) refers to this as becoming the *fair witness*. If you can stand back and let the feelings pass rather than identifying with them you can cultivate healthy and realistic self-talk about your feelings. You can come to tell yourself that "this too shall pass." Then when confronted with a difficult situation or bad times, you can avoid projecting your plight into the interminable future.

2. *Regain a sense of control.* Another method for overcoming always/never thinking is to regain a personal sense of control in those areas where you can exercise some control. You can thoughtfully survey your situation and identify actions that you might take to begin to improve things. The key is to focus on small, manageable steps that can begin the process of improvement. It is remarkable how much better you can feel when you are taking some action to help yourself. And, of course, as soon as you begin to do something you are defeating the logic of always/never thinking. You can strengthen a sense of hope by looking back at your own life, recalling the times you have overcome obstacles and dealt with tragedies, and then, regain your strength to do the same in the present.

3. *Use the "double standard" technique.* This technique is based on the idea that when it comes to explaining adverse events, we are often much harder on ourselves than we would be on our friends (Burns, 1999). We operate on a double standard. We have realistic and fair standards that apply to others whom we care about, and we encourage them to take a balanced perspective to negative events. In contrast, we set unrealistic standards for ourselves. To use this technique, ask yourself, "Would I say this to a close friend or family member with a similar problem? If not, what would I say to him or her?" The idea is to give yourself the same encouraging, empathic message you would give a friend.

All-or-Nothing Thinking

With all-or-nothing thinking, you see some fault in yourself or others and generalize beyond it to create a global evaluation. The reasoning goes something like this: "Because I made a mistake on this job I am a totally incompetent person." The same thinking is also applied to others. Because they don't live up to your expectations they are bad, inconsiderate people. With this type of all-or-nothing thinking, one negative behavior is enough to taint your entire perception of the person. This type of thinking increases and maintains anger, frustration, disgust, and hopelessness. It impairs self-esteem and inhibits your ability to solve problems, look for alternative solutions, and be aware of your positive aspects and those of others (Ellis, 2004).

Overcoming this type of fallacious all-or-nothing thinking is crucial for reducing stress. Changing your self-talk will help you overcome the habit of all-or-nothing thinking and use your emotional energy in much more constructive ways.

Strategies for Overcoming All-or-Nothing Thinking

1. *Apply logic.* One strategy is to apply logic. It does not follow that because others do something you don't like, they are worthless or despicable. Such thinking is illogical because you are using one piece of evidence to create a whole picture. Even if there is one aspect of a situation or person that you don't like, there are likely to be many more that are positive and likeable. Remind yourself to distinguish between "the deed and the doer"—a single behavior does not define a person's total worthiness.
2. *Make a balanced appraisal.* No matter how significant the error you or someone else makes, you can't ignore a person's, or your own, basic value as a human being. Using a "broader lens" allows you to feel less anger. By keeping a balanced perspective, you can deal more effectively with the incident or problem at hand. By freeing yourself from the grasp of all-or-nothing thinking, you can observe your own problem behavior as interesting, become aware of its causes and effects, and consider ways to do things differently in the future. In a similar vein, if you can avoid such negative judgments of others, you can focus instead on their specific behaviors and ask for and negotiate change.
3. *Catch and cease pit bull thoughts.* This is the term McKay and Sutker (2007) use for condemning judgments of ourselves and others. They use this term because these kinds of thoughts grab hold of your mind and keep it in a tight grip of contempt, accusation, and blame. Because these kinds of judgments happen so quickly that you are often not even conscious of them, recognizing and labeling these thoughts can serve as the prompt to stop "villainizing" yourself or someone else. This is a way to turn a villain into a mere mortal, albeit with some flaws.

Mind-Reading

Mind-reading concerns your thoughts and beliefs about the opinions of others. This type of self-talk is labeled "mind-reading" because you believe you know exactly what others are thinking about you. There are actually two types of mind-reading. The first involves assumptions regarding what others are perceiving, and the second involves beliefs about how others are evaluating you. In the first case, you imagine that others are noticing every aspect of your current mental, emotional, and physical state. If, for example, you are feeling anxious, you "know" that others are aware of your nervousness, tension, pounding heart, and sweaty palms.

In the second type of mind-reading, you believe you know how others are evaluating you. If they perceive your anxiety, then they are thinking that you are a nervous and weak person. You make yourself even more upset when you believe that these negative evaluations are unchangeable.

Mind-reading adds to your stress in a number of ways. First, it leads you to generate a number of the previously discussed types of self-talk. For example, if you believe that others can see your anxiety and evaluate you as incompetent, you may engage in horribilizing. Or you may engage in always-never thinking believing that others will always see you as ineffective and that you will never be accepted. Mind-reading also promotes a kind of negative self-watching, in which you are constantly concerned about your performance. You fear the slightest error, as it may worsen others' opinions of you. Accordingly, you become much more self-conscious and tense when you are around others and more likely to make mistakes. Consequently, mind-reading can isolate you from others, contributing to your inner turmoil and stress level.

Strategies for Eliminating Mind-Reading

1. *Challenge your assumptions.* Challenge the assumption that others are really able to perceive your inner states. The fact is, your inner signals of distress are much louder and more apparent to you than to others. You can feel the pounding of your heart and the shakiness of your limbs, but these same signals are barely perceptible to others.
2. *Be open to gaining insight.* A second assumption to challenge is the belief that others are automatically thinking something negative about you. Believing that others are seeing you only in a negative manner can be a projection of your own doubts and insecurities. Of course, there are instances where others do evaluate you negatively. Then it is important to cultivate a healthy attitude that what others think is not really important. A study of the lives of great and effective people reveals that they always had critics. You also need to remind yourself that people's opinions can change in surprising ways. Time and circumstance can bring the bitterest of enemies into close friendships.
3. *Look for the learning.* It is simply not healthy or logical to become too worried about the evaluations of others. At times you can gain valuable feedback and insight by listening to others, even if they do express a negative opinion. When you look for the learning, you can often gain something from the experience.

Learning to Modify Your Self-Talk

To become more adept at recognizing and then revising your self-talk during the often hectic flow of daily classroom life will require practice. A systematic procedure you can use to gain experience and skill in revising distressing self-talk is described in this section.

To begin rethinking your self-talk you need to remind yourself that when something happens to you, it is the way you assess the experience that determines your emotional reaction. If your thinking and assessment are automatic, you will have a stressful emotional response. If your thinking and assessment process is driven by more conscious self-talk you will have a more moderate emotional response, resulting in less stress.

Over time, these strategies for restructuring your responses to stressful situations work in three ways. They reduce the frequency and intensity of negative emotional

Personal Exercise: Examining the Quality of Your Daily Self-Talk

Activity Directions:

Step 1:   For one week, do the following two times per day:
a. Briefly describe an episode in which you experienced some upset.
b. Next, list statements and questions you said to yourself during and after this episode. One way to do this is to talk into your cell phone to record your self-talk. Most cell phones today have voice-activated apps that allow you to record messages to yourself.

Step 2:   At the end of the week:
a. Transcribe your self-talk word for word, categorizing it as either helpful or unhelpful.
b. Examine your unhelpful self-talk and categorize each as one of the six stress-producing categories discussed.
c. List your most common types of unhelpful self-talk.

Step 3:   For the coming week:
a. Choose one of your most common types of unhelpful self-talk.
b. Select one of the three strategies presented you think will be most helpful to begin talking to yourself in a more supportive way.
c. Use this strategy whenever you catch yourself using stress-producing self-talk.

Step 4:   You may want to continue this process for all of your identified types of unhelpful self-talk.

reactions, they turn off negative emotional reactions more quickly, and, eventually, they prevent them from occurring in the first place.

An example of both patterns of self-talk is shown in Figure 8.1.

The types of self-talk are categorized according to the six major categories described earlier. The emotional response is divided into the components of feelings, physiological changes, and behaviors. The feelings are rated on a Subjective Units of Distress Scale (SUDS) of 1–10, with 10 indicating the highest possible intensity.

In the top half of the figure are automatic stress-producing types of self-talk. In the bottom half, the types of self-talk are revised according to the perspectives described in the previous section. Thus, the emotional response is considerably moderated, the degree of stress is reduced, and the behavioral response is more likely to solve problems rather than to accentuate them.

An important point to make in this example is the individuality of your emotional patterns. Each person viewing this example will likely notice that certain types of

	Making Demands	Denial	Over-reaction	Always/ Never	All/ Nothing	Mind-reading	Response (Automatic)
Stress-producing Types of Self-talk	The principal shouldn't have fired me. He should have been more under-standing. He should know I have been trying to do my best. I should have handled the job better. I shouldn't have made any mistakes. Things like this just shouldn't happen.	I can't believe this happened. I can't understand why he fired me. How could I let something like this happen to me?	This is terrible. I can't handle it. It's awful. This is ruining me. It's killing me.	I'll never get another job. I'll never be able to hold a job. I'll always be a failure. I'll always feel this depressed and angry. I always make mistakes. I can never handle difficult situations.	I'm a real loser. I'm a total failure. I'm good for nothing My career is destroyed. The principal is a total jerk.	People can see how bad I feel. My neighbors think I'm a failure and they will put me down. All the people at work are bad-mouthing me. Everyone thinks I'm incompetent.	**Feelings*** Anger 9 Disgust 8 Frustration 8 Sadness 9 Hopelessness 9 **Physiology** Heart racing, diarrhea, mind racing, breath short, stomach in knots, neck hurts **Behavior** Yell at family. Avoid friends. Drink too much. Watch too much TV. Sleep a lot.
	Stating Preferences	**Acceptance**	**Perspective Setting**	**Objective Assessment**	**Balanced Appraisal**	**Challenging Assumptions**	**Response (Moderated)**
Stress-reducing Types of Self-talk	I prefer not to be fired. I would have liked the principal to be more under-standing. I'd like to have handled the job better. It would be nice if things like this didn't happen, but they do.	Did it happen? Yes, so I must accept that it has happened. The principal must have had some reason for firing me. Perhaps I do need to improve and maybe I can understand that.	This is unfortunate and certainly inconvenient but I can handle it even if I don't like it. Maybe there is even an opportunity for a positive outcome. Perhaps I can learn something from this situation. I might even find a better job. How will I feel about this in 6 years?	This too shall pass. My negative feelings will subside. Just because I may have done some-thing wrong on this job doesn't mean I'll always do things wrong. Let me think about what I can do to improve things from this point on. I'll focus on small manageable steps I can take.	I'm a fallible human being. I may make mistakes but this is just one thing and there are many things I do well. Essentially I'm OK. While this may be a setback, it doesn't mean my career is over. In fact, things might get better. Even though the principal fired me, I don't have to make him despicable. I can focus my energy in a more con-structive way.	I don't know for sure what others are thinking. If I want to know I can ask. Actually, they may be sympathetic or even indifferent, concerned with their own affairs. In any event, it doesn't matter, because others' opinions don't change who I am.	**Feelings*** Anger 3 Disgust 2 Frustration 2 Sadness 4 Hopelessness 1 **Physiology** Slight headache, some fatigue, unsettled stomach **Behavior** Initiate systematic job search. Start exercise program. Catch up on household projects. Evaluate work values and priorities.

*Subjective Units of Distress Scale (SUDS) 1-10

Figure 8.1. Types of Self-Talk for Being Fired from Teaching Job

self-talk are quite familiar and recognizable, while others are not. Recognizing your own individual response pattern will help you identify your particular sensitive areas.

This format can be used as a personal worksheet to examine a given emotional response and then to modify it. Doing this exercise will benefit you in at least three ways.

- First, it will help you to cope more effectively with a specific event.
- Second, it illustrates the experience of "witnessing" or observing your thought patterns so that you can then choose more helpful ones.
- Third, when you practice this written exercise several times, you will become more proficient in monitoring and changing your self-talk on an ongoing basis. In time, you will be able to notice your excessive negative reactions sooner, recognize your stress-producing self-talk, and switch to more helpful self-talk in the moment.

To do the following personal exercise, you need to identify an emotionally upsetting event that happened to you, such as a serious argument, a mistake at work, or someone failing to fulfill a promise. The more recent the event and the stronger your feelings about it, the better target it is for successful revision. Two separate worksheets are provided for this exercise in Figure 8.2 and 8.3.

Try to get yourself into a witnessing mode where you can to some extent observe your thinking and feeling responses. If you are feeling very emotional about the event, slow down your breathing and consciously relax. It is important to reduce the internal noise and distraction of a strong emotional response so that you can engage in constructive self-reflection.

As a general guideline in rating your feelings, you can consider that a rating of 6 or above represents the type of emotional response that creates stress. If you rate your feelings at an intensity of 4 or 5 it indicates you are coping to some degree. If the intensity level is at 3 or below you are coping fairly well, and you probably don't need to revise your self-talk.

The crucial point is that by changing your self-talk you can create a healthier and more constructive emotional response. Revising your self-talk is a very effective way to reduce the stress resulting from excessive emotional responding. The resultant healthy thinking is a skill that you will become better at the more you practice. This written exercise provides good practice. If you do this exercise several times, you will become more proficient at changing your self-talk on an ongoing basis. Over time, as you become aware of a stress-producing emotional reaction you will be able to more quickly revise your self-talk.

As you gain experience in analyzing your self-talk, you may notice that certain patterns seem to come up again and again. For example, you may find that you continually get caught up in over-reacting to events and then feel tense and anxious. Or, you may notice a tendency to engage in always-never thinking and find yourself feeling depressed and hopeless. We are all predisposed toward certain self-talk and the resulting emotional response.

Making Demands	Denial	Over-reaction	Always/ Never	All/ Nothing	Mind-reading	Response (Automatic)
						Feelings
						Physiology
						Behavior

Figure 8.2. Worksheet for Categorizing Stress-Producing Types of Self-Talk

Stating Preferences	Acceptance	Perspective Setting	Objective Assessment	Balanced Appraisal	Challenging Assumptions	Response (Moderated)
						Feelings
						Physiology
						Behavior

Figure 8.3.   Worksheet for Categorizing Stress-Reducing Types of Self-Talk

Personal Exercise: Changing Self-Talk

Activity Directions:

Step 1: First, decide on an emotionally upsetting event. If you are still feeling very emotional, breathe slowly and deeply to relax.

Step 2: Begin with the Worksheet for Categorizing Stress-Producing Types of Self-Talk. Once you have calmed yourself to the point where you can observe what is happening internally, describe your emotional response in the upper-right-hand column. Consider all three components of your emotional response—feelings, physiology, and behavior. First, list your feelings. If you are not sure what your feelings are, close your eyes and allow yourself to sense your spontaneous response to the event. Do you want to fight someone, or do you want to run away? Do you feel sickened, or do you want to cry? Such urges relate to the feelings of anger, fear, disgust, and sadness, respectively. Don't be surprised if there are a number of feelings. Most emotional responses are, in fact, a blend of feelings. In some cases there are layers of feelings. You may notice anger and then beneath that, hurt, and finally, sadness. Whatever feelings you have, they are yours and they provide valuable information in the process of self-reflection. Once you have established and identified your feelings, rate them according to intensity on a 1–10 scale.

Step 3: Now examine your physiological response. What is going on with your muscles? Do you notice patterns of tightening anywhere in your body? Do you feel your heart beating more rapidly, or is your stomach tied in knots? List all of the physical reactions of your emotional response.

Step 4: Next examine your behavioral response. What did you do in response to the event? Did you yell at someone or freeze up? Now you are ready to work with the six columns to identify your types of thoughts and beliefs.

Step 5: Review the descriptions for each category of stress-producing self-talk: (1) demands, (2) denial, (3) overreaction, (4) always-never thinking, (5) all-or-nothing thinking, and (6) mind reading.
- In the first column, list the rigid and inflexible demands that you are making of yourself, of others, and of life in general. Be aware of your thinking and see what kind of "shoulds" are setting off your response.
- In column two, examine the issue of denial. Are you accepting what has occurred? Can you begin to understand some of the possible causes for the event?
- In the third column, examine your reaction to the event. Are you telling yourself that the event is interesting, or are you engaging in overreacting and horribilizing about it?

- As you consider the fourth column, listen to the always-never thinking that may be going on inside your head. Are you projecting that this horrible state will always exist? Do you believe that you, another person, or the situation itself can never change?
- Move on to the fifth column and become aware of any all-or-nothing thinking. Are you describing either yourself or others as without value, totally unworthy of love, respect, or affection?
- Finally, in the last column, look for your patterns of mind-reading. Write down any attributions you are making regarding the perceptions of others or any negative evaluations that you believe others are formulating about you.

Step 6:   Now that you have filled in all the columns you have a good sense of the kinds of beliefs and self-talk that have created your stress-producing emotional response. Now you can begin to revise your self-talk to modify your emotional response. On the Worksheet for Categorizing Stress-Reducing Types of Self-Talk, work your way across the six categories, revising the old self-talk and writing new, more productive alternatives.
- In the demands column, restate your demands into more flexible wants and preferences.
- In the denial column, accept what has happened and begin to develop some insight.
- In the overreaction column, begin to formulate more realistic and accurate evaluations of the event.
- For your always-never thinking, create a more objective picture of future developments and note what you can do to start making things better right now.
- For your all-or-nothing thinking, replace global evaluations of yourself, others, and the situation and look for positive attributes that can be built on.
- In the mind-reading column compose more realistic self-talk about the perceptions and thoughts of others.

Step 7:   When you have written down the new self-talk statements in all six categories, read them over several times. At first they may seem quite different and hard to accept compared to your habitual, stress-producing self-talk that you have grown accustomed to repeating to yourself.

Step 8:   Using these new self-talk statements to evaluate the event, move on to the emotional response column. List your feelings and rate their intensity. Write down your physiological reactions and behavior. It is likely that you will notice a significant change in your emotional response. Strong negative feelings may well be reduced in intensity or disappear altogether. More adaptive feelings may arise, such as concern and interest instead of fear and anxiety. Physiological reactions may be much milder, and you may feel inclined to actions that will solve problems rather than create them.

CONVERTING OVERBEARING JUDGES TO REALISTIC GUIDES

In discussing the kinds of self-talk we use, Butler (2008) notes that we often use overbearing Judges rather than realistic Guides. She has developed a procedure for changing these Judges into a language of support that begins with developing an awareness of how we are driving, stopping, and confusing ourselves with our self-talk. The three categories of Judges are labeled Drivers, Stoppers, and Confusers. She advocates learning to replace your unhelpful Judges with Permitters to support learning to talk to yourself in a healthier and more facilitative way. Manning and Payne (1996) found that teachers who learned to counter their Judges with Permitters reported self-satisfaction that carried over into a more relaxed classroom.

A description of the three Judges along with Permitter self-talk for combating each of the Judges is provided in Table 8.2.

Learning the Language of Self-Support

To learn the language of self-support, Butler recommends a five-step process, each with an accompanying self-question.

Step 1:	Become aware and listen to what you are saying to yourself.
Self-Question:	*What am I telling myself?*
Step 2:	Evaluate whether your self-talk is supportive or destructive.
Self-Question:	*Is my self-talk helping me?*
	If not, then ask: *How can I change it so that it is healthier for me and for those around me?*
Step 3:	Identify what Driver, Stopper, or Confuser messages are maintaining your self-talk.
Self-Question:	*What types of messages are maintaining my self-talk?*
Step 4:	Support yourself by replacing your judging self-talk with permission and self-support.
Self-Question:	*What permission and self-support will I give myself?*
Step 5:	Develop your Guide and decide on an action plan that fits with your new supportive position.
Self-Question:	*What action will I take given my new supportive position?*

Awareness is the first step to break out of an unhelpful self-talk cycle. You can begin by keeping an accurate record of just how often your unhelpful self-talk occurs. There are certain cues that may signal unhelpful self-talk, such as feeling anxious or depressed, physical symptoms such as a fluttery stomach, sweaty palms, or tension headache, or avoidance thoughts or behaviors. External events such as receiving criticism or beginning a difficult project may evoke unhelpful self-talk. When you begin to notice the presence of unhelpful self-talk, interrupt your self-critical tirade with the firm statement, "Stop! This is not helping to talk to myself this way. Would I talk to a good friend this way?"

Step 2 begins the evaluation phase. As you answer for yourself whether your self-talk is helping and realize that it is not, then you can begin to disengage from it. You

Table 8.2   Drivers, Stoppers, and Confusers with Combating Permitter Self-Talk

DRIVERS: The unrealistic, relentless internal push to "get busy," "do it right," or "be strong."

Be Perfect	Pushes you constantly to perform at unreasonable levels. This type of judgmental thinking limits you to 100% or nothing. All or nothing attitude: *If I can't teach this perfectly, I won't try at all.*
Hurry Up	Pushes you to do everything quickly. This kind of thinking is one of the major contributors to Type A behavior: *I better hurry because all the other teachers are ahead of me in this book.*
Be Strong	Regards any need as a weakness to be overcome. Feelings of loneliness, sadness, or hurt are intolerable. Prevents you from asking for needed help: *I'm a new teacher. If I ask too many questions, they'll think I don't know what I'm doing.*
Please Others	Involves an intense fear of rejection, regardless of whether the disapproving person is important to you. You lose sight of your own feelings: *These students won't like me if I am too demanding. They have to like me.*
Try Hard	Impervious to the setting of appropriate limits for yourself. Taking on more and more responsibility without considering your own limitations. The inability to say no: *I have to be responsible, so I better agree to be on the new committee, too.*

Below are the permitter self-talk statements to combat unrealistic Driver self-talk.

PERMITTERS for Combating Driver Self-Talk

Driver	Permitter Self-Talk
Be Perfect	There are no perfect human beings. Why do I keep trying to be a perfect teacher? Being my best and accepting mistakes is a healthier way to teach.
Hurry Up	It's okay to take the time these students and I need. We will learn well what we are learning instead of trying to finish the book.
Be Strong	It's okay to have feelings and to express them. It is acceptable if I feel sad about where some of my students have to sleep at night.
Please Others	Pleasing others is rewarding, but it becomes a problem if I lose sight of my own feelings in exchange. I can please myself, too. I will lose who I am if I do not acknowledge my needs.
Try Hard	It's okay to recognize my own limits. I can give my responsibilities enough time and energy to succeed.

STOPPERS: Limiting messages that tell you "no," "don't," "only if." They interfere with your spontaneous self-expression. The stoppers keep you from asserting yourself.

Catastrophizing	Verbally rehearsing horrible events that might occur if you were to engage in certain behaviors. You exaggerate the risk of engaging in that behavior so much that you decide to do nothing: *If we go on field trips, the bus may break down, or the students may get unruly, or we may get too far behind in our other work.*
Negative Self-Labeling	Attaching arbitrary judgments to natural, healthy impulses: *I'd really like to tell my principal how much I appreciate all that she does, but she might think I'm trying to get something, so I won't.*
Rigid Requirements	Imposing a set of conditions that must occur before an action can take place. Usually begins with the word *if: If everyone will approve of my suggestion, then I'll speak out at our next faculty meeting.*

Table 8.2 *(Continued)*

Witch Messages	Restraining yourself with the word "Don't." Some examples are "don't change," "don't be yourself," "don't complain," "don't be different": *Don't complain because we aren't told ahead of time about afternoon faculty meetings.*

Below are the permitter self-talk statements to combat your Stopper self talk.

PERMITTERS for Combating Stopper Self-Talk

Stopper	Permitter Self-Talk
Catastrophizing	So what if? So what if the bus breaks down. They'll just send another one to take us. It might not be so pleasant but it won't be catastrophic, or even awful.
Negative Self-Labeling	Many good acts of mine are squelched because I call myself or my behavior bad names. When I start this again, I'll just ignore it!
Rigid Requirements	These *ifs* keep limiting my alternatives and block my feelings and behaviors. Next time I hear a rigid *if* I'll just go beyond it!
Witch Messages	I can assert my right to listen to and honor all aspects of myself.

CONFUSERS: Using confuser self-talk distorts your own reality. This kind of self-talk, like the other two, is a nonproductive way of talking to yourself.

Arbitrary Inference	Conclusion that is drawn without careful consideration of all the facts involved: *The student is not looking at me so she must not be listening.*
Misattribution	The direction of blame or responsibility is moved away from the real cause onto something or someone else: *That student makes me furious.*
Cognitive Deficiency	The failure to be aware of the complete picture; tunnel vision: *The reason Stewart is failing is because he does not concentrate.*
Over-generalization	Recognizing only the similarities between people or between events and ignoring differences. Racial, cultural, and gender prejudices are based on this confuser: *I'll bring some of my Sports Illustrated magazines to class for my boys to read.*
Either/or Thinking	Seeing everything as black or white, agree or disagree; no consideration is given for degrees or in-between ground: *I better decide if I am authoritarian or permissive.*
Vague Language	Using words that you have not defined clearly for yourself (e.g., success, happiness, wealth): *I just want to be successful in my teaching.*
Magnification	Overestimation of the importance of an event or a situation; blowing something out of reasonable proportion: *I am a terrible teacher if I allow that to happen.*

Below are the permitter self-talk statements to combat your distorted Confuser self-talk.

PERMITTERS for Combating Confuser Self-Talk

Confuser	Permitter Self-Talk
Arbitrary Inference	Be specific. When I say "I'm a failure as a teacher" what I really mean and should say is that half of my class failed their midterm examination.

Table 8.2 *(Continued)*

Misattribution	Students don't really make me furious. I choose to react in a negative way to their classroom behavior. What steps can I take to react in a more positive way? I am in control of my emotions; my students are not.
Cognitive Deficiency	What's the whole picture? A school problem is rarely so simple that it can be explained by one factor. What are other contributing factors to this problem?
Over-generalization	Watch it! Why did I assume that only the boys would want to read *Sports Illustrated*? Come to think of it, Sam would rather read poetry than play sports at recess.
Either/or Thinking	I can think in degrees, and in between the ends of the continuum. I will stop allowing others to categorize me so easily as either this or that. It often is not that simple and depends a great deal on the specific situation.
Vague Language	Success is in the eye of the beholder, just as beauty is. I need to be clear about how I'm defining success.
Magnification	Bring it down to size by dating and indexing. Dating means to tell precisely at what particular time something occurred (e.g., I was a terrible teacher last Friday when I was sick with the flu). Indexing means being specific about the uniqueness of each person or event (e.g., I am stricter than Ms. Jones during academic learning time.).

recognize that unhelpful self-talk produces feelings of anger, depression, anxiety, as well as undermines your problem-solving ability. This recognition is a very important step and helps you challenge a previously accepted way of talking to yourself. Now you are no longer going to accept it.

Step 3 is to identify the Driver, Stopper, and Confuser messages you are giving yourself. Once you become familiar with these critical Judges, you can start to notice and catch yourself when you are driving, stopping, and confusing yourself with these types of internal dialogues. If you can be more specific, it will help pinpoint the source of difficulty and direct you toward an alternative way of speaking to yourself. For example, "This is my day off and I've been calling myself lazy all day. I'm not going to spend it making myself hurry up." We are all too familiar with the tirades of self-criticism we deliver to ourselves each day. Learning a healthier way to support yourself means learning a new language.

For Step 4, it is important to recognize that at the core of all permission is a basic respect and trust of one's own feelings. When teachers do not respect themselves, they often do not respect others, including their students. In this step, it is helpful initially to prepare some self-talk statements to practice.

Step 5 involves the development of a concrete plan that promotes growth for your unique development without the added baggage of critical Judges. You may want to include a physiological component in your plan, like noticing where you are feeling tension in your body and releasing that tension, or taking deep breaths.

Personal Exercise: Becoming Aware of Your Personal Overbearing Judges

Activity Directions:

Step 1: a) From the list of five Driver judge messages (Be Perfect, Hurry Up, Be Strong, Please Others, Try Hard), identify one that causes a problem for you.
   b) From the list of four Stopper judge messages (Catastrophizing, Negative Self-Labeling, Rigid Requirements, Witch Messages), identify one that causes a problem for you.
   c) From the list of seven Confuser judge messages (Arbitrary Inference, Misattribution, Cognitive Deficiency, Overgeneralization, Either/or Thinking, Vague Language, Magnification), identify one that causes a problem for you.

Step 2: Designate one school week for collecting data. Decide on three specific times (e.g., mid-morning, lunch, right after students leave for the day). At your designated time, take a few minutes to recall and record any instances of using any of your three selected judges.

Step 3: At the end of the week, review the data you have collected to:
   a) Discover what judge you used most often.
   b) Identify any patterns or relationships you noticed.
   c) Use the insights gleaned from this exercise to follow the five-step program for learning the language of self-support.

A Stress Inoculation Strategy

Meichenbaum (1985) developed a preventative strategy he termed *stress inoculation.* This integrative strategy, in addition to cognitive-behavioral coping skills, incorporates relaxation training, rehearsal, and stress scripts. Stress scripts help you prepare for an encounter you know is going to be stressful. A central tenet of stress inoculation is the notion that many potential stressors allow for preparatory thoughts and actions that may either prevent anticipated negative incidents altogether or serve to reduce their magnitude and impact. Meichenbaum suggests that you will need to manage your self-talk at four stages as you work through a stressful encounter:

1. Preparing for the encounter
2. During the actual encounter
3. As you feel your anxiety or anger rising
4. Reflecting on how you handled the situation, both when the conflict is unresolved as well as when it is resolved and/or you coped successfully

Personal Exercise: Preparing for a Stressful Encounter

Activity Directions:

Step 1:   Prepare your own stress script by picking a few statements from Table 8.3 or writing your own for each of the four stages.
1. Preparing for the encounter

2. During the actual encounter

3. As you feel your anxiety or anger rising

4. Reflecting on: (a) An unresolved encounter

(b) A successfully resolved encounter

Step 2:   Rehearse your stress script until you have committed it to memory.

Step 3:   Try using your stress script the next time you are facing a potentially stressful encounter. It is best to practice using this strategy initially in situations that are not highly stressful. Once you have had some success you can move on to more challenging situations.

Personal Exercise: Inoculating Yourself Against Stress

Activity Directions:

Step 1:   Taking into account your personal qualities as well as your challenges, reflect on what school or classroom events or situations are most stressful for you.

Step 2:   Of the potential sources of job-related stress, identify the ones you are most susceptible to.

Step 3:   Consider what you could do to make yourself less vulnerable to these stressors.

Step 4:   Identify the one thing you can commit to doing to try to inoculate yourself against a source of stress that is potentially debilitating for you.

Table 8.3.   Stress Script for Dealing with Anger/Stress/Anxiety

Preparing for an Anxiety-Provoking Situation

I won't let this get me down.
I can follow my plan.
I can do this.
I can handle my anger.
I can control my thoughts.

I'm ready. I know how to deal with this.
I know what to do.
I know it's all up to me.
I will not argue.
It won't be easy, but I'm confident.

Reacting During the Encounter

Nothing can discourage me.
No one else can control me.
I'm not going to let this get to me.
Keep things in perspective.
It's not that important.
Keep smiling. Hang in there.

Stay cool.
I don't have to prove myself.
Accentuate the positive.
Don't blow this out of proportion.
I've got a handle on this situation.
Keep a sense of humor.

Coping with Anger Symptoms

I'm determined to handle this.
It won't get me anywhere to get angry.
I'm going to hold my ground, but I'm not going
   to get crazy.
Be constructive, not destructive.
I'm upset, but I'm handling myself pretty well.
I can't expect others to act the way I would.
No negative self-talk.
Easy does it.

I can feel my muscles starting to get tight.
Getting upset won't help.
Be respectful—don't blame.

Remember, I'm in control.
Don't counterattack—depersonalize.
Relax. Take a few deep breaths.
Slow down.

Reflecting on the Encounter

Unresolved conflict:
   I did not argue—that's progress.
   Remember to relax.
   I won't take it personally.
   It's not that serious.
   I got angry but I kept a lid on attacking.

Don't take it to heart.
This will take time to work out.
I won't worry about it.
I'm not going to let this get me down.
Life goes on.

Resolved conflict/successful coping:
   I did it!
   I really handled that well.
   I kept myself from getting angry.
   I'm getting better at this all the time.

I'm proud of myself.
It wasn't as bad as I thought.
I can control myself.

The following is an example of a teacher's stress-reducing self-talk statements at each stage in a stressful encounter.

   Preparing for an anger-provoking situation: "This is going to be upsetting, but I know how to deal with it."
   Reacting during the encounter: "If I just concentrate on breathing slowly, I can stay calm."
   Coping with angry feelings: "I can't expect my students to act the way I want them to. I can be annoyed, but I'm not going to get all bent out of shape."

Reflecting on the conflict:
When conflict is unresolved: "This is a difficult situation, but I'm going to keep working at it."
When conflict is resolved or coping is successful: "I actually got through that without getting angry. I guess I've been getting upset for too long when it wasn't necessary. I'm doing better at this all the time."

Table 8.3 has examples of self-talk statements you can use when dealing with potentially stressful encounters to manage your level of emotional arousal. The idea is to arm yourself with supportive self-talk for each of these four stages in preparation for an anticipated stressful encounter.

Chapter Nine

Learning to Quiet the Mind

Only in quiet waters things mirror themselves undistorted. Only in a quiet mind is adequate perception of the world.

—Hans Margolius

Stress management occurs on two levels: prevention and coping. Preventive strategies try to inoculate you against the harmful effects of stress-producing situations, while coping strategies attempt to minimize the effects of stressful situations so that you can cope more effectively. Strategies can be (1) physiological, dealing with the direct effect on the body, such as diet, exercise, or relaxation; (2) cognitive, or increasing awareness of, and redirecting, thought patterns and internal dialogue, or self-talk; or (3) behavioral, including overt behaviors or action steps taken to manage stressful situations, such as time management techniques to set long-term and short-term goals, monitor time spent, and prioritize activities. These types of strategies are often used in combination.

The techniques that have a direct effect on the body help you deal with the physical reactions the body has to stress. The mind is typically engaged in anxiety-producing thoughts that trigger the "fight-or-flight" response, keeping the body in a state of arousal. The body's other response is the "relaxation response," a state of lowered arousal that diminishes many adverse symptoms brought on by stress. While everyone needs some type of physiological stress-reducing strategies, it is especially important for teachers to have a way to quickly access the body's relaxation response.

Physiological stress-coping strategies that release the body's relaxation response include meditation, diaphragmatic or deep breathing, relaxation techniques, and visualization techniques. Hypnosis and creative imagery techniques such as guided fantasy and guided meditations are typically included here as well. Visualization techniques set the stage for listening to your unconscious and use the creative power of your imagination. Such techniques can be used for relaxation, problem solving, self-inquiry, or healing.

Some methods available to handle stress help you achieve mental balance by quieting the mind. In the yoga tradition, the mind stands between, and yet at the same time connects, our essential self with what is external (Harvey, 1988). The analogy often used is that the mind is like a lake. The bed of the lake is our essential or true self, the water is the mind "stuff," and the waves, currents, and turbulence in the water are our thoughts, feelings, and memories.

While meditation is a predominant strategy used to quiet the mind, other strategies that create an internal stillness that stop the flow of noise and interference endlessly parading through your mind can precipitate the relaxation response. In its normal state, your mind is preoccupied with an inner dialogue, which is an endless stream of commentary on your experiences. You need to find a way to catch yourself in the act of constructing your familiar internal stories so you can make the shift from thought to awareness of what is immediately happening. It is important for teachers to be able to catch themselves in the act of creating anxiety-producing storylines, especially when they are dealing with students whose behavior they find challenging.

As you learn to listen in on the internal dialogue lingering in your mind, observing your thoughts and becoming more aware of your feelings and actions, you can begin to surrender automatic ways of responding. The idea is to develop the capacity to create a quiet mind, totally free from thinking, interpreting, and replaying the past.

CULTIVATING MINDFULNESS

Today's challenge is to engage in the practice of daily conscious living—being mindful. This new paradigm for living beckons us to live our lives deliberately and mindfully, bringing our inner and outer worlds into balance. When we are in a balanced state, we are in a state that is the antithesis of being stressed. Research evidence clearly demonstrates that regular mindfulness practice positively impacts how our body and brain respond to stress.

The term *mindfulness* is fast becoming a household term. It seems to be everywhere we turn. In some ways, it is easier to understand mindlessness than mindfulness. We all wear mental blinders based on past experiences and assumptions without realizing it, cruising through life on automatic pilot, or mindlessly.

Mindfulness is a particular kind of attention encompassing a nonjudgmental awareness, openness, curiosity, and acceptance of internal and external present experiences. Mindfulness is attention to experience as it is happening—in the present moment. In Buddhist literature, this kind of attention is often referred to as "bear attention," or seeing things as they are with no shading from our past experiences. In other words, it is seeing things as they are without reference to the memory and mindset you bring to your experiences.

Mindfulness practice has been around for thousands of years. Relatively recently, it has been adopted by Western medicine to treat those suffering from chronic pain and those living with debilitating diseases. Mental health practitioners now use mindfulness practices to treat anxiety and depression. Even more recently, it is being advocated to help healthy individuals deal with bouts of stress and/or to help those with jobs where there is chronic stress, such as teaching. In the past decade, mindfulness practices are also making their way into elementary and secondary schools to help students deal more effectively with the stress in their lives.

Mindfulness can be initiated and enhanced by a variety of means, all of which seek to promote awareness and self-discovery on some level. Mindfulness can be cultivated through explicit practices that could be described as awareness expanding. There are literally hundreds of kinds of practices, including meditation, relaxation, concentration, visualization, forms of chanting and prayer, as well as movement-based practices such as yoga, tai chi, and qi gong.

Mindful awareness, which is sometimes used synonymously with mindfulness, means to be "aware of awareness," implying an awareness of self and the capacity to reflect. Smalley and Winston (2010), like many others, believe that integrating mindfulness into your life involves reflection. Siegel (2010), in his book *Mindsight*, likewise believes in the centrality of being reflective. According to Siegel, our five senses allow us to perceive the outside world. What some call our sixth sense allows us to perceive our internal bodily states (for example, a racing heartbeat, butterflies in our stomach). Siegel believes our ability to look within and perceive the mind by reflecting on our experiences is our seventh sense. He has coined the term *mindsight* to represent this essential seventh sense. He asserts that the power of reflection is at the core of mindsight. He identifies three very specific components of reflection that are at the heart of our mindsight abilities. He refers to these three fundamental components as the three legs of the tripod that stabilize our mindsight lens: *openness*, *observation*, and *objectivity*.

With openness we are receptive to whatever comes into our awareness, not clinging to preconceived ideas about how things *should* be. We see things as they are rather than trying to make them how we want them to be, giving us the power to recognize limiting judgments. Observation is the ability to perceive the self simultaneously with an experience. It is actually self-observation, offering a way to disengage from automatic behaviors and habitual responses, opening up the possibility of finding ways to alter them. Objectivity allows us to have a thought or feeling and not become swept away by it. It is the ability of the mind to be aware that its present activities—our thoughts, feelings, memories, beliefs, and intentions—are temporary and, more importantly, they are not the totality of who we are (for example, I am not angry, rather I am feeling angry). Objectivity allows us to develop what some refer to as discernment. With discernment we can see that a thought or feeling is just mental activity, not absolute reality. One part of discernment is the ability to be aware of how we are being aware. According to Siegel, if we can develop this "meta-awareness," or awareness of awareness, it can liberate us from our automatic reactions.

It is important to acknowledge that the capacities of being open, objective, and self-observing are all hallmarks of being a reflective practitioner. Developing mindfulness or having mindsight are concepts that overlap substantially with the tenants of reflective practice discussed previously. The more reflective teachers are, the more they can access a broader perspective for interpreting student behavior to refrain from reactive judgments.

Research Evidence for Mindfulness

Being mindful has a positive impact on both physical health and psychological well-being. Feelings of anxiety and depression lessen, well-being improves, and relationships to self and others are healthier. In their book, *Fully Present: The Science, Art, and Practice of Mindfulness*, Smalley and Winston (2010) report that research exploring mindfulness is demonstrating that repeated practice leads to a whole host of positive outcomes. Some of these include the following changes:

- lowering stress
- boosting the body's immune system to fight disease
- reducing chronic physical pain
- managing negative emotions
- coping with painful life events
- expanding self-awareness to expose harmful reactive patterns
- increasing positive emotions
- enhancing relationships with self and others
- improving attention and concentration

Research is now beginning to elucidate the various pathways through which mindfulness may exert its effects on the brain (attention, working memory, cognitive control, emotion regulation) and the body (symptom reduction, greater physical well-being, immune function enhancement). Brain research suggests that higher levels of mindfulness are associated with enhanced emotional awareness and understanding, increased ability to control emotional reactions, and greater capacity to alter unpleasant moods (Baer, Smith, Hopkins, Krietemeyer, & Toney, 2006; Brown, Ryan, & Creswell, 2007; Creswell, May, Eisenberger, & Lieberman, 2007; Feltman, Robinson, & Ode, 2009; Greeson, 2009). Researchers have also found that more hours of mindfulness practice translate into greater capacity for self-regulation of attention (Moore, Gruber, Derose, & Malinowski, 2012; Jha, Krompinger, & Baime, 2007).

While earlier research focused on studying more experienced mindfulness practitioners, some recent research shows that brief training in a mindfulness practice can also produce similar increases in the ability to self-regulate attention (Dickenson et al., in press; Moore et al., 2012). For teachers who already have a very full plate, investing a minimal amount of time to learn a mindfulness practice could have a huge payoff given that the ability to regulate internal experiences in the present moment appears to translate into good overall mental health.

This line of research supports the position that regular mindful awareness practice changes how your body and brain respond to stress, strengthening brain connections to reduce reactivity, supporting self-reflection and self-regulation (Davidson & Begley, 2012; Siegel, 2010). This has important implications for teachers in that teachers who develop their capacity for mindfulness may be better equipped to communicate, monitor, and manage their emotions, which can reduce the emotional exhaustion that is often the precursor to burnout.

Researchers have posited that through regularly practicing mindfulness you may broaden your awareness horizons so that you come to interpret stressful life events in a more empowering way, leading to substantially less stress. By learning to observe your thoughts, feelings, and sensations nonjudgmentally you can break the chain of reactions that negative emotions set in motion, piggybacking on one another to quickly "catastrophize" a situation. While practicing mindfulness engenders a "transitory" state of mindfulness, when engaged in over time, it may accrue into "trait" mindfulness; that is, it may become a general propensity to exhibit nonjudgmental awareness in everyday life (Chambers, Gullone, & Allen, 2009; Garland et al., 2010). In other words, by engaging in an ongoing mindfulness practice, you build up sustaining resources that may make it easier for you to tap into a more positive state when stress comes at you. Researchers have also found that as mindfulness increases so does the capacity for positive reappraisal, a coping strategy for recasting a negative event in a more positive light (Garland, Gaylord, & Fredrickson, 2011; Modinos, Ormel, & Aleman, 2010).

As mentioned before, your nervous system has two basic modes: It fires up or quiets down. When you are in a reactive state, your brain stem signals the "fight-freeze-flight" survival reflex. In this state, even neutral comments may be taken as fighting words. On the other hand, an attitude of receptivity activates a different branch of the brain stem as it sends messages to relax the muscles of the face and vocal chords and normalizes blood pressure and heart rate. Siegel explains that such a receptive state literally turns on the social engagement system that connects you to others.

According to Siegel, the development of attention through mindfulness meditative exercises is a crucial aspect of inner balance. Mindfulness helps you regulate your internal state, including your immune system, your emotions, your attention, and even your interpersonal interactions. This is because mindfulness promotes the growth of integrative fibers in the brain, which are what's needed for regulation across all these domains. Siegel tells us that integration is the fundamental mechanism of self-regulation. The natural outcome of integration is compassion, kindness, and resilience. Because being mindful is associated with perspective taking, emotional communication, and forgiveness, teachers who practice mindfulness are more capable of providing the emotional support that many students need.

Calming the Body Through Meditation

One avenue for calming the body and developing mindfulness is the practice of meditation. Meditation is an umbrella term that encompasses a wide variety of practices. Some of the most popular include mindfulness meditation, Transcendental meditation, and Zen meditation. While techniques differ, all types of meditation share the common goal of training an individual's attention and awareness so that consciousness becomes more finely tuned to events and experiences in the present.

In meditation you create an observation point from which you can begin to notice your thoughts and then let go of your old dialogues. Developing a quiet mind is having a way of pulling into yourself to create a state of awareness. Joan Borysenko (1987) calls it creating an observation point from which you can witness and let go of your old dialogues. John Welwood (1990) calls it returning to a state of simple presence, noticing your thoughts and then letting them go. Jon Kabat-Zinn (1994) calls it deepening and refining your attention and awareness so that you come to realize your path of life is unfolding, moment by moment. They are all advocates of mindfulness meditation as the vehicle for creating such a state.

Meditation is actually an activity of attention and concentration, not relaxation. Relaxation is a by-product of meditation, much as it is of other focused activities such as athletics, dance, or sex. There are many styles and methods of meditation, but in virtually all forms of meditation, two elements are involved, concentration and relaxation.

There are many aids to concentration that can be used, like a bell or gong, or incense. You can also concentrate on a flame, or your breath. One focusing tool often recommended to anchor the mind is a *mantra* that you say softly over and over to yourself. A mantra can be a sound, a word, or a phrase. A mantra can be:

- A neutral sound, that is having no association, like the number *one*
- A sound with a pleasant association, like *mmm*
- A word that evokes personal meaning, such as a reminder as in *pause* or *focus*
- A significant message, like *It's not important* or *This too shall pass*

A commonly recommended mantra in the Hindu tradition is *Om* (pronounced aum), a sacred symbol representing the Universal, the All, or the One. While a mantra can be used to help create a meditation state, it can also be used as a cue to monitor your awareness and regulate your mind when it starts to take off with a life of its own down memory lane, replaying the ever present old tapes.

Meditation can be any activity that keeps attention fixed in the present moment, allowing you to transcend your normal state of consciousness. When you block out everything but the focal point commanding your attention, you are in a meditation state. It is a state of deep concentration, in which you are totally engrossed, fully present.

Meditation is different from relaxation training in several ways. Meditation involves witnessing events and experiences as they present themselves on a moment-to-moment basis. Relaxation training involves the pursuit of a "state of reduced autonomic arousal." Relaxation may be a by-product of meditation, but it is not an objective of the practice. Second, relaxation is taught as a stress management technique to be used during stressful or anxiety-provoking situations. Meditation, in contrast, is not a technique used in stressful situations; rather, it is conceived as cultivating "a way of being." Relaxation techniques are discussed later in this chapter.

Research Evidence for Meditation

The purported benefits of meditation are many, including the capacity to pay attention to the present moment, the ability to recognize emotions as they surface, enhanced self-awareness, and stress reduction. Research evidence is mounting to support these contentions. Brain research also indicates that regular meditation effects brain functions, literally changing the brain. A regular meditation practice can enhance the brain's capacity for perception, awareness, attention, and self-monitoring (Brewer et al., 2011; Cahn & Polich, 2006; Lutz, Slagter, Dunne, & Davidson, 2008; Pagnoni & Cekic, 2007; Siegel, 2010). These results overlap considerably with outcomes on mindfulness discussed in the previous section. This is because meditation is one of the primary routes for becoming more mindful.

There is a growing body of research indicating that meditation reduces negative mental health symptoms, including anxiety and depression (Baer, 2003; Greeson & Brantley, 2008). Meditation can also enhance well-being by cultivating self-compassion and empathy (Brown et al., 2007; Murphy & Donovan, 1997; Singer & Lamm, 2009; Tang et al., 2007). The practice of meditation impacts regions of the brain involved with empathetic responses. Researchers speculate that the capacity to cultivate compassion, which involves regulating thoughts and emotions, may also be useful for preventing aggressive behavior and bullying in children and adolescents (Lutz, Brefczynski, Johnstone, & Davidson, 2008). As with other mindfulness practices, developing a meditation practice over time may allow you to shift into a state of mind in which coping with stress takes less effort. That is, it may build up resilience for facing stressful situations.

MINDFULNESS-BASED STRESS REDUCTION (MBSR)

Mindfulness-based stress reduction (MBSR) is one of the most widely used mindfulness training programs since its development by Jon Kabat-Zinn at the University of Massachusetts Medical Center in 1979. MBSR is a standardized program initially created in an effort to integrate mindfulness meditation with contemporary clinical and psychological practices. While originally developed as a group-based program for patients with chronic pain, in the last couple of decades it has been advocated for helping healthy people reduce their stress.

Although MBSR and cognitive-behavioral therapy (CBT) discussed earlier share some similar attributes and can be used in conjunction, they are different in several ways. While both methods work to achieve results by changing thought patterns, CBT labels negative thoughts and feelings as disruptive and emphasizes replacing them, and MBSR encourages acceptance of the thoughts without dwelling on them. MBSR is not regarded as a treatment per se; rather, it is considered preventative, providing a new way of thinking and functioning.

The main feature of MBSR is the cultivation of mindfulness, allowing you to act more reflectively rather than impulsively. MBSR teaches you to observe situations and thoughts nonjudgmentally without reacting to them impulsively, helping to "stay in the moment" by developing awareness of inner and outer experiences.

MBSR merges the following three different techniques.

1. Mindfulness meditation, which involves both mindful attention on the breath as well as on other perceptions, and a state of nonjudgmental awareness of the stream of thoughts and distractions that continuously flow through the mind.

Participants are taught to sit in meditation and to focus in the present and not think about anything other than simply existing. They are taught to keenly observe their thoughts and emotions but then to let them pass without judging them or becoming immersed in them. Participants are also encouraged to incorporate meditation into their daily lives so that routine activities become a meditative practice, for example, eating.

2. Body scan, which involves a gradual sweeping of attention through the entire body from head to foot, noncritically focusing on any sensation or feeling in body regions and using periodic suggestions on breath awareness and relaxation.

A body scan is performed by first focusing attention on the breath and then on each section of the body. During a body scan, participants methodically think about each body part, observe their sensations, and then intentionally relax each body part.

3. Hatha yoga practice, which includes breathing exercises, simple stretches, and posture designed to strengthen and relax the musculoskeletal system.

In Hatha yoga the postures are generally gentle and can be performed by individuals of varying fitness levels. The concept behind Hatha yoga is that the mind focuses on the posture rather than being occupied with distracting thoughts.

MBSR is a structured program consisting of an eight-week course in which participants meet once a week for a two-and-a-half-hour session and one eight-hour day. Participants are taught mindfulness-based meditation, Hatha yoga, and to perform a body scan. Participants are given daily homework assignments of meditation, yoga, and inquiry exercises to increase their observation power. Participants are also asked to set aside approximately 45 minutes per day to practice MBSR in addition to the classes. This entails doing mindfulness-based meditation, yoga, and journaling to store their thoughts and feelings. Participants use CDs or audiotapes provided to guide them at home in meditation and yoga.

As an illustration, we have all experienced thoughts about an argument or unpleasant experience lingering in our mind well after it has occurred. Imagine you are preparing dinner and becoming increasingly angry over an argument you had earlier that day. You could let the anger prevail, or you could acknowledge that you were thinking about the argument, let that feeling pass, and focus your attention on your breath and dinner. If you chose the latter, you would eventually become immersed in the task and not think about anything else but breathing and cooking. You would experience a sense of calmness. This is living in the moment, and it is what MBSR teaches.

Research Findings on MBSR

There is an impressive array of research confirming the effectiveness of MBSR. Much of the earlier research on MBSR was conducted with samples with a variety of physical and psychological diagnoses. Decades of research has shown MBSR reduces stress, increases mindfulness, and improves quality of life (Carmody & Baer, 2008; Grossman, Niemann, Schmidt, & Walach, 2004; Kabat-Zinn, 2003). Research with clinical samples shows decreased anxiety and depression as well as decreased rumination, or a dwelling on negative thoughts (Jain et al., 2007; Ramel, Goldin, Carmona, & McQuaid, 2004).

More recent research on MBSR confirms similar benefits for healthy individuals. In a meta-analysis of 10 studies, researchers concluded that MBSR is an equally effective program for reducing stress in healthy people (Chiesa & Serretti, 2009). Similarly, studies of healthcare professionals demonstrate reduced stress, increased coping, and improved empathy after completing a MBSR program (Beddoe & Murphy, 2004; Galantino, Baime, Maguire, Szapary, & Farrar, 2005). Also studying healthy samples, Shapiro and colleagues found MBSR decreased levels of stress, anxiety, and depression (Oman, Shapiro, Thoresen, Plante, & Flinders, 2008; Shapiro, Brown, & Biegel, 2007; Shapiro, Schwartz, & Bonner, 1998). In addition, MBSR significantly increased positive mood (Shapiro et al., 2007), forgiveness (Oman et al., 2008), and self-compassion (Birnie, Speca, & Carlson, 2010; Shapiro et al., 2007).

Similar to research reported earlier, MBSR affects brain functioning. Studying healthy, meditation-naïve participants that underwent the MBSR program, researchers found measurable changes in brain regions associated with memory, sense of self, empathy, and stress (Holzel et al., 2011). Participants reported spending on average 27 minutes per day practicing mindfulness exercises. This level of time commitment may be doable even for a teacher's jam-packed schedule. These researchers found increases in gray-matter density in the part of the brain known to be important for learning and memory, and in brain structure associated with compassion and introspection. Reductions in stress were also correlated with decreased gray-matter density in the part of the brain that plays an important role in anxiety and stress.

Other researchers have also found positive changes for novice meditators with MBSR training, finding increased activation in the brain area associated with positive emotions (Davidson et al., 2003). More importantly for teachers, MBSR increases the capacity for empathy (Beddoe & Murphy, 2004; Galantino et al., 2005; Holzel et al., 2011; Klatt, Buckworth, & Malarkey, 2008). Empathy is defined by Rogers (1961) as the capacity to understand, be sensitive to, and feel what another is feeling as well as the ability to communicate this sensitivity to the person. Clearly, this is an important character strength for teachers to develop, and mindfulness training is one path for doing so.

Research on Mindfulness with Teachers and Students

Mindfulness programs designed especially for teachers are starting to emerge. The Cultivating Awareness and Resilience in Education (CARE) professional development program is intended to help teachers bring a more mindful approach to their teaching and to reduce their stress. CARE targets enhancing teacher well-being, classroom climate, and students' prosocial behavior through participation in a series of four day-long sessions. Teachers participating in CARE report increased levels of mindfulness and well-being. They also respond more effectively to challenging student behavior, which both improves classroom climate and reduces stress (Jennings, Snowberg, Coccia, & Greenberg, 2012).

The Inner Resilience Program (IRP) is designed to improve the stress management of both teachers and their students. The IRP is an intensive year-long program consisting of yoga training and practice, the Nurturing the Inner Life (NTIL) Series exploring a variety of reflective approaches for managing stress, and a weekend residential retreat offering rejuvenation as well as practical strategies for staying calm within the turbulence of teaching. A recent evaluation of IRP showed impressive results, including increased teacher mindfulness and relational trust, greater student autonomy, decreased student frustration, and especially pronounced improvement for students identified as at risk for reacting to stressful situations in destructive ways (Lantieri, Kyse, Harnett, & Malkmus, 2011).

Although there has been little research with teachers taught the MBSR program, a study was conducted by the Center for Mindfulness Research and Practice in the United Kingdom with primary teachers (Gold et al., 2010). The MBSR course was delivered immediately following the school day, as eight 2.5-hour weekly sessions and a "silent day" conducted on a Saturday. Results indicated that 10 of the 11 participants experienced reductions in stress, depression, and anxiety. With less intensive training, researchers taught a simple meditation technique to student teachers during four 45-minute sessions, and found that participants showed significantly reduced emotional, physical, and behavioral manifestations of stress symptoms compared to the control group (Winzelberg & Luskin, 1999).

Research is beginning to accumulate on the effectiveness of mindfulness practices for school-age populations. For example, some of the programs with research confirming their effectiveness include *A Still Quiet Place* (Saltzman, in press) for kindergarteners, InnerKids (Flook et al., 2010) and the MindUp Program (Schonert-Reichl & Lawlor, 2010) for elementary and secondary students, as well as programs earmarked for parents and kids to take together (Saltzman & Golden, 2008; Singh et al., 2010).

A review of research studies on the effect of meditative practices implemented with youth aged 6 to 18 years in school, clinic, and community settings from 1982 to 2008 identified 16 empirical studies (Black, Milam, & Sussman, 2009). Among these studies, the types of meditation included mindfulness meditation, transcendental meditation, MBSR, and mindfulness-based cognitive therapy. Based on their review, the authors concluded that meditation is an effective intervention for the treatment of physiological, psychological, social, and behavioral symptoms among a school-age sample. Researchers found a mindfulness practice taught to preadolescents and early adolescents resulted in less aggressive and oppositional behavior toward teachers, greater attention in class, and more positive emotions, including more optimism (Schonert-Reichl & Lawlor, 2010).

There have also been some impressive results with students having a variety of diagnoses. For example, adolescents with ADHD following participation in an eight-week mindfulness training program reported improvements in ADHD, anxiety, and depressive symptoms (Zylowska et al., 2008). Research on 102 adolescents with various psychiatric diagnoses who were taught the MBSR program found that participants reported reduced symptoms of anxiety, depression, and physical distress, as well as increased self-esteem. Even more notable was the finding that clinicians documented a significant increase over the control group in the number of adolescents who were no longer clinically depressed or anxious (Biegel, Brown, Shapiro, & Schubert, 2009).

Encouraging results have also been obtained with relatively short training periods. For example, studying adolescents diagnosed with learning disabilities, researchers found that a mindfulness intervention significantly reduced anxiety. In addition, there was a decrease in teacher ratings of student problem behaviors (Beauchemin, Hutchins, & Patterson, 2008). These results were obtained in 5- to 10-minute sessions, five days per week for five weeks. With school-referred students diagnosed with a conduct disorder, researchers found a decrease in aggressive behavior and bullying (Singh et al., 2007). These results were obtained in 15-minute sessions, three times per week for a four-week period, with greater decreases occurring during the 25 weeks of practice that followed training.

Learning to Meditate

One of the most prevalent routes to developing mindfulness is through mindfulness-based meditation. This process trains the mind to function in a nonjudgmental minute-to-minute mode. Mindfulness meditation involves three core elements (Shapiro, Carlson, Astin, & Freedman, 2006):

Intention involves consciously and purposefully regulating attention.

Attention is the ability to sustain attention in the present moment without interpretation or evaluation.

Attitude is a frame of mind brought to mindfulness meditation, commonly described as open, acceptant, and nonjudgmental.

While meditation may initially be a deliberative practice, over time the emotional and bodily awareness that results from meditation may produce an increase in daily positive emotion, which in turn may interrupt a stressor before it fully unfolds and help buffer against future stressors. This means that meditation has the power to reduce stress, not only in the moment but also over the long haul. By bringing your focus to the present moment and negating thoughts of the past or future, you become attuned to the awareness that there is nothing you can do at this current moment about what has already happened or what's going to happen. In meditation, you find solace right here in the present, which provides a major source of stress relief.

According to Kempton (2011), one of the benefits of a meditation practice is that creative solutions to problems present themselves naturally when you enter a certain state of quiet. She also suggests that a regular meditation practice helps you hold steady in times of emotional turmoil.

General Guidelines for Developing a Meditation Practice

In order to embark on a formal mindfulness-based meditation practice, you will need to carve out some time on a regular, daily basis. The general recommendation is to meditate in preparation for activity; for example, before you go to work rather than after you may already be stressed. You need to make sure you won't be interrupted, and choose a comfortable chair. It is best to keep your spine straight because the little effort that it will take to keep your spine straight will help you to stay awake. Some people become so relaxed that they may nod off to sleep while meditating, but the idea is to be awake in a unique way. If you do go to sleep, usually five minutes of meditation afterward will make you wide awake. For some people, meditating makes them feel very awake—so much so that if they meditate before bedtime, they have trouble getting to sleep.

To get started, you will need to find 10 to 20 minutes in your daily routine. Before breakfast is an ideal time for most people. Commit yourself to a specific length of practice, and stick to it. Time yourself by glancing periodically at a clock or watch, but don't set an alarm. Set aside time to practice once, or preferably twice a day. Make this a gentle process, a relaxing time. Don't worry about how well you are doing, or get upset if you are distracted (Benson, 1997).

There are many ways to meditate, and every world culture has developed one or more techniques. You should choose a simple core practice and do it daily until it becomes a habit. Your core practice is your base, your foundation for turning the mind inward. Following a basic technique helps you set up the discipline of a regular practice and teaches you how to get your body comfortable, find inner focus, and keep your mind from running rampant. As you continue, you begin to experience periods of quiet, even contentment (Kempton, 2011).

To get you started, the following section provides several sets of simple instructions used by experts in the field. Experiment with each of them to discover which method seems to work best for you.

Basic Method 1:

This method was developed by Jon Kabat-Zinn, founder of the first hospital-based stress reduction clinic in the country at the University of Massachusetts Medical Center. It is the first method taught to those at the clinic. He is also the author of many books on mindfulness, including *Wherever You Go, There You Are* (1994) and *Coming to Our Senses: Healing Ourselves and the World Through Mindfulness* (2006).

1. Assume a comfortable posture lying on your back or sitting. Close your eyes if it feels more comfortable.
2. Bring your attention to your belly, feeling it rise or expand gently on the inbreath and fall or recede on the outbreath.
3. Keep the focus on your breathing, "being with" each inbreath and outbreath for its full duration, as if you were riding the waves of your own breathing.
4. Every time you notice that your mind has wandered off the breath, notice what it was that took you away, then bring your attention back to your belly and the feeling of the breath coming in and out.
5. Practice this exercise for 15 minutes at a convenient time every day, for one week, to begin to experience how it feels to incorporate a disciplined breathing practice into your daily routine.

Basic Method 2:

This method is suggested by Richard Davidson, one of the world's premier neuro-scientists, director of the Laboratory for Affective Neuroscience, and coauthor of *The Emotional Life of Your Brain: How Its Unique Patterns Affect the Way You Think, Feel, and Live—and How You Can Change Them* (Davidson & Begley, 2012).

1. Choose a time of day when you are the most awake and alert.
2. Sit upright on the floor or a chair, keeping the spine straight and maintaining a re-laxed but erect posture so you do not get drowsy. You can do this practice with your eyes open or closed, depending on which feels most comfortable.
3. Focus on your breathing, on the sensations it triggers throughout your body. Notice how your abdomen moves with each inhalation and exhalation.
4. Focus on the tip of the nose, noticing the different sensations that arise with each breath.
5. When you notice that you have been distracted by unrelated thoughts or feelings that have arisen, simply return your focus to your breathing.

6. Try this for 5 to 10 minutes at a sitting, ideally twice a day.
7. As you feel more comfortable, increase the length of time.

Methods three and four incorporate the common practice of using a mantra as a focusing tool.

Basic Method 3:

This method was developed by Herbert Benson and is the standard set of instructions used at the Mind/Body Medical Institute at Harvard Medical School. He is also the author of the classic book, *Beyond the Relaxation Response* (1984).

1. Pick a focus word or short phrase that is firmly rooted in your personal belief system. For example, *The Lord is my shepherd* or, simply, *one, peace,* or *love.*
2. Sit quietly in a comfortable position.
3. Close your eyes and relax your muscles.
4. Breathe slowly and naturally, repeating your focus word or phrase silently as you exhale.
5. Throughout, assume a passive attitude. When thoughts come to mind, simply say to yourself "Oh, well" and gently return to the repetition.
6. Continue for 10 to 20 minutes. You may open your eyes to check the time.
7. When you finish, sit quietly for a minute or so, at first with your eyes closed and later with your eyes open.
8. Do not stand up until one or two minutes have passed.
9. Practice this technique once or twice a day.

Basic Method 4:

This method is described in *Self-Directed Behavior,* now in its 10th edition (Watson & Tharp, 2012).

1. Designate 10 or 15 minutes to begin practicing.
2. Sit in a comfortable chair with your spine straight in a quiet room away from any interruptions.
3. Let your hands fall into your lap, close your eyes, and relax your muscles. Breathe slowly and naturally.
4. Pay no attention to the world outside your body. It is easiest to do this if you have something to focus your mind on, such as a mantra.
5. Keep softly repeating your selected mantra to yourself. Breathe in first and then say your mantra as you breathe out.
6. When you first sit down and begin to relax, you will notice thoughts coming into your mind. After a minute or two, begin to say the mantra to yourself slowly.
7. As you say the mantra to yourself, other thoughts will come. After a while you may realize that you've been so busy with these thoughts that you haven't said your mantra in several minutes. When you become aware of this, just return to the mantra.
8. Don't fight to keep thoughts out of your mind; instead, let them drift through. This is not a time for working out solutions to problems or thinking things over. Allow thoughts other than the mantra to drift in, and drift out again, smoothly as the flowing of a river. Keep returning to the mantra and you will relax.
9. When your designated time is up, sit quietly for a minute or so with your eyes closed, and then gradually open your eyes.

Personal Exercise: Experimenting with Basic Meditation Methods

Activity Directions:

Step 1:   Designate a total of one month to experiment with each of the four basic meditation methods. Allot one week for each method.

Step 2:   Allocate 15 minutes per day, preferably every day, but minimally five days per week. It is best to designate the same time period every day. During your designated time, practice the selected method.

Step 3:   Identify the method that seems to be most beneficial for you, and make this method your practice.

Step 4:   Aim to practice every day, and when you can, more than once a day. Gradually increase the length of time you practice.

PRACTICING MINDFULNESS AS A PATHWAY TO MANAGING EMOTIONS

Smalley and Winston (2010) assert that being mindful does not change your life; it changes your *relationship to life*. Mindfulness certainly doesn't make all your problems go away, but it may give you the fortitude to face your problems from a source of contentment. Regular mindfulness practice builds the capacity to cope with stressors as they come at you. Some suggest that mindfulness brings a sense of meaning and purpose to life by cultivating an appreciation of the nonseparation of self and others coming to understand our interconnectedness.

Mindfulness serves as a tool to heighten self-awareness. For example, you might become more aware of the negative impact of gossiping, or your own inner critic. One of the things I became aware of through years of mindfulness practices was my habit of talking to myself, using my last name when I was being self-critical and using my first name when I was being self-accepting (e.g., *Larrivee, you are such a jerk for being sucked in again to someone else's agenda* versus *It's okay, Barb, to disappoint someone to align with your own integrity.*)

The brain naturally responds to sensations with emotions first and rational thought later. It's a kind of default setting that kicks in automatically unless you can purposefully train your mind to operate differently. As discussed previously, we have the capacity to rewire our brains, meaning our brains can be changed in both structure and function with practice and experience. Our brain changes as a consequence of experiences we create through repeated thoughts, feelings, and actions. The relationship is circular—experience shapes our brain and our brain shapes our experiences.

Practicing mindfulness offers a pathway to managing your emotions, rather than being managed by your emotions. Not being able to manage the emotional stress of teaching is one of the primary reasons teachers become dissatisfied and decide to leave teaching.

When you practice mindfulness you notice what's happening as it's happening and consciously take a brief pause between registering what's happened and doing something with or about it. Training the mind to pay attention to breathing improves your ability to pay attention to the experience of feeling. The time it takes to complete one cycle of inhalation and exhalation gives your thinking mind the chance to catch up with your feeling. Pausing buys you time for your thoughts to catch up and collaborate with your emotions so you can choose how you want to respond. Emotions come and go, often taking you by surprise. This is especially important for a teacher because when a situation stirs up a strong emotion, a teacher doesn't get to simply walk away until the emotion subsides. She must stay in the classroom with her students.

In their book *Mindful Teaching and Teaching Mindfulness: A Guide for Anyone Who Teaches Anything*, Schoeberlein and Sheth (2009) contend that "practicing mindfulness when you're not swept away by emotion is the precursor to applying mindfulness in the midst of real-life situations" (p. 69). The greater your ability to notice your emotions as soon as possible, the more likely you are to pause, think, and act mindfully. When you take time to experience your thoughts and feelings with a present-centered, nonjudgmental attitude, you begin to see such patterned behaviors for what they are and they naturally subside, rather than drive you to react in ways you may later regret.

Mindfulness Practices

Some mindfulness practices include setting intentions, developing rituals, pausing for brief moments of mindfulness, and movement-based practices.

Setting Intentions

Setting an intention prompts you to activate a particular quality or strength, such as patience. Intentions can focus on behaviors, thoughts, or feelings. Setting an intention primes your mind to be focused throughout the day as you shift among your many activities of the school day.

Setting intentions provides a way to purposefully cultivate awareness, such as taking one breath before responding to a student's challenging behavior. Although you may be tempted to set a broad intention, you are more likely to actually follow through if you set a smaller intention (Schoeberlein & Sheth, 2009). For example:

Instead of setting an intention to be patient in your third period class, set an intention to be patient with a particular student who tends to press your buttons.

Rather than telling yourself to stay calm, set an intention to close your door and take a few minutes to practice mindful breathing right before your lunch or break period.

It is more helpful to give yourself specific details that include *how*, *when*, and *where* you will apply the intent. For example, to transition out of your teaching role:

> At the end of the day (when) I will sit at my desk (where) and practice deep breathing for five minutes (how).

When you set more achievable goals, you are more likely to experience success. As you become more familiar with the act of setting intentions, you can keep shifting your attention to a goal requiring more and more effort.

Schoeberlein and Sheth also recommend developing a practice to acknowledge the experience of shifting from sleep into conscious awakeness. The idea is to receive the day with a welcoming acknowledgment. This could be something as minimal as setting an intention to savor your breakfast rather than shoving down your food while you're running out the door.

Developing Rituals

You could also create a daily ritual. Creating a ritual develops a familiar routine. Rituals are activities that you do the same time and in the same way each time you do them. This might be something as simple as standing in front of the window for a brief moment to greet whatever kind of day nature has provided. Or, it may be establishing a daily routine of sitting up in your bed and meditating for 20 minutes before getting out of bed.

The morning can be the most negative time of day for many people, so it may be helpful to get your day off to a good start. By developing a morning ritual, you can proactively set the tone for your day. With the constant influx of negative news from the media, having a begin-the-day uplifting ritual as the first thing you do can make a world of difference. Here are a few ways to start the day mindfully.

> Develop the ritual of beginning your day with a statement of appreciation. For example, "Today I am grateful for the time I'm going to spend with my friend Fran."

> Begin the day with a wish for the day: At the beginning of each day, make a wish for something positive to happen that day.

> Begin each day with a short inspirational message: Read a different life-enhancing message providing food for thought.

A daily ritual can be incorporated into an already routine part of your day. Ideally, it would be the same time every day. For example, as the last thing you do before crawling into bed, you can set one of the following rituals.

> Recount your day by remembering three things that you are grateful for. One rendition of this ritual could be to make the practice of having at least one of the things you are grateful for be particular to that day, while the other two may be general, such as good health.

> Recap the day on a positive note by appreciating someone else's act of kindness toward you by completing the following: "The most helpful thing someone did for me today was . . ."

Acknowledge something you've done to improve our world.

Designate a brief period at the end of each day to think about a way you contributed to the betterment of your students, school, community, or the world at large.

Practice Mindfulness by Following the "R" List

Winner (2008) in his book *Take the Stress Out of Your Life* offers some very simple things that you can do that will go a long way to reduce stress. Based on practicing mindfulness, he offers his "R" list:

1. **Resist Not:** Don't get stressed about being stressed.
2. **Relax:** Take a few deep breaths.
3. **Refocus:** Place full attention on your current activity.
4. **Repeat:** Repeat one to three frequently throughout the day.
5. **Regain Perspective:** When everything seems to be going wrong, focus on what is right.
6. **Reframe:** Look for the opportunity to learn from a challenging situation.
7. **Relationships:** Seek social support from friends and family.
8. **Reconsider:** Reconsider some of your choices and make changes in your work and home environment to reduce stress.

Another strategy he offers is to follow little stressors throughout the day with pausing for a "moment of mindfulness." This will keep minor hassles from snowballing into full-blown wipeouts by the end of the day.

Movement-based Mindfulness Practices

Moving your body through these specific poses and movements are mindfulness practices because they help take your mind off the stresses of your life. They also improve your balance and flexibility and can improve your peace of mind in general.

Tai chi and qi gong (pronounced "chee goong") are traditional Chinese movement exercises for developing focus and mental clarity. They are based on two ideas:

- Energy, called *chi* or *qi*, is defined as an inner energy or "life force" that is said to animate living beings. It flows through the body along "energy pathways" called *meridians*. If the flow of chi is blocked or unbalanced at any point on a pathway, it is believed to cause illness.
- Good health results when energy forces are in balance. You do tai chi and qi gong movements in an attempt to help restore the body's balance. They increase energy flow through gentle, repeated movements.

Tai chi is a graceful series of movements. Tai chi involves a system of soothing movements done either very slowly or quickly to help move the body's chi. Qi gong involves different movements. Some common qi gong movements include raising and lowering the arms, moving the head from side to side, and gently rubbing the ears, feet, and hands. Both are used as ways to combine meditation and movement as a practice to improve and maintain health. Because tai chi and qi gong require you to move your body just right as you glide through a variety of positions, it is best to learn them from a qualified instructor rather than from a book or video.

Another type of physical activity that can help develop mindfulness and relieve stress is the ancient practice of yoga. The stretching and deep breathing that yoga provides relieves muscle tension while improving flexibility, agility, and balance. Yoga is safe for people who are generally healthy, but you should check with your doctor before starting yoga if you have joint problems, neck or back pain, osteoporosis, high blood pressure, or are at risk for blood clots.

The concentration yoga requires helps get your mind off stressful situations in your life. There are many different styles of yoga. Hatha yoga is a common style that is not too physically demanding and involves moving through specific poses while breathing in a focused and controlled manner.

While you can learn yoga from books, videotapes, or DVDs, here again because yoga requires you to move your body precisely as you flow through different positions, getting feedback from a qualified instructor is preferable to trying to learn yoga on your own. Also, practicing yoga with like-minded people in a class makes it more enjoyable—and there is the added benefit of social support.

THE POWER OF THE BREATH

Breathing techniques are a cornerstone of many traditions of meditation. According to Dr. Andrew Weil, author of numerous books on health and healing, there is no single more powerful, or more simple, daily practice to further your health and well-being than breathwork (Weil, 1997/2006). Luskin and Pelletier (2005) consider deep breathing to be the most important life skills in their research-based stress management program, which has a proven record of success for reducing stress and lowering the risk of heart disease. Most people take breathing for granted. Breathing is automatic, and it doesn't require much thought as you go about your busy day. You also may not give much thought to how breathing affects your health, but it does.

The importance of breathing has also been validated in the now well-known long-term Framingham Study of cardiovascular health and longevity. It turns out that the best predictor of longevity isn't your genes, your nutrition, or how much exercise you get. It's your breathing. A measure called FEV1 is the volume of air you can expel in one second. The better your lungs work, the more volume of air you can blow out in one second. This study showed that FEV1 did a better job of predicting healthy longevity than other factors such as nutrition and exercise.

Technically, breathing gets oxygen into your body and brain when you inhale and gets carbon dioxide out of your body when you exhale. Your brain automatically controls breathing, including the size and frequency of each breath, based on signals from sensors in the lungs. On average, a person breathes in and out from 12 to 20 times a minute. Your lungs have no muscles of their own for breathing. The diaphragm is the major muscle of breathing. When you inhale, the diaphragm flattens downward, creating more space in the chest cavity for the lungs to fill. When you exhale, the diaphragm relaxes and returns to its dome shape. Although the diaphragm functions automatically, you can learn to control its movement, which is one very important way you can relax.

Although the mind has the power to control the body, it is influenced by the body. Mental anxiety is not possible whenever you are in a relaxed state. By maintaining an even, steady breath you maintain a state of physiological balance. This means you can achieve a significant degree of control over your emotions by learning to regulate the breath.

On a more subtle level, awareness of the breath can lead to control over the actual events within the stream of consciousness itself. This is surprisingly simple and direct. Most of us are locked into our thinking process, which manifests itself in an almost constant chatter within the mind. Left uncontrolled, this chatter is a great source of stress, as the mind constantly jumps from past to future with little focus on the here and now. This problem-solving aspect of the mind's working, if not focused on an immediate problem, will create a problem to solve. This is done through anticipation, and it is the basis for fear, which triggers an alarm response.

By bringing the focus of attention to the feeling of the breath as it enters your nostrils you can stop this chatter immediately. In more psychological terms, you move from a thinking, abstract mode of being to a more pristine, perceptual mode of being. This simple technique of breath awareness gradually leads to a greater degree of control over thoughts and to a greater sensitivity to both internal and external events. Over time, you become more able to act and respond more effectively.

The breath is within your power to alter. You just have to become aware of that power and use it for your benefit. Teachers can practice breathing techniques at school and/or at home as a way to quiet the mind. Simply by using breaks from teaching, such as recess or lunch, to observe themselves breathing slowly and deeply, harried teachers can reconnect with the more natural rhythm of their bodies.

Methods of Breathing

There are two primary methods of breathing, *chest breathing* and *diaphragmatic breathing*. Most people breathe by expanding and contracting their chests (chest breathing). Diaphragmatic breathing involves a slight in-and-out movement of the abdomen, pushing out when you inhale and pulling in when you exhale. It is also referred to as *deep*, *relaxed*, or *belly* breathing.

Most adults breathe shallowly by expanding only their chests. Some believe this may be an adaptation to stress. Infants and children usually use diaphragmatic breathing. It is a better method for breathing because it allows for the most effective exchange of oxygen and carbon dioxide with the least amount of effort (Smith, 1985). Deep breathing is easy to learn and requires minimal discipline to master. It can also help you to remain alert, energetic, and productive. Deep breathing can also be helpful for headaches, anxiety, high blood pressure, or difficulty sleeping (Smith, 2005).

When you feel stressed, you often find yourself taking short, gasping breaths, but this is something you have direct control over. You can consciously try to restore your breath to its usual steady rhythm, breathing just a little deeper than usual, but not taking deep, shuddering breaths. This is important because the body has a particular need for oxygen when stressed.

Because breathing is so integral to managing stress, breathing exercises are an important part of any effective stress management program. An easy way to learn diaphragmatic breathing from the Stress Free for Good program is described at the end of this chapter.

RELAXATION TECHNIQUES

Relaxation training is effective for lowering stress and anxiety (Bernstein, Borkovec, & Hazlett-Stevens, 2000). Individuals typically report that different techniques are more or less effective for different symptoms, so the general recommendation is to learn several approaches and then do your own experimenting. The research on stress in general indicates that the number of coping resources one has available predicts how well a person will cope. Having a repertoire of resources available increases the confidence and expectation of being able to cope effectively with whatever stressors may come along.

Relaxation techniques are easy to learn, but they do require a commitment to practice. The method used is less important than the amount of practice you devote to learning the technique. You should choose a method of relaxation that is pleasant so that you will actually practice. Trying several approaches increases the likelihood that you will find one or more that work particularly well for you in a variety of situations.

Relaxation is both a mental and physical response—a feeling of calmness and serenity, and a state of muscular release. Many of the physical symptoms of stress come from the muscle tension it produces. Being able to maintain a single focus of attention is impeded by residual tensions in either the body or the mind. Paradoxically, the ability to relax is prevented by the very same factors that give rise to the need to relax.

Consciously directed relaxation techniques achieve relaxation more rapidly and thoroughly than other indirect methods that you might use to relax, such as taking a nap, reading a book, or watching TV or a movie. Part of this simply has to do with your attention: If you pay attention to something, you can do it better. If you read a book to relax, you may relax, but your mind is still paying attention to the book. Relaxation is enhanced if you pay attention to the relaxation process itself. This attentiveness is the basis for what are called "relaxation techniques." In general, what these techniques have in common is the focus of your attention on various parts of the body to develop an awareness of the sensations of tension or relaxation arising from these areas, coupled with an intent to relax.

There are actually two separate components to most relaxation techniques. First, the focus of attention is placed on a neutral or relaxing image to remove stress-inducing thoughts from the mind. Just doing this will help interrupt the cycle of tension, and the muscles will begin to relax, especially as the flux of constantly changing thoughts begins to quiet down. Second, the process of physical relaxation is facilitated if the focal point for attention is the body itself, particularly the areas reflecting tension, such as within certain muscles. Moving your awareness from point to point throughout the muscles of the body is a way to give release to the mental restlessness arising from tension without interrupting the overall process of relaxation.

When you tense your muscles repeatedly under stress, you can develop headaches, neck stiffness, and back and jaw pain. The goal is to learn to produce relaxation at the first sign of tension. As you learn to recognize the signs of tension, you can quickly produce tension release, that is, relaxation. You use the first signs of tension as your cue to relax and interrupt the tension process early in its sequence.

Relaxation should be a systematic, conscious, and comfortable process. First you need to find a quiet place to lie down, preferably on a carpeted floor or padded mat on the floor. Then loosen any tight clothes and remove your shoes. A classic relaxation posture in yoga is known as the corpse pose. For this position, you lie on your back and close your eyes, placing your feet a comfortable distance apart. Your arms should be away from the sides of your body with palms upward and fingers gently curled. Lie in a symmetrical position with your head, neck, and trunk aligned.

Deep Muscle Relaxation

One method for learning to relax is to use deep muscle relaxation. Take a moment now to try relaxing your hand and arm or your jaw muscles. By doing so you realize how much energy is tied up in excess muscular tension. The personal exercise provided is designed to relax the skeletal muscles, eliminate fatigue and strain, and energize both mind and body.

Progressive Muscle Relaxation (PMR)

Many people don't realize that they are tensing their muscles during stress and have trouble allowing their muscles to totally relax. Progressive muscle relaxation (PMR) is designed specifically to reduce muscle tension through focused attention. In PMR you move progressively through the major areas of the body, alternately making your muscles tense and then relaxed. The idea is to learn the difference between these two states so that you can better recognize tension in your body and use PMR to relax. PMR has been a well-accepted method for relaxation since it was developed in the late 1930s (Jacobson, 1938). PMR is more difficult to learn, but it can produce a deeper and longer-lasting state of relaxation (Bernstein et al., 2000; Harris, 2003). Some find it especially pleasant to practice before going to sleep.

The general idea is to first tense a muscle group and then relax it so that the muscle relaxes more deeply than before the muscle was tensed. You repeat this process around your entire body in order to learn to recognize what tension and relaxation feel like. You focus your attention on each muscle group as you work through the various muscle groups so that you get a good sense of what each feels like when it is tense and when it is relaxed.

Initially, you will need to tape the directions. Eventually, you will want to memorize the specific muscle groups and the exercises for each, committing the instructions to memory so you can relax quickly at any time or place by following your own self-instructions. The idea is to master this practice so that in stressful situations in daily life you can notice your body's tension, identify the tense muscle groups, and relax them.

Personal Exercise: Deep Muscle Relaxation

Activity Directions: During this exercise keep your mind alert and concentrated on your breath as you progressively relax the muscles. The exercise should take about 10 minutes.

Lie in the corpse posture with eyes gently closed. Inhale and exhale through the nose slowly, smoothly, and deeply. There should be no noise, jerks, or pauses in the breath; let the inhalations and exhalations flow naturally without exertion in one continuous movement. Keep the body still. Mentally travel through the body and relax the top of the head, forehead, eyebrows, space between the eyebrows, eyes, eyelids, cheeks, and nose. Exhale and inhale completely four times.

Relax the fingertips, fingers, hands, wrists, lower arms, upper arms, shoulders, upper back, and chest. Concentrate on the center of the chest, and exhale and inhale completely four times.

Relax the stomach, abdomen, lower back, hips, thighs, knees, calves, ankles, feet, and toes. Exhale as though your whole body is exhaling, and inhale as though your whole body is inhaling. Expel all your tension, worries, and anxieties; inhale vital energy, peace, and relaxation. Exhale and inhale completely four times.

Relax the toes, feet, ankles, calves, thighs, knees, hips, lower back, abdomen, stomach, and chest. Concentrating on the center of the chest, exhale and inhale completely four times.

Relax the upper back, shoulders, upper arms, lower arms, wrists, hands, fingers, and fingertips. Exhale and inhale completely four times.

Relax the fingertips, fingers, hands, wrists, lower arms, upper arms, shoulders, neck, chin, jaw, mouth, and nostrils. Exhale and inhale completely four times.

Relax the cheeks, eyelids, eyes, eyebrows, space between the eyebrows, forehead, and the top of the head. Exhale and inhale completely four times.

Now, for 60 seconds, let your mind be aware of the calm and serene flow of the breath. Let your mind make a gentle, conscious effort to guide your breath so that it remains smooth, calm, and deep.

Personal Exercise: Practicing Progressive Muscle Relaxation

Activity Directions: First you will need to make an audiotape combining the general directions with the specific exercise for each individual muscle group. Choose a private place, quiet and free of interruptions and distractions. Sit comfortably in a chair, and be well supported by the chair so that you don't have to use your muscles to support yourself. Or, you may prefer to lie down. You may want to close your eyes. The basic procedure below for each muscle group is the same (Watson & Tharp, 2012).

For each muscle group:

- Tense the muscle.
- Hold for five seconds, noticing the tension.
- Now release and let the tension slide away.
- Notice the warmth of relaxation.
- Repeat: Tense> hold> notice tension> release> notice warmth of relaxation
- Repeat: Tense> hold> notice tension> release> notice warmth of relaxation

After moving through this sequence for each muscle group, tense all the muscles together, holding for five seconds, release, and take a deep breath, saying "relax" as you breathe out slowly. Repeat two more times.

Progressive Relaxation Instructions for Each Muscle Group

Muscle Group	Tension Exercise
1. The dominant hand	Make a tight fist.
2. The other hand	
3. The dominant arm	Curl your arm up; tighten the bicep.
4. The other arm	
5. Upper face and scalp	Raise eyebrows as high as possible.
6. Center face	Squint eyes and wrinkle nose.
7. Lower face	Smile in a false, exaggerated way; clench teeth.
8. Neck	a. Pull head slightly forward, then relax. b. Pull head slightly back, then relax.
9. Chest and shoulders	a. Pull shoulders back until the blades almost touch then relax. b. Pull shoulders forward all the way, then relax.
10. Abdomen	Make abdomen tight and hard.
11. Buttocks	Tighten together.
12. Upper right leg	Stretch leg out from you, tensing both upper and lower muscles.
13. Upper left leg	
14. Lower right leg	Pull toes up toward you.
15. Lower left leg	
16. Right foot	Curl toes down and away from you.
17. Left foot	

Initially, the exercises take 20 to 30 minutes. As you become more proficient, less and less time will be needed. When you release the muscle tension, rather than relaxing the tension gradually, you should let it go instantly so that your muscles become suddenly limp (Smith, 2005). If you have an injury or other problem with any of these muscle groups, skip over them. If you have high blood pressure, talk to your doctor before doing PMR. Achieving results will require daily practice for several weeks.

STRESS-FREE LIFE SKILLS

In the time-pressured world of teachers, they need quick and practical stress relievers. The Stress Free for Good program offers 10 easy-to-learn, simple, and practical "LifeSkills." They take 10 minutes or less to learn, can be practiced in about a minute, and work in less than ten seconds. These LifeSkills include exercises that create a state of physical relaxation while remaining mentally alert, practices that help to maintain emotional stability while under stress, strategies to create greater peace, and tools that show you how to recognize and appreciate the many positives and blessings that surround you.

Luskin and Pelletier (2005) are pioneers in mind-body medicine and have more than a combined total of 40 years of clinical and research experience in the area of stress management and developing emotional well-being. Based on research conducted at the Stanford University School of Medicine, they created a research-based stress reduction program. Their book, *Stress Free for Good: 10 Scientifically Proven Life Skills for Health and Happiness*, describes these essential LifeSkills. Their research found these LifeSkills broad enough to help almost everyone who has tried the Stress Free for Good program. They have been tested in both rigorous research trials and in clinics throughout the United States and have proven successful for reducing stress levels, lowering risks and incidence of heart disease, as well as improving mood and quality of life.

They are presented in order of the simplest to learn to the more complicated.

10 Stress-Free LifeSkills

1. Breath from your belly (take deep breaths from your diaphragm).
2. Appreciate what you have (be grateful).
3. Tense to relax (tense and then relax different muscles of your body).
4. Visualize success (picture yourself being successful).
5. Slow down (become totally focused on what you are doing).
6. Appreciate yourself (honor your own worth, value, and contributions).
7. Practice smiling (remind yourself of why you do what you do—and smile).
8. Stop doing what doesn't work (try a different solution to get better results).
9. Say no (don't allow others to overburden you).
10. Accept what you can't change (find a way to make peace with what is).

Once you learn these skills, each LifeSkill takes from about 1 minute to as little as 15 seconds to put into practice. With practice, your mind and body will feel positive results in about 6 to 10 seconds. Long-term practice of the LifeSkills will enhance the results of your daily practice. While improvement begins immediately, the timetable for mastering these skills can be a lot longer. Based on their knowledge of our current scientific understanding of how the brain and nervous systems function, Luskin and Pelletier say it can often take from 10 to 12 weeks to uncover a dysfunctional way of seeing, thinking, or behaving and replace it with a new approach. This timetable has proven accurate for many aspects of life in which you want to learn a new skill or develop a new habit (for example, physical fitness, dieting, developing an athletic skill, changing a behavior pattern).

Some of these strategies have already been discussed in previous sections of this book. Several more that involve expressing appreciation and gratitude will be covered in the final chapter. Three of these LifeSkills have nearly instantaneous results—breathing deeply, putting a smile on your face, and visualizing success. The next section describes these three "instant stress-busters" in more detail.

Three Instant Stress-Busters

Belly breathing. Because our body is designed for self-preservation, it gears up to face danger within one heartbeat. By increasing the depth and decreasing the rate of your breathing, you signal to your body that the threat has passed and the body can calm down. That's why the simplest and most direct form of stress management is to change your shallow, rapid breathing to deep, slow breathing. Belly breathing acts like a control switch to shut down the stress response. You have to practice belly breathing for between 6 and 10 seconds for the "all-clear" message to register in the

---

Personal Exercise: Practicing Belly Breathing

Activity Directions: The recommendation is to practice every day, sometimes for 5 to 10 minutes at a time. Your practice sessions could be done while you're sitting in your car, watching TV, walking for exercise, or sitting at the computer.

1. As you inhale, imagine that your belly is a big balloon that you are slowly filling with air.
2. Place your hands on your belly while you slowly inhale.
3. Watch your hands as they rise with your inbreath.
4. Watch your hands fall as you slowly breathe out, letting the air out of the balloon.
5. As you exhale, keep your belly relaxed.
6. Take at least three more slow and deep breaths, keeping your attention on the rise and fall of your belly.

brain. Typically, this is between three and four breaths. Learning to breathe slowly, fully, and deeply is the cornerstone LifeSkill. The personal exercise shows you how to practice belly breathing.

Practice smiling. Recent brain research has found that smiling stimulates the production of endorphins in the brain. Endorphins are naturally occurring opiates that relieve pain and give a sense of pleasure, peace, and well-being. A smile is the expression of contentment and joy. When you feel happy, you smile. No other part of the body registers such a visible change.

When a child smiles at you, do you find yourself automatically smiling back? It turns out that we actually have a built in "empathy" response that is part of the wiring of the human brain. Brain research has revealed that we mirror the emotions we perceive in others (Singer & Lamm, 2009). Try the personal exercise to see for yourself.

A word of caution is in order here. It cannot be an inauthentic, frozen, or sticky-sweet smile; rather, it needs to be a genuine smile fed by actually experiencing a positive emotion.

Visualize success. This LifeSkill teaches you to visualize a successful outcome to a problem by picturing that outcome in your mind. Your ability to visualize better solutions to stressful situations can be the missing link between those problems and effective solutions. Most of us are unaware of the power in our images. Your body reacts to whatever picture you create in your mind. For example, your body reacts to your worry of having total chaos in your classroom by tensing up. When you have a picture of this in your mind's eye, your body reacts as if it were really happening.

According to Luskin and Pelletier, the muscles of the back are particularly sensitive, rendering back pain a common response to stress. Headaches and back pain are tools the body uses to bring the problem to our attention. They cite research supporting the value of positive visualization for reducing pain, improving physical functioning, and boosting mental outlook for those suffering from a multitude of physical symptoms. In fact, one study with individuals suffering from tension headaches found those using imagery were three times more likely to report major pain reduction compared to those using other interventions.

We think not just in words but with all our senses. These mental images are very powerful, and they can be used either to stress you out or calm you down. When you

---

Personal Exercise: Try a Smile

Activity Directions:

Try a smile right now. Think of the good you do every day with your students, and smile. Hold that smile for about 10 seconds. Feel better? Not only do you smile when you feel happy, you also feel happy when you smile. They apparently go hand-in-hand. If you find you have a hard time smiling out of the blue, just think of a loved one and remember the last time you saw him or her laughing. This image alone is enough to make you smile.

Personal Exercise: Visualizing Success

Activity Directions:

Think about what is happening in your classroom, or with a particular student, that you want to improve. Take a few belly breaths. Picture in your mind your situation turning out the way you would like it to. Once you get a clear picture, describe to yourself what the picture shows you about succeeding. Imagine that you navigated your day in your classroom well. See yourself driving home from school with a smile on your face, congratulating yourself for managing the day so well. Now, you can begin to make a plan for how you can put into practice what you saw.

have a picture of yourself as overworked, exhausted, and underappreciated you feel like a failure and picture yourself as one. It's like wearing a big red F on your forehead.

Visualizing success works in two distinct ways: It relaxes and calms the body and it allows you to create better solutions to your problems by helping you to plan and anticipate creative outcomes to problems. To best use this skill, you first need to become clear about your goals. You need to be able to say exactly what it is you want to improve. Then you can brainstorm ideas that might move you in the direction of success. Try the personal exercise to practice this LifeSkill.

It's best to start small and then gradually move on to your bigger challenges. You will need to practice this exercise at least three times for the problem you are tackling, more if it is a serious one. You can practice this skill by picturing yourself having a successful day or class period. See yourself getting through your classroom routines more efficiently, and think of specific ways you might be more successful. Picture yourself as a teacher who is quite capable of being effective. Now, picture a truly perfect school day. Describe exactly what this kind of day looks like in your eyes.

Now you're ready to make a plan for how you might carry out your positive image, taking it from a fantasy to reality. Think about some ideas that might work better than what you're doing now. Consider what specific steps are involved, and lay out the order in which these steps would need to be taken. When you have a reasonable plan of action, rehearse your plan in your imagination.

Luskin and Pelletier say this whole process takes less than 10 minutes. That's the time it takes to go from feeling helpless to having options, from feeling overwhelmed to experiencing hope. This process may allow you to find wisdom that has been unavailable when you were tense and stressed, allowing you to access ideas you have never thought of before. Visualizing yourself being successful may help you figure out what it will take to actually create that experience. The critical step here is to move from insight to action as you visualize a new way to deal with your daily stressors.

Although visualization can be very powerful, of course, it doesn't work equally well for everyone. You will need to experiment to see if you reap its potential benefits.

Chapter Ten

How to Thrive and Flourish: Sustaining Resilience, Optimism, and Hope

The emerging field of positive psychology explores and analyzes positive emotions, personal characteristics, and environments in order to identify situations that lead to human beings thriving and flourishing (Seligman & Csikszentmihalyi, 2000). In other words, positive psychology is the scientific study of what makes life most worth living. As president of the American Psychological Association (APA), Martin Seligman marshaled in this "new" psychology in 1998.

Research indicates that fewer than 20% of adults in the United States report that they are flourishing (Keyes, 2002). According to Fredrickson (2008), many appear to be languishing; that is, feeling as if they are "stuck in a rut" or "wanting more." Increasingly psychological well-being is viewed as not only the absence of mental disorder but also the presence of positive psychological resources. Some of these include positive emotion, life satisfaction, happiness, purpose in life, self-acceptance, positive relations, and autonomy.

What triggered the birth of positive psychology was Seligman's assertion that the majority of efforts in psychology since the 1940s had focused on human problems and how to remedy them, neglecting the study of what can go right. Traditionally, the goal of psychology has been to relieve human suffering. Positive psychology attempts to shift the assumptions of psychology away from embracing a disease model of human nature that views people as flawed and fragile victims of bad environments and/or genetics.

Positive psychology challenges such a disease model, calling for as much focus on strengths as on weaknesses, as much interest in building the best things in life as in repairing the worst, and as much attention to fulfilling the lives of healthy people as healing the wounds of the distressed (Seligman, 2002). The field of positive psychology is divided into three related topics: 1) positive experiences (happiness, pleasure, gratification, fulfillment), 2) positive individual traits (strengths of character, talents, interests, values), and 3) enabling positive institutions (families, schools, businesses, communities, societies). The theory is that positive institutions facilitate the development and display of positive traits, which in turn facilitate positive experiences (Peterson & Park, 2003).

Although Seligman is credited with the term *positive psychology*, it was first used not by him, but by Abraham Maslow, in 1954. In many ways, positive psychology builds on key tenets of humanistic psychology. Carl Rogers's (1951) client-centered therapy, for example, was based on the theory that people could improve their lives by expressing their authentic selves. And Maslow (1954/1970) identified traits of self-actualized people that are similar to the character strengths identified in positive psychology. Positive psychology was originally conceived as a way to advance well-being and optimal functioning in healthy people, focusing on positive emotions and building strengths.

BUILDING CHARACTER STRENGTHS

Based on their research conducted to categorize character virtues and strengths across 40 countries, Peterson and Seligman (2004) found a surprising amount of similarity across cultures, with a strong cross-cultural convergence of six core virtues. They dubbed these the "High Six." These six overarching virtues are endorsed by almost every culture across the world.

They distinguished two conceptual levels. The first is virtues, or the broad, core characteristics. They argue that these are universal, perhaps grounded in biology through an evolutionary process. They posit that these virtues are what allow human beings to struggle against, and to triumph over, what is darkest within us. Arrien (2011) describes virtues as the qualities that support the inherent goodness that resides in each of us.

The second level is character strengths, the psychological ingredients, processes, or mechanisms, that define the virtues. They are the distinguishable routes to displaying the virtue. For example, the virtue of humanity can be achieved through such strengths as kindness, love, and social or emotional intelligence. Table 10.1 shows the classification scheme with six categories of virtues with 24 corresponding character strengths.

Based on their research, Peterson and Seligman (2004) found that the five most commonly endorsed strengths are kindness, fairness, authenticity, gratitude, and open-mindedness. They have also found strengths "of the heart"—zest, gratitude, hope, and love—to have greater association with life satisfaction than the more cerebral strengths of curiosity and love of learning (Park, Peterson, & Seligman, 2004).

Certain virtues had real "staying power." Justice and humanity were the most reliably consistent across every tradition. Temperance and wisdom finished a close second based on their survey of the cultures with long literary traditions. Transcendence was fifth, and courage last. These general traits, virtues, or values that predispose individuals to the (psychological) good life appear to be universal, whether termed positive mental health, well-being, self-actualization, psychosocial maturity, or authentic happiness (Peterson & Seligman, 2004).

Seligman (2002) originally used the term *authentic happiness* to extend happiness beyond the "feel-good" connotation of the term *happiness* itself to include engagement and meaning as elements of the "good life." His years of previous research and

Table 10.1. Virtues with Corresponding Character Strengths

1. **Wisdom and Knowledge**
   Creativity
   Curiosity
   Open-mindedness
   Love of learning
   Perspective
2. **Courage**
   Authenticity
   Bravery
   Persistence
   Zest
3. **Humanity**
   Kindness
   Love
   Social intelligence or emotional intelligence
4. **Justice**
   Fairness
   Leadership
   Teamwork
5. **Temperance**
   Forgiveness
   Modesty
   Prudence
   Self-regulation
6. **Transcendence**
   Appreciation of beauty and excellence
   Gratitude
   Hope
   Humor
   Religiousness

that of colleagues revealed a major shortcoming in studying happiness. As it turns out, happiness actually boils down to a single dimension, *life satisfaction*. This is mainly due to the measurement used in most studies that simply asks individuals to rate how satisfied they are with their life (on a 1 to 10 scale). Researchers report that, averaging over many, many people, the mood you are in determines more than 70% of how much life satisfaction you report.

In research on happiness, three distinct routes to happiness have been explored: positive emotion and pleasure, engagement, and meaning (Seligman, 2002). Research suggests that the most satisfied people are those who orient their pursuits toward all three, with the greatest weight carried by engagement and meaning (Peterson, Park, & Seligman, 2005). As defined by Seligman, the term *authentic happiness* refers jointly to positive emotion, engagement, and meaning.

Interestingly, pleasure seems to be the least consequential pathway to a content, satisfied life. Gratification stems from doing activities we like, that engage us fully without self-consciousness, creating what Csikszentmihalyi (1990) calls a "flow" experience. This kind of deeply involving and gratifying experience depends on our capacity to develop our authentic talents, strengths, and virtues. Research in positive psychology reveals that recognizing, honoring, and developing our strengths is the most important way to instill a true sense of engagement (Lopez & Snyder, 2003; Peterson & Seligman, 2004).

Finding a sense of meaning or purpose in life is another essential element that contributes to our feelings of happiness and well-being. Developing such a sense rests on our ability to use our strengths and virtues in the service of something much larger than ourselves (Seligman, Steen, Park, & Peterson, 2005). These larger domains might be focusing on children, family, disease, spirituality, social justice, or the environment. Such altruistic actions are also deeply tied to our sense of satisfaction.

In his book, *Gross National Happiness*, Brooks (2008) argues that what is crucial to well-being is not how cheerful you feel or how much money you make; rather, it is the meaning you have created and your sense of "earned success"—the belief that you have created value in your life or others' lives. And who has greater potential for earned success than a teacher? What could create more value than having a positive impact on the children you teach every day of your career?

According to Brooks, we find meaning in providing unconditional love for children. Paradoxically, our happiness is raised by our very willingness to have our happiness lowered through years of tantrums and backtalk. Willingness to accept unhappiness from children (and students) is a source of happiness. Parents focus on the golden moments while forgetting the more frequent travails. Seligman, a father of eight himself, says that parents are seeking far more than happy feelings, asserting that if this is all we wanted our species would have died out long ago. We have children to pursue other elements of well-being, such as meaning in life and nurturing relationships. In a similar vein, teachers reap great pleasure from the sparks of hope they see ignited in their students.

Just as an athlete exercises certain muscles to become stronger, the theory is that people who use their strengths regularly will function better in life. The field of positive psychology now embraces a variety of strategies and interventions that encourage identifying and further developing your own character traits, positive emotions, and experiences.

Seligman and colleagues have developed a series of personal exercises intended to build character strengths and cultivate positive emotions. They have conducted extensive research online with hundreds of participants who were asked to record their responses to five exercises done every night for one week. Participants also completed baseline and follow-up assessments to gauge the impact of these exercises. Results

Personal Exercise: Using Your Signature Strengths

Activity Directions:

Identify your top five strengths (by taking an inventory of character strengths online at www.authentichappiness.org). Then use one of these top five strengths in a new and different way daily.

showed that after six months, those completing the character strengths exercise were significantly happier and less depressed than the control group.

The online inventory of character strengths now has two versions, the Brief Strengths Test containing only 24 items and the Values in Action Institute (VIA) Survey of Character Strengths with 240 items. You get a more complete picture by taking the lengthier survey. After completing the survey, you receive a report that ranks the 24 strengths by the degree to which they characterize you. The report also features your top five strengths and encourages you to reflect on which ones truly resonate for you—which strengths, when you act on them, make you come alive. This self-reflection is how you locate your "signature" strengths among your top five.

We all have our own set of unique strengths and limitations. Using the categories of cognitive, social, emotional, and physical provides another way of thinking about your strengths and limitations. These categories are defined below, with a strength example for each.

Cognitive:	Intellectual functioning, characteristics of the mind.
	A cognitive strength is the ability to be open-minded.
Social:	The relationship you have with others.
	A social strength is kindness.
Emotional:	The relationship you have with yourself.
	An emotional strength is self-regulation.
Physical:	Pertaining to your body.
	A physical strength is stamina.

Completing the personal exercise may help you create a clearer picture of how you see yourself.

If in this exercise you listed many more limitations than strengths, you are probably expecting too much of yourself. If you are the kind of person who dwells on your own limitations, this likely means you are overly judgmental and critical of others as well. The problem lies not in recognizing your limitations but in your "overindulgence" of these so that they have a disproportionate influence on how you view yourself as well as your behavior toward others.

Each of us is a unique combination of strengths and limitations. Successful, happy people dwell on their strengths, not their weaknesses, and this is what you should be doing. As you become more adept at recognizing and expressing your own strengths you will be more likely to recognize and acknowledge the strengths of others, particularly your students. When teachers focus on their own strengths, they will also focus on the strengths, not the limitations, of their students. Using all four areas (cognitive, social, emotional, physical) helps teachers see a total person and transfer this holistic view to finding strengths in their students.

Another interesting twist on acknowledging and building character strengths is Arrien's (1993) notion about ways that we receive acknowledgment in our lives. As a cultural anthropologist, her research across many cultures led her to identify four ways people are acknowledged. These four ways are universal and are related to skill, appearance, character, and impact. We may have been acknowledged or appreciated by others because of our appearance (physical attributes, style), the skills we have

Personal Exercise: Assessing Your Strengths and Limitations

Activity Directions:

Step 1: Take a few minutes and think about your own strengths and limitations. Use the categories of cognitive, social, emotional, and physical to guide your thinking. Divide a sheet of paper in half and write your strengths in the top half of the page and your limitations in the bottom half.

Step 2: Now look over your list and answer the following questions:
Have you listed more strengths than weaknesses?
Have you listed more weaknesses than strengths?
Do you have a majority of items in one or more of the four categories?
What can you say about this picture of yourself?

Step 3: Next, look back over your list of limitations. Some examples of limitations you might have listed are shy, uncoordinated, or slow. Now, change the item to be purely descriptive. For example, rather than saying "shy" you might say, "When I am with people I don't know, I don't like to initiate a conversation." Revise the item so that it is limited to a particular situation where the trait occurs. Take some time and revise each of the limitations, keeping the following guidelines in mind: (1) eliminate any words that have a negative connotation, (2) be specific and factual, and (3) relate the weakness to a specific situation.

Step 4: Finally, look back over your list of strengths and see if there are any you have overlooked. Think of kind words your family or friends have said to you and make sure these are included. Go even a step further and take these isolated words and write complete sentences, creating a more accurate description of yourself. For example, if you used the word musical to initially describe yourself, your revision might be "I have a beautiful voice and I love to sing."

developed (leadership, emotional intelligence), our character strengths (authenticity, persistence), or the impact we have had on others (kindness, hope). She asserts that we have all been acknowledged for different assets, and this lifelong acknowledgment is a significant part of our identity.

Arrien goes on to say that the area(s) in which we have received little acknowledgment (some may say reinforcement) is the area we learn to pay less attention to in our lives, and so it stays underdeveloped. She recommends identifying which area you may have neglected and trying to build that area. The next exercise asks you to reflect on how you have been acknowledged in your life.

Personal Exercise: How Have You Been Acknowledged in Your Life?

Activity Directions:

Step 1:   The four areas that we typically receive acknowledgment from others are relative to our skills, appearance, character, and impact. Think about how you have been acknowledged in each of these areas.

Step 2:   In which of the four ways have you been most acknowledged in your life?

Step 3:   In which of the four ways have you been least acknowledged in your life?

Step 4:   As a result of the acknowledgment you have received throughout your life, what have you paid less attention to that you may want to begin paying more attention to now?

In doing this exercise myself, I gained the insight that I have been acknowledged most for my impact on others, next by the skills I have mastered, and third by my appearance. The area I have received the least acknowledgment in my life is character. This new awareness has heightened my consciousness regarding character strengths I want to embrace.

PROMOTING WELL-BEING

Well-being is a vague expression that is hard to define. While it may be difficult to fully grasp all it entails, everyone seems to be jumping on the bandwagon to promote it. It is fast seeping into popular consciousness.

Holmes (2005), writing about teacher well-being, offers the following definition:

Well-being requires harmony between mind and body. It implies a sense of balance and ease with the myriad dimensions of life. When we feel a sense of well-being, we are not under-stimulated and bored, nor are we suffering under the burden of excessive stress and pressure. We have a sense of control over our work and even over our destiny in life. (p. 6)

Although in the past, the mind-body connection had been rejected by modern medicine, increasingly research undeniably shows the extent of the influence that the mind can have over physical and emotional well-being. As discussed in previous chapters, well-being is not simply the opposite of stress; it entails far more.

The span of well-being is all-encompassing. For the purposes of defining the scope of well-being both in the classroom and the wider context of life, Holmes divides it into four categories:

- Physical well-being
- Emotional well-being
- Mental and intellectual well-being
- Spiritual dimensions of well-being

Everyone most likely has a clear sense of what physical well-being entails. Emotional well-being is more difficult to define. The following quote captures the essence of this domain.

> We either make ourselves miserable, or we make ourselves strong. The amount of work is the same.
>
> —Carlos Castaneda

Mental and intellectual well-being encompass the mind-set of continuous professional and personal development. It refers to those factors that must be present in order to feel a sense of intellectual well-being in the work that you do. At its core, it is the notion of being a lifelong learner. For teachers, it means keeping your passion to teach alive.

Within the conception of spiritual well-being, the term *spirit* need not be dependent on a particular religious belief, or even with some realm above and beyond the here and now. What is most important is what spiritual well-being means for each individual. Those writing about spiritual well-being typically describe it as an experience that extends beyond the material world. It also tends to be linked to the desire to become in some way a fuller, more complete person as well as embracing a sense of greater good. One useful way to conceive of spirituality may be as a thread running through our lives that gives purpose and meaning.

From Authentic Happiness to Well-Being to Flourishing

Being in a state of well-being is not merely being symptom- or disorder-free. Mental health and mental illness are not two ends of one continuum; rather, they constitute separate dimensions of human functioning (Keyes, 2005). Well-being is a state of mind in which you are not languishing in life; you are flourishing.

Over the past 10 years, Seligman's research has led him to extend his original conception of authentic happiness and to advocate for well-being. He now embraces the concept of well-being, replacing his earlier use of the term *authentic happiness*. In his latest book, *Flourish: A Visionary New Understanding of Happiness and Well-Being*, he explains that while happiness is a real thing, well-being is a construct (Seligman, 2011a). Well-being has five distinct and measurable elements, each of which contributes to a sense of well-being. They include the original three that comprised authentic happiness plus two new dimensions. He refers to these as the five pillars of his latest version of positive psychology, and they are what it takes to lead what he calls a "life of profound fulfillment." Enjoying positive emotion, being engaged with the things and people you care about, having meaning in your life, achieving your work goals, and maintaining positive relationships are the five elements needed to flourish.

Research in the realm of positive psychology over the past two decades aspires to promote well-being by building positive strengths through intentional interventions that aim to cultivate positive feelings, thinking, and behaviors. Researchers studying dimensions of happiness over the past 20 years have discovered that it is how we choose to view the world that is key. Research consistently bears out that, once basic needs are met, greater income does not significantly boost happiness (Brooks, 2008).

Most of us operate under the assumption that there is a fixed, genetically determined set point for happiness—a "feel-good" gene that you either have or you don't have. Actually, that's only half true. About 50% of our tendency toward being happy and optimistic is genetic (Lyubomirsky, 2007). The other 50% is totally up for grabs. Roughly 40% is influenced by attitudes and behaviors, and the remaining 10% by circumstances. Because nearly half of our happiness quotient lies in the way we think and act, we have the power to influence how we feel and behave. With this much of the individual differences in happiness determined by what we do, by exerting intentional effort we can both preserve happiness and become happier (Lyubomirsky, Sheldon, & Schkade, 2005; Sheldon & Lyubomirsky, 2004).

According to Lyubomirsky (2011), both the joys of loves and triumphs, and the sorrows of losses and humiliations, fade with time. The process by which people become accustomed to a positive or negative event such that its emotional effect is weakened over time is labeled *hedonic adaptation* in the psychological literature (Frederick & Loewenstein, 1999). Research indicates that adaptation is faster in response to positive than negative experiences. That is, although both positive and negative emotions do not sustain themselves, the positive emotions fade more quickly. The impact of everyday negative events is more powerful and longer lasting than that of positive events (Lawton, DeVoe, & Parmelee, 1995; Nezlek & Gable, 2001; Sheldon, Ryan, & Reis, 1996).

A line of research that may also shed light on the "bad is stronger than good" phenomenon is the positivity (good-to-bad) ratios that distinguish flourishing individuals, couples, and groups. Such ratios generally range from 3–1 to 5–1 (Fredrickson, 2009; Fredrickson & Losada, 2005). Fredrickson, in her book *Positivity: Top-Notch Research Reveals the 3-to-1 Ratio That Will Change Your Life*, presents convincing data in support of this ratio. According to Fredrickson, below a 3–1 ratio positivity may be overwhelmed by the greater potency of negativity, whereas at or above a 3–1 ratio positivity gains adequate strength to overcome negativity.

In classrooms, a ratio of at least 5 to 1 positive to negative comments to students has long been the advocated standard. Happily married couples, for example, are characterized by ratios of approximately 5–1 in their positive verbal and emotional expressions to each other, as compared to very unhappy couples who display ratios of less than 1–1 (Gottman, 1994). The same optimal ratio of 5–1 characterizes the verbal comments of profitable and productive versus less profitable and productive business teams (Losada, 1999). These findings seem to suggest that the blow of one bad emotion, comment, or event can match or undo that of three or more positive ones.

Wilson and Gilbert (2008) propose that people engage in a sequential process of attending, reacting, explaining, and ultimately adapting to events. They break adaptation into three processes.

First, people are less likely to attend to positive as opposed to negative events.

Second, people have weaker emotional reactions to positive events.

Finally, it is less difficult and less time-consuming to explain or make sense of positive than negative events.

In other words, positive affect signals to individuals that things are going well and that they may continue engaging with their environment. Negative affect, by contrast, warns people of potential danger or unpleasantness in the environment to which they must respond (for example, attack, flee, conserve resources). Because survival is much more dependent on urgent attention to potential dangers than on passing up opportunities for positive experiences, it is more adaptive for "bad to be stronger than good" (Baumeiser, Bratslavsky, Finkenauer, & Vohs, 2001).

Learning to adapt to circumstantial changes in response to both favorable and unfavorable life changes is essential for maintaining happiness and well-being. The process involves both facilitating coping in the negative domain and enhancing happiness and well-being in the positive domain. Maintaining well-being then calls for activating or accelerating adaptation when your fortunes have turned for the worse and slowing down adaptation when they have turned for the better.

One avenue for facilitating coping with negative emotions is through expressive writing. Research substantiates the value of systematically analyzing and coming to terms with traumas, stressors, and hurt feelings by writing about them (Lyubomirsky, Sousa, & Dickerhoof, 2006; Pennebaker, 1997). Pennebaker has conducted numerous studies demonstrating how emotional disclosure through writing can promote both mental and physical health (Pennebaker, 1993, 1997; Pennebaker & Chung, 2007). Writing is inherently a structured process that forces you to organize and integrate thoughts, reflect on what causes what, create a coherent narrative about yourself, and consider systematic, step-by-step solutions (Pennebaker, Mayne, & Francis, 1997; Pennebaker & Seagal, 1999).

Writing is an effective strategy because it can reduce how often and how intensely you experience intrusive thoughts about negative experiences by helping you make sense of them, find meaning in them, and get past them. Some research suggests that men accrue more benefits than women by expressing thoughts about a stressful event through writing (Smyth, 1998). This may be because men do not have the same opportunities as women to engage in emotional expression in their normal social network.

The Importance of Enhancing Positive Emotions

Until recently, most research for reducing stress focused on a "negative affect pathway" by regulating the harmful effects of stress-related emotions such as hostility, anger, despair, and guilt. More recent research incorporates a "positive affect pathway" that can serve to protect, restore, and sustain well-being during periods of stress.

Research is accumulating that indicates maintaining positive affect is beneficial to health (see reviews by Lyubomirsky, 2011; Moscowitz, 2011; Tugade, 2011).

What is significant about strategies for maintaining positive emotional states is that often such strategies are not directed at the immediate stressors, but elsewhere at other positive events or conditions within a person's life—past, present, or anticipated. Positive events and emotions can co-occur with negative ones, and positive emotions can help sustain efforts to cope with ongoing stress.

Fredrickson (2001) has put forth the "broaden-and-build" theory of positive emotions that asserts that people's daily experiences of positive emotions compound over time to build up enduring personal resources. These resources can be cognitive, psychological, social, or physical. Positive emotions produce more expansive options for action (Fredrickson & Branigan, 2005). On the other hand, negative emotional states are associated with narrow and fixated thinking and action.

The broadening function of positive emotions is useful for developing a repertoire of coping strategies to be kept in store until needed to cope with stress. For instance, experiences of gratitude increase awareness of social connections. When feeling a sense of gratitude, you think about the many ways people are important in your life. According to the theory, the outgrowth of positive emotions, like gratitude, is more expansive thinking and a greater breadth of action that helps to build personal resources, including coping resources.

Deliberately cultivating positive emotions and appreciating "run-of-the-mill" daily events help people cope with their stress. Positive emotions, in turn, can provide the needed psychological lift to help people continue and move forward in their lives even when they are under stress. Positive emotions can have a lasting "undoing effect" on negative emotions.

As we have all experienced, the smell of the ocean or the feel of warmth from a hot cup of tea can be soothing and elicit feelings of contentment. When undergoing a stressful experience, such sensory experiences can activate positive emotions that help coping, even outside of one's conscious awareness. Through the automatic process of perception, sensory experiences can activate a positive state interrupting the trajectory of a stressful episode before it can fully unfold (Tugade, 2011). This phenomenon is the basis of conventional wisdom to "smell the roses."

Research suggests that strategies that elicit positive emotions are beneficial for coping not only in the short run, but can also have long-lasting benefits. Individuals may initially use positive emotions strategically while coping with a stressful situation, actively cultivating positive emotions to regulate distress. To the extent that this same strategy is enacted over time, the conscious strategy can become automatic (Bargh & Chartrand, 1999). Using positive emotions to cope then can be likened to mastering any skill. With repeated practice, the skill becomes automatic, requiring only minimal attention or cognitive effort. In other words, frequently enacting positive emotions can actually expand your outlook in ways that, little by little, can reshape who you are.

Research shows that positive emotions are advantageous during the process of recovery from negative experiences (Fredrickson, 2001; Fredrickson & Cohn, 2008). Even brief or minor positive emotions, thoughts, and events marshaled in the face of adversity can build resilience by helping people bounce back from stressful experiences (Keltner & Bonnano, 1997; Ong, Bergeman, Bisconti, & Wallace, 2006).

Although research with teachers is limited, there is some evidence showing the benefit of a positive emotional state. A recent study found that teachers who experience positive emotions in their classrooms are more skilled at regulating their emotions (Brackett, Palomera, Mojsa-Kaja, Reyes, & Salovey, 2010). Likewise, teachers who are high in *positive affectivity*, defined as a general tendency to experience pleasant feelings such as enthusiasm and excitement and to react to life events in hopeful and encouraging ways, experience low levels of burnout (Carson et al., 2011; Kahn et al., 2006). Research simiiarly shows that the capacity to consciously summon a positive emotional state in the classroom is negatively related to burnout (Barber et al., 2011; Carson et al., 2011; Näring et al., 2006; Tsouloupas et al., 2010).

Practices to Enhance Positive Emotions

As a general strategy, the idea is to actively try to delay the normal adaptation period for a positive emotional experience by developing explicit practices. Examples of such practices include cultivating gratitude and "appreciative attention," such as deliberately savoring an enjoyable moment. There is a rapidly expanding research literature base on these and other practices, including acts of kindness, forgiveness, deliberately reminiscing, and positive reappraisal as well as such contemplative practices as yoga and meditation as a means for boosting positive emotional states.

Effortful strategies and practices can instill new ways of thinking and behaving to preserve well-being in the face of stress and trauma and produce potentially lasting increases in well-being in their absence. The many strategies that are now accumulating have three things in common (Fredrickson & Levenson, 1998; Fredrickson, Mancuso, Branigan, & Tugade, 2000).

1. They direct attention to positive aspects and away from negative aspects of experiences.
2. They keep positive experiences fresh; that is, varied and novel.
3. They produce or preserve a stream of positive emotions, thoughts, and events that serve to thwart negative states.

As an example of the effect of novelty, individuals who performed different acts of kindness every week were found to display an upward trajectory for happiness during a 10-week intervention and four weeks after, relative to those who performed similar acts of kindness each week (Boehm, Lyubomirsky, & Sheldon, 2008).

As discussed earlier, while research indicates that it is valuable to try to systematically analyze and come to terms with stressful experiences, the opposite recommendation applies to the domain of positive events. Wilson and Gilbert (2005, 2008) propose that attempting to understand and make sense of positive experiences is likely to hinder the savoring of these experiences because such attempts transform the experiences from something novel and extraordinary to something predictable and ordinary. The implication is that you should not try to think too much about or make sense of your successes and windfalls. In other words, you should savor, not try to explain.

A recent meta-analysis of the effects of 51 interventions targeted to positive affect outcomes showed significant increases in well-being, including positive affect, hope, life satisfaction, and happiness, as well decreases in depression (Sin & Lyubomirsky, 2009). Such strategies as diverse as practicing optimistic thinking, replaying positive experiences, writing gratitude letters, and socializing have been shown to increase well-being in nonclinical samples (Fordyce, 1983; Lyubomirsky, Dickerhoof, Boehm, & Sheldon, 2011; Ruini, Belaise, Brombin, Caffo, & Fava, 2006). Building character strengths and tending positive emotions are also especially effective for preventing future relapse for formerly depressed people (Seligman, Rashid, & Parks, 2006).

Positive emotions and happiness are associated with and promote numerous successful life outcomes (Lyubomirsky, King, & Diener, 2005; Snyder & Lopez, 2006). These include:

- Superior physical and mental health
- Enhanced creativity and productivity
- Work success
- Higher income
- More prosocial behavior
- Stronger interpersonal relationships

Through a multitude of studies, Lyubomirsky and other researchers have zeroed in on specific behaviors that build happiness and cultivate optimism. In Lyubomirsky's (2007) book, *The How of Happiness: A Scientific Approach to Getting the Life You Want*, some of the research-based strategies leading to happiness include:

- Count Your Blessings
  Jotting down a list helps you to realize that there are more good things about your life than you thought.
- Look Again
  Take another look to try to find the bright side to a situation.
- Don't Stew
  Dwelling on problems or comparing yourself unfavorably to others will just keep you miserable.
- Get Lost
  Getting so involved in something that you lose track of time gives your brain a chance to recharge.
- Remember When
  Think back to times when you felt happy. Those memories can infuse your everyday actions with joy.
- Pursue a Long-Neglected Goal
  Maybe you love photography but have been putting off taking that photography class you've always planned to take.
- Cope Calmly
  Manage stress in healthy, calm ways, like walking or talking to friends.
- Forgive
  Let go of anger and resentment toward those who have hurt you.

Personal Exercise: Acknowledging Three Good Things

Activity Directions:

Every evening, write down three good things that happened that day. In addition, provide a causal explanation for why you think each good thing happened.

Most people tend to dwell on negative events and emotions and ignore the positive ones. To counteract this tendency, a way to reverse the focus is to proactively implement strategies aimed at shifting attention to more positive aspects of life. For example, taking a mental spotlight each night to scan over the events of the day, thinking about what went right or compiling an "I did it" list instead of the usual "to do" list (Kauffman, 2006).

Seligman and colleagues found that a similar exercise highlighting daily positive events done every night for one week reaped benefits. Even after six months, those completing the personal exercise acknowledging three goal things were significantly happier and less depressed than the control group.

Several studies have found that exerting high levels of effort to practice a positive-emotion strategy, and continuing to practice it even after the intervention is over, results in greater improvements in well-being as well as depression (Lyubomirsky et al., 2011; Seligman et al., 2005). It also appears that a "shotgun" approach, in which individuals practice multiple positive-emotion enhancing intervention activi-

Personal Exercise: Aligning with What's Important

Activity Directions:

Step 1:   a) Think about all the roles you have.
           b) Make a list here. Try to get to 10.

Step 2:   Now, reflect on the following questions:
           a) Is there a role that's important to me that I have been neglecting lately?
           b) Have I done something I really enjoy recently?
           c) Have I done anything relating to something I care deeply about in the last month?

Step 3:   Within the next few days, do something that relates to one of these questions.

Step 4:   Revisit these questions at least once a month.

ties, may be more effective than engaging in only one activity (Sin & Lyubomirsky, 2009; Seligman et al., 2005). This means that you may see the most benefit trying out multiple and different positive strategies. With this in mind, try the personal exercise which asks you to think about all the roles you have in your life. As an example, you might be a mother, daughter, sister, wife, friend, teacher, student, counselor, mentor, and volunteer.

Expressing Gratitude

In her most recent book, *Living in Gratitude*, Angeles Arrien (2011) defines gratitude as the acknowledgment of the positive things that come your way that you did not actively work toward or ask for. Gratitude is a feeling of thankfulness and appreciation. It might be expressed toward other people, nature, or your God. The association between intentionally noting things for which one is grateful and increased well-being is well-supported by research (Arrien, 2011; Emmons, 2007; Fredrickson, 2006; Lyubomirsky, Sheldon, & Schkade, 2005). Studies demonstrate that keeping a gratitude journal is associated with higher positive affect, lower negative affect, fewer physical symptoms, better sleep quality, and greater satisfaction with life compared to control conditions (Emmons & McCullough, 2003). Gratitude also predicts greater daily positive affect in war veterans suffering from post-traumatic stress disorder (Kashdan, Uswatte, & Julian, 2006).

Seligman and colleagues found in their online research with 411 participants that conducting a "gratitude visit" derived positive results. Participants wrote a letter of gratitude and then delivered it. This is the next personal exercise.

This gratitude visit exercise initially created the most positive change of all five exercises examined, with participants reporting being significantly happier and less depressed. This change was sustained for one month, but not in the six-month follow-up. One interpretation of this finding might be that the powerful impact of explicitly expressing gratitude weans after one month. In order to sustain its effect, similar expressions of gratitude may need to be conducted at least on a monthly basis.

Given that middle school is a stressful transitional period for many students, researchers tested a gratitude intervention (Froh, Sefick, & Emmons, 2008). Classes were randomly assigned to compose gratitude lists, compose hassles lists, or no intervention. Students in the gratitude and hassles groups listed activities daily for two weeks. Results indicated that students compiling gratitude lists showed significantly

---

Personal Exercise: Making a Gratitude Visit

Activity Directions:

Write a letter to someone who has been especially kind to you, but whom you have never thanked, explaining why you feel grateful for what he/she did or said. Deliver the letter to the person.

greater gratitude and school satisfaction compared to the other two groups, and significantly lower negative affect compared to students compiling hassles lists.

CULTIVATING OPTIMISM AND HOPE

Much research supports the numerous benefits of maintaining an optimistic outlook (Fredrickson, 2009; Seligman, 2006). Optimistic people are healthier, more successful, more socially engaged, and live longer (Seligman et al., 2005). There are clear benefits to being an optimist. Optimists tend to both earn more and save more, and they have healthier lifestyles (Seligman, 2006).

Analyzing questionnaire data as well as the verbatim content of speeches and writing, Buchanan and Seligman (1995) assessed "explanatory style" as either optimistic or pessimistic. They discovered that people who don't give up interpret setbacks as transitory (for example, "This won't last forever."). Accordingly, optimists bounce back quickly from setbacks. Optimism is the antithesis of helplessness. Seligman believes optimism is the primary route to expanding personal control.

Optimists take action whereas pessimists give up. Consequently, pessimists suffer more stress than optimists, who cope better with stress. Optimists believe that their actions matter. On the other the hand, pessimists feel helpless and believe that nothing they do will matter. Optimists try to do something, while pessimists lapse into passivity. The following quote portrays the world of difference between an optimist and a pessimist.

An optimist expects his dreams to come true; a pessimist expects his nightmares to.

—Hermann Hesse

Optimists take better care of themselves and act on medical advice. Studies of optimism and heart disease show that optimism is strongly related to protection from cardiovascular disease (Giltay, Geleijnse, Zitman, Hoekstra, & Schouten, 2004; Kubzansky, Sparrow, Vokonas, & Kawachi, 2001; Tindle et al., 2009). This is true even when correcting for all the traditional risk factors, such as obesity, smoking, excessive alcohol use, high cholesterol, and hypertension (Seligman, 2011a). Researchers studying heart disease patients report that optimists are more likely to take vitamins, eat low-fat diets, and exercise, thereby reducing their overall risk for heart problems.

Optimistic individuals have the capacity to sustain resilient efficacy beliefs in the face of difficulty. Teachers who believe that an outcome is within reach will successfully handle negative experiences because they are certain that the outcome is still attainable (Usher & Pajares, 2008). Conversely, teachers who make less optimistic appraisals of their teaching competencies believe their odds for success are tenable. Holding this belief, such teachers will more easily fall victim to setbacks and discouragement and will forsake challenges that may well have been within their reach.

Optimism and Stress

Seligman (2011b) maintains that how people react to extreme stress and adversity is normally distributed. On one end are those who fall apart into post-traumatic stress disorder (PTSD), depression, and even suicide. They go from sadness to depression to a paralyzing fear of the future. In the middle are most people who at first react with symptoms of depression and anxiety, but within a month or so are back where they were before the stressful event. In other words, they are resilient.

At the other end are about one-third of the people who show post-traumatic growth (PTG), also more recently referred to as stress-related growth (SRG). They, too, first experience depression and anxiety, but within a year they are better off than they were before the trauma. After a brief period of malaise they bounce back and have grown because of their experience. Research indicates that those who are optimistic are more likely to experience SRG (Affleck & Tennen, 1996; Bellizzi, 2004; Tedeschi & Calhoun, 2004; Updegraff & Marshall, 2005).

Research reveals that the distinguishing characteristic of people who don't give up is optimism. Optimists construe setbacks as temporary, local, and changeable (for example, "This too shall pass; It is just one situation; I can do something to change this."). According to Seligman, after 30 years of research we have learned not only how to distinguish those who will grow after failure from those who will collapse but also how to build the set of skills necessary to turn their most difficult experiences into catalysts for personal growth.

Seligman's research suggests that resilience can be taught, and it can be taught by teaching people to think like optimists. He has coined the term *PERMA* as a label for the skills that are the building blocks of resilience and growth. This acronym stands for positive emotion, engagement, relationships, meaning, and accomplishment. These are the same elements discussed earlier as the new five pillars of positive psychology and what it takes to flourish in life (Seligman, 2011a).

Trauma and Burnout as Catalysts for Transformation

Following intense periods of stress a major psychological shift, or transformation, frequently occurs. As a potential answer to why trauma and turmoil can trigger psychological transformation, Taylor (2012) explains that when stress or anxiety are constant over a long period and build up to a high enough intensity, they have the effect of "dissolving psychological attachments."

Under normal circumstances most of us are psychologically attached to our hopes and ambitions for the future, our beliefs and ideas about life and the world, and our image of ourselves, including our sense of status, appearance, and accomplishments. These become attached to our sense of self. There are also more tangible attachments, such as possessions, jobs, and roles (for example, parent, wife, teacher). These feed the psychological construct of self-image, supporting a sense of identity and providing a sense of well-being and security. They are the building blocks of the sense of "self." We feel like "someone" because we have hopes, beliefs, status, a job, possessions, and the approval of others.

The significant point is that during states of trauma or high stress, these psychological attachments, or at least some of them, are dissolved. This is the very reason why a person suffers despair or depression—because the constructs the person has been dependent on to sustain well-being have been removed, the "scaffolding" that supports a sense of identity has fallen away. Hopes and beliefs are shown to be illusions; possessions and status have been taken away. As a result, the person feels naked and lost, as if his or her identity has been destroyed. But, paradoxically, at this very point he or she is close to a state of liberation that melds into acceptance. This is the psychological explanation for why a person can actually become a "new" person after experiencing extreme stress.

Such transformations frequently bring about a permanent change in identity, crystallizing a new psychological state that is akin to self-actualization, or even "enlightenment." This state may be latent, but only able to form once the normal psyche dissolves as a structure.

In a recent study, Taylor (2012) interviewed 32 individuals who experienced psychological transformation following periods of intense turmoil and trauma in their lives. The types of turmoil these individuals experienced included intense stress and upheaval, depression, bereavement, serious illness, becoming disabled, alcoholism, and encounters with death. The majority of them reported undergoing a permanent psychological transformation. The most prevalent characteristics of their new state of being included increased well-being, intensified perception, a sense of connection, improved relationships, a less materialistic and more altruistic attitude, decreased cognitive activity, and reduced fear of death. The relevance here is that teacher burnout has this transformative potential.

Teacher Burnout and Hope

Burnout cannot only signal despair, it can also usher in hope. Recognized and attended to, burnout can become a positive energy force, signifying that the time has come for a cease and desist action, a hard look at yourself, and a change to something new.

The positive potential that burnout can ignite is aptly expressed in the following comment (Pines, Aronson, & Kafry, 1981):

> While burnout can be an extraordinarily painful and distressing experience, as with any difficult event, if properly handled it can not only be overcome, it can be the first step toward increased self-awareness, enriched human understanding, and a precursor of important life changes, growth and development. Accordingly, people who have experienced burnout and have overcome it almost invariably end up in a better, fuller, more exciting life space. (p. 3)

Woods and Carlyle (2002) conducted a series of detailed, longitudinal interviews with a group of secondary teachers all clinically diagnosed as suffering from stress. Their research revealed a noticeable measure of self-renewal among most of the sample. Thirteen of the 21 teachers felt enhanced in some way, and for them, the self-renewal process was an empowering experience. The journey was indeed an emotional one. For all of these teachers, extreme and traumatic emotions were experienced—yet there was light at the end of the tunnel.

There is an important distinction between hope and optimism. The following quote aptly expresses that distinction.

Hope is definitely not the same thing as optimism. It is not the conviction that something will turn out well, but the certainty that something makes sense, regardless of how it turns out. It is hope, above all, that gives us strength to live and to continually try new things, even in conditions that seem hopeless.

—Vaclav Havel

The process of coping with stress can be the impetus to develop new capacities and skills. When stress occurs, your old way of doing things comes into question because it is inadequate or limited. The uncertainty that stress creates can lead to more closely observing and examining your behavior. Choosing to stay with your familiar, comfortable way of doing things just keeps you in a stressful state.

Personal growth and development occur not just through gains but through losses as well. Losing bad habits, self-defeating beliefs, an outgrown definition of yourself, or a pessimistic worldview may be necessary steps in developing the internal resources needed to cope with stress. Stress can be the opportunity to lose well-ingrained destructive habits and modes of behavior and to exercise a different choice. Stress and burnout have the potential to transform a teacher, being the catalyst for a new course of action.

Epilogue

Based on the many years spent preparing this book and the compelling research now available, an ideal personal stress reduction program should be fivefold.

THE FIVEFOLD TEACHER STRESS REDUCTION PLAN

First, have an instant stress-buffer in your repertoire, such as deep breathing, emitting a genuine smile, or visualizing being successful.

Second, develop the habit of a daily ritual to create, preserve, and restore a positive state of mind.

Third, embark on or maintain a lifestyle mindfulness practice (for example, meditation, yoga, tai chi).

Fourth, keep challenging your self-defeating beliefs and their accompanying stress-producing self-talk by confronting them and replacing them with ones that are more life-enhancing.

Fifth, in your classroom strive to be reflective, authentic, and mindful to nurture and sustain the relationships you have with your students.

It is my hope that I have inspired you to take action—today!

References

Abel, M. H., & Sewel, J. (1999). Stress and burnout in rural and urban secondary school teachers. *Journal of Educational Research, 92*(5), 287–93.

Adelmann, P. K. (1995). Emotional labor as a potential source of job stress. In S. L. Sauter, & L. R. Murphy (Eds.), *Organizational risk factors for job stress* (pp. 371–81). Washington, DC: American Psychological Association.

Affleck, G., & Tennen, H. (1996). Construing benefits from adversity: Adaptational significance and depositional underpinnings. *Journal of Personality, 64,* 899–922.

Aldwin, C. M. (2007). *Stress, coping, and development: An integrative perspective* (2nd ed.). New York: Guilford Press.

Aldwin, C. M., & Gilmer, D. F. (2004). *Health, illness, and optimal aging: Biological and psychosocial perspectives.* Thousand Oaks, CA: Sage.

Aldwin, C. M., Sutton, K. J., Chiara, G., & Spiro, A., III. (1996). Age differences in stress, coping, and appraisal: Findings from the Normative Aging Study. *Journal of Gerontology: Psychological Sciences, 51B,* 179.

Aldwin, C. M., Sutton, K. J., & Lachman, M. (1996). The development of coping resources in adulthood. *Journal of Personality, 64*(4), 91–113.

Allen, T. D., Herst, D. E., Bruck, C. S., & Sutton, M. (2000). Consequences associated with work-to-family conflict: A review and agenda for future research. *Journal of Occupational Health Psychology, 5*(2), 278–308.

Alliance for Excellent Education. (2005). *Teacher attrition: A costly loss to the nation and to the states.* Washington, DC: Author.

American Psychological Association. (2012). *Stress in America: Our health at risk.* Washington, DC: American Psychological Association.

Anderson, M. (2010). *The well-balanced teacher: How to work smarter and stay sane inside the classroom and out.* Alexandria, VA: ASCD.

Argyris, C. (1964). *Integrating the individual and the organization.* New York: Wiley.

Arrien, A. (1993). *The four-fold way: Walking the paths of the warrior, teacher, healer, and visionary.* San Francisco: Harper Collins.

Arrien, A. (2011). *Living in gratitude: A journey that will change your life.* Boulder, CO: Sounds True.

Ashforth, B. E., & Humphrey, R. H. (1993). Emotional labor in service roles: The influence of identity. *Academy of Management Review, 18*(1), 88–115.

Aspinwall, L. G., & Taylor, S. E. (1997). A stitch in time: Self-regulation and proactive coping. *Psychological Bulletin, 121*(3), 417–36.

Avtgis, T. A., & Rancer, A. S. (2008). The relationship between trait verbal aggressiveness and teacher burnout syndrome in K–12 teachers. *Communication Research Reports, 25*(1), 86–89.

Azar, B. (1998). Split-second evaluations shape our moods, actions. *APA Monitor, 29*(9), 13–15.

Baer, R. A. (2003). Mindfulness training as a clinical intervention: A conceptual and empirical review. *Clinical Psychology: Science and Practice, 10*(2), 125–43.

Baer, R. A., Smith, G. T., Hopkins, J., Krietemeyer, J., & Toney, L. (2006). Using self-report assessment methods to explore facets of mindfulness. *Assessment, 13,* 27–45.

Baker, J. A. (2006). Contributions of teacher-child relationships to positive school adjustment during elementary school. *Journal of School Psychology, 44*(3), 211–29.

Baker, J. A., Grant, S., & Morlock, L. (2008). The teacher-student relationship as a developmental context for children with internalizing or externalizing behavior problems. *School Psychology Quarterly, 23*(1), 3–15.

Bakker, A. B., & Demerouti, E. (2007). The Job Demands-Resources model: State of the art. *Journal of Managerial Psychology, 22,* 309–28.

Bakker, A. B., Hakanen, J. J., Demerouti, E., & Xanthopoulou, D. (2007). Job resources boost work engagement, particularly when job demands are high. *Journal of Educational Psychology, 99*(2), 274–84.

Bakker, A. B., Van Emmerik, I. J. H., & Euwema, M. C. (2006). Crossover of burnout and engagement in work teams. *Work & Occupations, 33,* 464–89.

Bandura, A. (1997). *Self-efficacy: The exercise of control.* New York: W. H. Freeman.

Barber, L. K., Grawitch, M. J., Carson, R. L., & Tsouloupas, C. N. (2011). Costs and benefits of supportive versus disciplinary emotion regulation in teachers. *Stress and Health, 27*(3), 173–87.

Bargh, J. A., & Chartrand, T. L. (1999). The unbearable automaticity of being. *American Psychologist, 54*(7), 462–79.

Bas, G. (2011). Teacher student control ideology and burnout: Their correlation. *Australian Journal of Teacher Education, 36*(4), 84–94.

Baumeister, R. F., Bratslavsky, E., Finkenauer, C., & Vohs, K. D. (2001). Bad is stronger than good. *Review of General Psychology, 5*(4), 323–70.

Beaman, R., & Wheldall, K. (2000). Teachers' use of approval and disapproval in the classroom. *Educational Psychology, 20*(4), 431–446.

Beatty, J. (2000). *The human brain: Essentials of behavioral neuroscience.* Thousand Oaks, CA: Sage.

Beauchemin, J., Hutchins, T. L., & Patterson, F. (2008). Mindfulness meditation may lessen anxiety, promote social skills, and improve academic performance among adolescents with learning disabilities. *Complementary Health Practices Review, 13*(1), 34–45.

Beck, A. (1976). *Cognitive therapy and the emotional disorders.* New York: International Universities Press.

Beck, A., Emery, G., & Greenberg, R. (2005). *Anxiety disorders and phobias.* New York: Basic Books.

Beddoe, A. E., & Murphy, S. O. (2004). Does mindfulness decrease stress and foster empathy among nursing students? *Journal of Nursing Education, 19,* 26–35.

Bellizzi, K. M. (2004). Expressions of generativity and posttraumatic growth in adult cancer survivors. *International Journal of Aging and Human Development, 58*(4), 267–87.

Benson, H. (1984). *Beyond the relaxation response.* New York: Time Books.

Benson, H. (1997). *The relaxation response.* New York: Harper Paperbacks.

Ben-Ze've, A. (2000). *The subtlety of emotions.* Cambridge: MIT.

Bernard, M. E. (1988). Classroom discipline and the effective self-management of teacher stress. *S. E. T. materials for teachers.* Melbourne: New Zealand/Australian Councils for Educational Research.

Bernard, M. E., & Joyce, M. R. (1984). *Rational-emotive therapy with children and adolescents.* New York: Wiley.

Bernstein, D. A., Borkovec, T. D., & Hazlett-Stevens, H. (2000). *New directions in progressive relaxation training: A guidebook for helping professionals.* New York: Praeger.

Bibou-Nakou, I., Stogiannidou, A., & Kiosseoglou, G. (1999). The relation between teacher burnout and teachers' attributions and practices regarding school behavior problems. *School Psychology International, 20*(2), 209–17.

Biegel, G. M., Brown, K. W., Shapiro, S. L., & Schubert, C. M. (2009). Mindfulness-based stress reduction for the treatment of adolescent psychiatric outpatients: A randomized clinical trial. *Journal of Consulting and Clinical Psychology, 77*(5), 855–66.

Billingsley, B. S. (1993). Teacher retention and attrition in special and general education: A critical review of literature. *Journal of Special Education, 27*(2), 137–74.

Birnie, K., Speca, M., & Carlson, L. E. (2010). Exploring self-compassion and empathy in the context of mindfulness-based stress reduction (MBSR). *Stress and Health, 26*(5), 359–72.

Black, D. S., Milam, J., & Sussman, S. (2009). Sitting-meditation interventions among youth: A review of treatment efficacy. *Pediatrics, 124*(3), 532–41.

Blackmore, J. (1998). The politics of gender and educational change: Managing gender or changing gender relations? In A. Hargreaves, A. Lieberman, M. Fullan, & D. Hopkins (Eds.), *International handbook of educational change* (Vol. 5, pp. 460–81). Dordrecht: Kluwer Academic Publishers.

Blase, J., & Kirby, P. (1991). *Bringing out the best in teachers: What effective principals do.* Newbury Park, CA: Corwin Press.

Bocchino, R. (1999). *Emotional literacy: To be a different kind of smart.* Thousand Oaks, CA: Corwin Press.

Boehm, J. K., Lyubomirsky, S., & Sheldon, K. M. (2008). Spicing up kindness: The role of variety in the effects of practicing kindness on improvements in moods, happiness, and self-evaluations. Manuscript in preparation.

Bondy, E., Ross, D. D., Gallingane, C., & Hambacher, E. (2007). Creating environments of success and resilience: Culturally responsive classroom management and more. *Urban Education, 42*(4), 326–48.

Bono, J. E., & Vey, M. A. (2005). Toward understanding emotional management at work: A quantitative review of emotional labor research. In C. E. Hartel, W. J. Zerbe, & N. M. Ashkanasy (Eds.), *Emotions in organizational behavior* (pp. 213–33). Mahwah, NJ: Lawrence Erlbaum.

Borysenko, J. (1987). *Minding the body, mending the mind.* New York: Bantam Books.

Bower, S. A., & Bower, G. H. (2004). *Asserting yourself: A practical guide for positive change* (2nd ed.). New York: Da Capo Press.

Boyle, G. J., Borg, M. G., Falzon, J. M., & Baglioni, A. J. J. (1995). A structural model of the dimensions of teacher stress. *British Journal of Educational Psychology, 65*(1), 49–67.

Brackett, M. A., Palomera, R., Mojsa-Kaja, J., Reyes, M. R., & Salovey, P. (2010). Emotion-regulation ability, burnout, and job satisfaction among British secondary-school teachers. *Psychology in the Schools, 47*(4), 406–17.

Brewer, J. A., Worhunsky, P. D., Gray, J. R., Tang, Y., Weber, J., & Kober, H. (2011). Meditation experience is associated with differences in default mode network activity and connectivity. *Proceedings of the National Academy of Sciences, 108*(50), 20254–59.

Brock, B. L. (1999). Perceptions of teacher burnout in Catholic schools. *Catholic Education: A Journal of Inquiry and Practice, 2*, 281–93.

Brookfield, S. D. (1995). *Becoming a critically reflective teacher.* San Francisco: Jossey-Bass.

Brooks, A. C. (2008). *Gross national happiness: Why happiness matters for America and how we can get more of it.* New York: Basic Books.

Brophy, J. (1996). *Teaching problem students.* New York: Guilford Press.

Brophy, J. (2006). History of research on classroom management. In C. Evertson & C. Weinstein (Eds.), *Handbook of classroom management: Research, practice, and contemporary issues* (pp. 17–43). Mahwah, NJ: Lawrence Erlbaum.

Brophy, J., & McCaslin, M. (1992). Teachers' reports of how they perceive and cope with problem students. *Elementary School Journal, 93*(1), 3–68.

Brotheridge, C., & Grandey, A. (2002). Emotional labor and burnout: Comparing two perspectives on "people work." *Journal of Vocational Behavior, 60*(1), 17–39.

Brotheridge, C., & Lee, R. T. (2002). Testing a conservation of resources model of dynamics of emotional labor. *Journal of Vocational Behavior, 7*, 57–67.

Brotheridge, C., & Lee, R. T. (2003). Development and validation of the emotional labour scale. *Journal of Occupational and Organizational Psychology, 76*, 365–79.

Brouwers, A., & Tomic, W. (2000). A longitudinal study of teacher burnout and perceived self-efficacy in classroom management. *Teaching and Teacher Education, 16*(2), 239–52.

Brown, D. F. (2003). Urban teachers' use of culturally responsive management strategies. *Theory into Practice, 42*(4), 277–82.

Brown, D. F. (2004). Urban teachers' professed classroom management strategies: Reflections of culturally responsive teaching. *Urban Education, 39*(3), 266–89.

Brown, G. W., & Harris, T. O. (1989). Depression. In G. W. Brown, & T. O. Harris (Eds.), *Life events and illness* (pp. 49–93). New York: Guilford Press.

Brown, K. W., Ryan, R. M., & Creswell, J. D. (2007). Mindfulness: Theoretical foundations and evidence for its salutary effects. *Psychological Inquiry, 18*(4), 211–37.

Brown, M., & Ralph, S. (1998). The identification of stress in teachers. In J. Dunham, & V. Varma (Eds.), *Stress in teachers: Past, present and future* (pp. 37–56). London, UK: Whurr Publishers.

Bubb, S., & Early, P. (2004). *Managing teacher workload work-life balance and well-being*. London: Paul Chapman.

Buchanan, G. M., & Seligman, M. E. P. (1995). Explanatory style and heart disease. In G. M. Buchanan, & M. E. P. Seligman (Eds.), *Explanatory style* (pp. 255–82). Hillsdale, NJ: Lawrence Erlbaum.

Burisch, M. (2002). A longitudinal study of burnout: The relative importance of dispositions and experiences. *Work and Stress, 16*, 1–17.

Burke, R. J., & Greenglass, E. (1995). A longitudal study of psychology burnout in teachers. *Human Relations, 48*(2), 187–202.

Burke, R. J., Greenglass, E. R., & Schwarzer, R. (1996). Predicting teacher burnout overtime: Effects of work stress, social support, and self-doubts on burnout and its consequences. *Anxiety, Stress, and Coping, 9*, 261–75.

Burns, D. D. (1999). *Feeling good: The new mood therapy* (2nd ed.). New York: HarperCollins.

Butler, A. C., Chapman, J. E., Forman, E. M., & Beck, A. T. (2005). The empirical status of cognitive-behavioral therapy: A review of meta-analyses. *Clinical Psychology Review, 26*(1), 17–31.

Butler, E. A., Egloff, B., Wilhelm, F. H., Smith, N. C., Erickson, E. A., & Gross, J. J. (2003). The social consequences of expansive suppression. *Emotion, 3*(1), 48–67.

Butler, P. E. (1991). *Talking to yourself: Learning the language of self-affirmation*. San Francisco: HarperSanFrancisco.

Butler, P. E. (2008). *Talking to yourself: How cognitive behavior therapy can change your life*. Charleston, SC: BookSurge Publishing.

Buyse, E., Verschueren, K., Doumen, S., Van Damme, J., & Maes, F. (2008). Classroom problem behavior and teacher-child relationships in kindergarten: The moderating role of classroom climate. *Journal of School Psychology, 46*(4), 367–91.

Byrne, B. M. (1999). The nomological network of teacher burnout: A literature review and empirically validated model. In R. Vandenberghe, & A. M. Huberman (Eds.), *Understanding and preventing teacher burnout: A sourcebook of international research and practice* (pp. 15–37). Cambridge, UK: Cambridge University Press.

Cacioppo, J. T., Bernston, G. G., Larsen, J. T., Poehlmann, K. M., & Ito, T. A. (2000). The psychophysiology of emotion. In M. Lewis, & J. M. Haviland-Jones (Eds.), *Handbook of emotions* (2nd ed., pp. 173–91). New York: Guilford Press.

Cahill, L., & McGaugh, J. (1998). Mechanisms of emotional arousal and lasting declarative memory. *Trends in Neuroscience, 21*, 294–99.

Cahn, B. R., & Polich, J. (2006). Meditation states and traits: EEG, ERP, and neuroimaging studies. *Psychological Bulletin, 132*(2), 180–211.

Caine, R. N., & Caine, G. (1997). *Unleashing the power of perceptual change: The potential of brain-based teaching*. Alexandria, VA: Association for Supervision and Curriculum Development.

Caine, R. N., & Caine, G. (2011). *Natural learning for a connected world: Education, technology, and the human brain*. New York: Teachers College Press.

Caine, R. N., Caine, G., McClintic, C., & Klimek, K. (2009). *12 brain/mind learning principles in action*. Thousand Oaks, CA: Corwin Press.

Calkins, S. D., & Bell, M. (2010). *The developing human brain: Development at the intersection of emotion and cognition*. Washington, DC: American Psychological Association.

Cano-García, F. J., Padilla-Muñoz, E. M., & Carrasco-Ortiz, M. A. (2005). Personality and contextual variables in teacher burnout. *Personality and Individual Differences, 38*(4), 929–40.

Carlson, B. C., & Thompson, J. A. (1995). Job burnout and job leaving in public school teachers: Implications for stress management. *International Journal of Stress Management, 2*(1), 15–29.

Carmody, J., & Baer, R. A. (2008). Relationships between mindfulness practice and levels of mindfulness, medical and psychological symptoms and well-being in a mindfulness-based stress reduction program. *Journal of Behavioral Medicine, 31*(1), 23–33.

Carson, R. L., Plemmons, S., Templin, T. J., & Weiss, H. M. (2011). "You are who you are": A mixed method study of affectivity and emotional regulation in curbing teacher burnout. In G. M. Reevy & E. Frydenberg (Eds.), *Personality, stress, and coping: Implications for education* (pp. 239–65). Charlotte, NC: Information Age Publishing.

Carson, R. L., Templin, T. J., & Weiss, H. M. (2006). *Exploring the episodic nature of teachers' emotions and its relationship to teacher burnout.* Paper presented at the Annual Meeting of the American Educational Research Association, San Francisco.

Carstensen, L. L., Pasupathi, M., Mayr, U., & Nesselroade, J. R. (2000). Emotional experience in everyday life across the adult life span. *Journal of Personality and Social Psychology, 79*(4), 644–55.

Cecil, M. A., & Forman, S. G. (1988). *Effects of stress inoculation training and coworkers support on teacher stress.* Paper presented at the Annual Meeting of the National Association of School Psychology, Chicago.

Center, D. B., & Callaway, J. M. (1999). Self-reported job stress and personality in teachers of students with emotional or behavioural disorders. *Behavioural Disorders, 25*(1), 41–51.

Chambers, R., Gullone, E., & Allen, N. B. (2009). Mindful emotion regulation: An integrative review. *Clinical Psychology Review, 29*(6), 560–72.

Chang, M. L. (2009a). An appraisal perspective of teacher burnout: Examining the emotional work of teachers. *Educational Psychology Review, 21*(3), 193–218.

Chang, M. L. (2009b). *Teacher emotion management in the classroom: Appraisals, regulations, and coping with emotions.* Unpublished doctoral dissertation.

Chen, E., Hanson, M. D., Paterson, L. Q., Griffin, M. J., Walker, H. A., & Miller, G. E. (2006). Socioeconomic status and inflammatory processes in childhood asthma: The role of psychological stress. *Journal of Allergy & Clinical Immunology, 117*(5), 1014–20.

Chiesa, A., & Serretti, A. (2009). Mindfulness-based stress reduction for stress management in healthy people: A review and meta-analysis. *Journal of Alternative & Complementary Medicine, 15*(5), 593–600.

Chorney, L. A. (1998). Self-defeating beliefs and stress in teachers. *Dissertation Abstracts International, 58*, 2820.

Cinamon, R. G., & Rich, Y. (2005). Work-family conflict among female teachers. *Teaching and Teacher Education, 21*(4), 365–78.

Clark, C. M., & Peterson, P. L. (1986). Teachers' thought processes. In M. C. Wittrock (Ed.), *Handbook of reading research on teaching* (pp. 255–96). New York: Macmillan.

Clausen, K. W., & Petruka, D. R. (2009). Tending the garden: Case studies in school stress. *Clearing House, 82*(4), 187–92.

Clore, C. L., & Centerbar, D. B. (2004). Analyzing anger: How to make people mad. *Emotion, 4*(2), 139–44.

Clunies-Ross, P., Little, E., & Kienhuis, M. (2008). Self-reported and actual use of proactive and reactive classroom management strategies and their relationship with teacher stress and student behavior. *Educational Psychology, 28*(6), 693–710.

Conderman, G., & Stephens, J. T. (2000). Voices from the field: Reflections from beginning special educators. *Teaching Exceptional Children, 33*(1), 16–21.

Cooley, E., & Yovanoff, P. (1996). Supporting professionals at-risk: Evaluating interventions to reduce burnout. *Exceptional Children, 62*(4), 336–55.

Cooper, C. L., & Kelly, M. (1993). Occupational stress in head teachers: A national UK study. *British Journal of Educational Psychology, 63*(1), 130–43.

Creswell, J. D., May, B. M., Eisenberger, N. I., & Lieberman, M. D. (2007). Neural correlates of dispositional mindfulness during affect labeling. *Psychosomatic Medicine, 69*(6), 560–65.

Csikszentmihalyi, M. (1990). *Flow: The psychology of optimal experience.* New York: Harper & Row.

Curwin, R. L., & Mendler, A. N. (1988). *Discipline with dignity.* Alexandria, VA: Association for Supervision and Curriculum Development.

Damasio, A. (1999). *The feeling of what happens: Body and emotion in the making of consciousness.* New York: Harcourt Brace.

Damasio, A. (2003). *Looking for Spinoza: Joy, sorrow, and the feeling brain.* New York: Harcourt.

David, D., Szentagotai, A., Eva, K., & Macavei, B. (2005). A synopsis of rational emotive behavior therapy (REBT): Fundamental and applied research. *Journal of Rational-Emotive & Cognitive-Behavioral Therapy, 23*, 175–221.

Davidson, R. J., & Begley, S. (2012). *The emotional life of your brain: How its unique patterns affect the way you think, feel, and live—and how you can change them.* New York: Hudson Street Press.

Davidson, R. J., Kabat-Zinn, J., Schumacher, J., Rosenkratz, M., Muller, D., & Santorelli, S. F. (2003). Alterations in brain and immune function produced by mindfulness meditation. *Psychosomatic Medicine, 65*, 564–70.

Davis, M., Eshelman, E. R., & McKay, M. (2008). *The relaxation and stress reduction workbook* (3rd ed.). Oakland, CA: New Harbinger.

Day, C., Sammons, P., & Gu, Q. (2008). Combining qualitative and quantitative methodologies in research on teachers' lives, work, and effectiveness: From integration to synergy. *Educational Research, 37*(6), 330–42.

Deci, E. L., & Ryan, R. M. (1985). *Intrinsic motivation and self-determination in human behavior.* New York: Plenum.

Deci, E. L., & Ryan, R. M. (2000). Self-determination theory and the facilitation of intrinsic motivation, social development, and well-being. *American Psychologist, 55*(1), 68–78.

Deci, E. L., & Ryan, R. M. (2008). Facilitating optimal motivation and psychological well-being across life domains. *Canadian Psychology, 49*(1), 14–25.

de Lange, A. H., Taris, T. W., Kompier, M. A. J., Houtman, I. L. D., & Bongers, P. M. (2003). "The very best of the millennium": Longitudinal research and the demand-control-(support) model. *Journal of Occupational Health Psychology, 8*, 282–305.

Deiro, J. A. (1996). *Teaching with heart. Making healthy connections with students.* Thousand Oaks, CA: Corwin Press.

Delpit, L. (1995). *Other people's children.* New York: New Press.

Delpit, L. (2003). Educators as "seed people" growing a new future. *Educational Researcher, 32*(7), 14–21.

deMarrais, K., & Tisdale, K. (2002). What happens when researchers inquire into difficult emotions? Reflections on studying women's anger through qualitative interviews. *Educational Psychologist, 37*(2), 115–23.

Derryberry, D., & Tucker, D. M. (1994). Motivating the focus of attention. In P. M. Neidenthal & S. Kitayama (Eds.), *The heart's eye: Emotional influences in perception and attention* (pp. 167–96). San Diego, CA: Academic Press.

Detweiler, J., Rothman, A., Salovey, P., & Steward, W. (2000). Emotional states and physical health. *American Psychologist, 55*(1), 110–21.

Devine, J., & Cohen, J. (2007). *Making your school safe: Strategies to protect children and promote learning.* New York: Teachers College Press.

Diamond, M. (1988). *Enriching heredity: The impact of the environment on the anatomy of the brain.* New York: Free Press.

Dickenson, J., Berkman, E. T., Arch, J., & Lieberman, M. D. (in press). Neural correlates of focused attention during a brief mindfulness induction. *Social Cognitive and Affective Neuroscience.*

Diefendorff, J. M., Croyle, M. H., & Gosserand, R. H. (2005). The dimensionality and antecedents of emotional labor strategies. *Journal of Vocational Behavior, 66*(2), 339–57.

Dimsdale, J. E. (2008). Psychological stress and cardiovascular disease. *Journal of the American College of Cardiology, 51*(13), 1237–46.

Dohrenwend, B. P. (2000). The role of adversity and stress in psychopathology: Some evidence and its implications for theory and research. *Journal of Health & Social Behavior, 41*(1), 1–19.

Dorman, J. (2003). Testing a model for teacher burnout. *Australian Journal of Educational & Developmental Psychology, 3*, 35–47.

Dorz, S., Novara, C., Sica, C., & Sanavio, E. (2003). Predicting burnout among HIV/AIDS and oncology health care workers. *Psychology and Health, 8*(5), 677–84.

Drago, R. W. (2007). *Striking a balance: Work, family, life.* Boston: Economic Affairs Bureau.

Duckworth, M. P., & Mercer, V. (2006). Assertiveness training. In J. E. Fisher & W. T. O'Donohue (Eds.), *Practitioner's guide to evidence-based psychotherapy* (pp. 80–92). New York: Springer Science & Business.

Duijts, S. F., Zeegers, M. P., & Borne, B. V. (2003). The association between stressful life events and breast cancer risk: A meta-analysis. *International Journal of Cancer, 20*(107), 1023–29.

Dunham, J., & Varma, V. (1998). *Stress in teachers: Past, present and future.* London: Whurr Publishers.

Durlak, J. A., Weissberg, R. P., Dymnicki, A. B., Taylor, R. D., & Schellinger, K. B. (2011). The impact of enhancing students' social and emotional learning: A meta-analysis of school-based universal interventions. *Child Development, 82*(1), 405–32.

Durr, J. (2008). *Identifying teacher capacities that may buffer against teacher burnout.* Unpublished doctoral dissertation, The Ohio State University, Columbus OH.

Dworkin, A. G. (1986). *Teacher burnout in the public schools: Structural causes and consequences for children.* Albany, NY: State University of New York Press.

Efklides, A., & Volet, S. (2005). Feelings and emotions in the learning process [Special issue]. *Learning and Instruction, 15*(5), 377–415.

Egyed, C. J., & Short, R. J. (2006). Teacher self-efficacy, burnout, experience and decision to refer a disruptive student. *School of Psychology International, 27*(4), 462–74.

Ekman, P. (1992). An argument for basic emotions. *Cognition and Emotion, 6,* 169–200.

Elias, M. J., & Schwab, Y. (2006). From compliance to responsibility: Social and emotional learning and classroom management. In C. Evertson & C. Weinstein (Eds.), *Handbook of classroom management: Research, practice, and contemporary issues* (pp. 309–41). Mahwah, NJ: Lawrence Erlbaum.

Ellis, A. (1973). *Humanistic psychotherapy: The rational-emotive approach.* New York: Julian Press.

Ellis, A. (2001). *Overcoming destructive beliefs, feelings, and behaviors: New directions for rational emotive behavior therapy.* Amherst, NY: Prometheus Books.

Ellis, A. (2004). *The road to tolerance: The philosophy of rational emotive behavior therapy.* Amherst, NY: Prometheus Books.

Ellis, A., & Bernard, M. E. (1984). *Rational-emotive approaches to the problems of childhood.* New York: Plenum.

Ellis, A., Gordon, J., Neenan, M., & Palmer, S. (2003). *Stress counseling: A rational emotive behavior approach* (2nd ed.). London: Sage.

Ellis, A., & Harper, R. A. (1961). *A guide to rational living.* North Hollywood, CA: Wilshire Books.

Ellis, A., & Harper, R. A. (1975/1997). *A new guide to rational living.* North Hollywood, CA: Wilshire Books.

Emmons, R. A. (2007). *Thanks! How the new science of gratitude can make you happier.* New York: Houghton Mifflin.

Emmons, R. A., & McCullough, M. E. (2003). Counting blessings versus burdens: An experimental investigation of gratitude and subjective well-being in daily life. *Journal of Personality and Social Psychology, 84,* 377–89.

Entwisle, D. R., & Alexander, K. L. (1988). Factors affecting achievement test scores and marks of black and white first graders. *Elementary School Journal, 88*(5), 449–71.

Erb, C. S. (2002). *The emotional whirlpool of beginning teachers' work.* Paper presented at the Annual Meeting of the Canadian Society of Studies in Education, Toronto, Canada.

Esteve, J. M. (2000). The transformation of the teachers' role at the end of the twentieth century: New challenges for the future. *Educational Review, 52*(2), 197–207.

Evers, W. J. G., Tomic, W., & Brouwers, A. A. (2004). Burnout among teachers: Students' and teachers' perceptions compared. *School Psychology International, 25*(2), 131–48.

Eysenck, M. W. (1997). *Anxiety and cognition.* Hove, East Sussex, England: Psychology Press.

Farber, B. A. (1984). Stress and burnout in suburban teachers. *Journal of Educational Research, 7*(6), 325–31.

Farber, B. A. (1991). *Crisis in education: Stress and burnout in the American teacher.* San Francisco: Jossey-Bass.

Feltman, R., Robinson, M. D., & Ode, S. (2009). Mindfulness as a moderator of neuroticism-outcome relations: A self-regulation perspective. *Journal of Research in Personality, 43*(6), 953–61.

Feng, L. (2006). *Combating teacher shortages: Who leaves, who moves, and why.* Unpublished doctoral dissertation, Florida State University.

Fisher, G. G. (2002). Work/personal life balance: A construct development study. Doctoral dissertation, Bowling State University. *Dissertation Abstract International, 63*(1–B), 575.

Fives, H., Hamman, D., & Olivarez, A. (2007). Does burnout begin with student-teaching? Analyzing efficacy, burnout, and support during the student-teaching semester. *Teacher and Teacher Education, 23*(6), 916–34.

Flook, L., Smalley, S. L., Kitil, M. J., Galla, B. M., Kaiser-Greenland, S., Lockec, J., Ishijima, E., & Kasari, C. (2010). Effects of mindful awareness practices on executive functions in elementary school children. *Journal of Applied School Psychology, 26*(1), 70–95.

Folkman, S., & Lazarus, R. S. (1985). If it changes it must be a process: Study of emotion and coping during three stages of a college examination. *Journal of Personality and Social Psychology, 48*, 150–70.

Folkman, S., & Lazarus, R. S. (1988). *Manual for the ways of coping questionnaire.* Palo Alto, CA: Mind Garden.

Fontana, D., & Abouserie, R. (1993). Stress levels, gender and personality factors in teachers. *British Journal of Educational Psychology, 63*, 261–70.

Fordyce, M. W. (1983). A program to increase happiness: Further studies. *Journal of Counseling Psychology, 30*, 483–98.

Forman, S. G. (1981). Stress-management training: Evaluation of effects on school psychological services. *Journal of School Psychology, 19*, 233–42.

Forman, S. G. (1982). Stress management for teachers: A cognitive-behavioral program. *Journal of School Psychology, 20*, 180–86.

Forman, S. G. (1990). Rational-emotive therapy: Contributions to teacher stress management. *School Psychology Review, 19*(3), 315–21.

Frederick, S., & Loewenstein, G. (1999). Hedonic adaptation. In D. Kahneman, E. Diener, & N. Schwarz (Eds.), *Well-being: The foundations of hedonic psychology* (pp. 302–29). New York: Russell Sage Foundation.

Fredrickson, B. L. (2001). The role of positive psychology: The broaden-and-build theory of positive emotions. *American Psychologist, 56*(3), 218–26.

Fredrickson, B. L. (2004). Gratitude, like other positive emotions, broadens and builds. In R. A. Emmons & M. E. McCullough (Eds.), *The psychology of gratitude* (pp. 145–66). New York: Oxford University Press.

Fredrickson, B. L. (2008). Promoting positive affect. In M. Eid & R. J. Larsen (Eds.), *The science of subjective well-being* (pp. 449–68). New York: Guilford Press.

Fredrickson, B. L. (2009). *Positivity: Top-notch research reveals the 3-to-1 ratio that will change your life.* New York: Three Rivers Press.

Fredrickson, B. L., & Branigan, C. (2005). Positive emotions broaden the scope of attention and thought-action repertoire. *Cognition & Emotion, 19*(3), 313–32.

Fredrickson, B. L., & Cohn, M. A. (2008). Positive emotions. In M. Lewis, J. Haviland, & L. F. Barrett (Eds.), *Handbook of emotions* (3rd ed., pp. 777–96). New York: Guilford Press.

Fredrickson, B. L., & Levenson, R. W. (1998). Positive emotions speed recovery from the cardiovascular sequelae of negative emotions. *Cognition and Emotion, 12*, 191–220.

Fredrickson, B. L., & Losada, M. F. (2005). Positive affect and the complex dynamics of human flourishing. *American Psychologist, 60*(7), 678–86.

Fredrickson, B. L., Mancuso, R. A., Branigan, C., & Tugade, M. M. (2000). The undoing effect of positive emotions. *Motivation and Emotion, 24*, 237–58.

French, J. R. P., Caplan, R. D., & Van Harrison, R. (1982). *The mechanism of job stress and strain.* Chichester, England: Wiley.

Freudenberger, H. J. (1974). Staff burnout. *Journal of Social Issues, 30*(1), 159–64.

Friedman, A. A., & Reynolds, L. (2011). *Burned in: Fueling the fire to teach.* New York: Teachers College Press.

Friedman, I. A. (1995). Student behavior patterns contributing to teacher burnout. *Journal of Educational Research, 88*(5), 281–89.

Friedman, I. A. (2000). Burnout in teachers: Shattered dreams of impeccable professional performance. *Journal of Clinical Psychology, 56*(5), 595–606.

Friedman, I. A. (2006). Classroom management and teacher stress and burnout. In C. Evertson & C. Weinstein (Eds.), *Handbook of classroom management: Research, practice, and contemporary issues* (pp. 925–44). Mahwah, NJ: Lawrence Erlbaum.

Friedman, I. A., & Farber, B. A. (1992). Professional self-concept as a predictor of teacher burnout. *Journal of Educational Research, 86*(1), 28–35.

Friesen, D., Prokop, C., & Sarros, J. (1988). Why teachers burn out. *Educational Research Quarterly, 12*(3), 9–19.

Froh, J. J., Sefick, W. J., & Emmons, R. A. (2008). Counting blessings in early adolescents: An experimental study of gratitude and subjective well-being. *Journal of School Psychology, 46*(2), 213–33.

Froyen, L. A., & Iverson, A. M. (1999). *Schoolwide and classroom management: The reflective educator-leader.* New York: Merrill.

Galantino, M. L., Baime, M., Maguire, M., Szapary, P. O., & Farrar, J. T. (2005). Short communication: Association of psychological and physiological measures of stress in health-care professions during an 8-week mindfulness mediation program: Mindfulness in practice. *Stress and Health, 21*, 255–61.

Gardner, H., Csikszentmihalyi, M., & Damon, W. (2001). *Good work: When excellence and ethics meet.* New York: Basic Books.

Garland, E. L., Fredrickson, B. L., Kring, A. M., Johnson, D. P., Meyer, P. S., & Penn, D. L. (2010). Upward spirals of positive emotions counter downward spirals of negativity: Insights from the broaden-and-build theory and affective neuroscience on the treatment of emotion dysfunctions and deficits in psychopathology. *Clinical Psychology Review, 30*, 849–64.

Garland, E. L., Gaylord, S. A., & Fredrickson, B. L. (2011). Positive reappraisal mediates the stress-reductive effects of mindfulness: An upward spiral process. *Mindfulness, 2*, 59–67.

Gaziel, H. H. (1995). Sabbatical leave, job burnout and turnover intentions among teachers. *International Journal of Lifelong Education, 14*(4), 331–38.

Gazzaniga, M. S., Ivry, R. B., & Mangun, G. R. (2002). *Cognitive neuroscience: The biology of the mind* (2nd ed.). New York: Norton.

Geving, A. M. (2007). Identifying the types of student and teacher behaviours associated with teacher stress. *Teaching and Teacher Education, 23*(5), 624–40.

Giallo, R., & Little, E. (2003). Classroom behaviour problems: The relationship between preparedness, classroom experiences and self-efficacy in graduate and student teachers. *Australian Journal of Educational and Developmental Psychology, 3*, 21–34.

Giltay, E., Geleijnse, J., Zitman, F., Hoekstra, T., & Schouten, E. (2004). Dispositional optimism and all-cause and cardiovascular mortality in a prospective cohort of elderly Dutch men and women. *Archives of General Psychiatry, 61*, 1126–35.

Girdano, D. A., Everly, G. S., & Dusek, D. E. (1996). *Controlling stress and tension.* Boston: Allyn & Bacon.

Glasser, W. (1986). *Control theory in the classroom.* New York: Harper & Row.

Glasser, W. (1998). *The quality school: Managing students without coercion.* New York: Harper & Row.

Gmelch, W. (1983). Stress for success: How to optimize your performance. *Theory into Practice, 22*(1), 7–14.

Goddard, R., O'Brien, P., & Goddard, M. (2006). Work environment predictors of beginning teacher burnout. *British Educational Research Journal, 32*(6), 857–74.

Golby, M. (1996). Teachers' emotions: An illustrated discussion. *Cambridge Journal of Education, 26*(3), 423–34.

Gold, E., Smith, A., Hopper, L., Herne, D., Tansey, G., & Hulland, C. (2010). Mindfulness-based stress reduction for primary school teachers. *Journal of Child and Family Studies, 19*(2), 184–89.

Gold, Y. (1988). Recognizing and coping with academic burnout. *Contemporary Education, 59*(3), 142–45.

Gold, Y., Roth, R. A., Wright, C. R., & Michael, W. B. (1991). The relationship of scores on the Educators Survey, a modified version of the Maslach Burnout Inventory, to three teaching-related variables for a sample of 132 beginning teachers. *Educational and Psychological Measurement, 51*, 429–38.

Goleman, D. (1995). *Emotional intelligence: Why it can matter more than IQ.* New York: Bantam.

Gottman, J. M. (1994). *What predicts divorce? The relationship between marital processes and marital outcomes.* Hillsdale, NJ: Lawrence Erlbaum.

Gottman, J. M., Katz, L. F., & Hooven, C. (1997). Introduction to the concept of meta-emotion. In J. M. Gottman, L. F. Katz, & C. Hooven (Eds.), *Meta-emotion: How families communicate emotionally* (pp. 3–8). Mahwah, NJ: Lawrence Erlbaum.

Grandey, A. A. (2003). When "the show must go on": Surface acting and deep acting as determinants of emotional exhaustion and peer-rated service delivery. *Academy of Management Journal, 46*(1), 86–96.

Grant-Vallone, E. J., & Donaldson, S. I. (2001). Consequences of work-family conflict on employee well-being over time. *Work and Stress, 15*, 214–26.

Grayson, J. L., & Alvarez, H. K. (2008). School climate factors relating to teacher burnout: A mediator model. *Teaching and Teacher Education, 24*(5), 1349–63.

Greenglass, E. R. (1991). Burnout and gender: Theoretical and organizational implications. *Canadian Psychology, 32*, 562–70.

Greenglass, E. R. (2002). Proactive coping. In E. Frydenberg (Ed.), *Beyond coping: Meeting goals, vision, and challenges* (pp. 37–62). New York: Oxford University Press.

Greenglass, E. R. (2007). Teaching and stress. In G. Fink (Ed.), *Encyclopedia of stress* (pp. 713–17). San Diego, CA: Academic Press.

Greenglass, E. R., Burke, R. J., & Konarski, R. (1997). The impact of social support on the development of burnout in teachers: Examination of a model. *Work and Stress, 11*, 267–78.

Greenglass, E. R., Fiksenbaum, L., & Burke, R. J. (1996). Components of social support, buffering effects and burnout: Implications for psychological functioning. *Anxiety, Stress and Coping, 9*, 185–97.

Greenhaus, J. H., Collins, K. M., & Shaw, J. D. (2003). The relation between work-family balance and quality of life. *Journal of Vocational Behavior, 63*, 510–31.

Greeson, J. M. (2009). Mindfulness research update: 2008. *Complementary Health Practice Review, 14*(1), 10–18.

Greeson, J. M., & Brantley, J. (2008). Mindfulness and anxiety disorder: Developing a wise relationship with the inner experience of fear. In F. Didonna (Ed.), *Clinical handbook of mindfulness* (pp. 171–88). New York: Springer.

Gregory, A., Cornell, D., & Fan, X. (2011). The relationship of school structure and support to suspension rates for black and white high school students. *American Educational Research Journal, 48*(4), 904–34.

Griffith, J., & Steptoe, A., & Cropley, M. (1999). An investigation of coping strategies associated with job stress in teachers. *British Journal of Educational Psychology, 69*, 517–31.

Grissmer, D. W., & Kirby, S. N. (1992). *Patterns of attrition among Indiana teachers*. Santa Monica, CA: RAND.

Gross, J. J. (1998). The emerging field of emotion regulation: An integrative review. *Review of General Psychology, 2*(3), 271–99.

Gross, J. J. (1999). Antecedent- and response-focused emotion regulation: Divergent consequences for experience, expression, and physiology. *Journal of Personality and Social Psychology, 74*(1), 224–37.

Gross, J. J. (2002). Emotion regulation: Affective, cognitive, and social consequences. *Psychophysiology, 39*, 281–91.

Gross, J. J. (2009). *Handbook of emotion regulation*. New York: Guilford Press.

Gross, J. J., & John, O. P. (2002). Wise emotion regulation. In L. Feldman Barrett & P. Salovey (Eds.), *The wisdom of feelings: Psychological processes in emotional intelligence* (pp. 297–318). New York: Guilford Press.

Gross, J. J., & John, O. P. (2003). Individual difference in two emotion regulation processes: Implications for affect, relationships, and well-being. *Journal of Personality and Social Psychology, 85*, 348–62.

Gross, J. J., & John, O. P. (2004). Healthy and unhealthy emotion regulation: Personality processes, individual differences, and lifespan development. *Journal of Personality, 72*, 1301–34.

Gross, J. J., & Levenson, R. W. (1993). Emotional suppression: Physiology, self-report, and expensive behavior. *Journal of Personality and Social Psychology, 64*, 970–86.

Gross, J. J., Richards, J. M., & John, O. P. (2006). Emotion regulation in everyday life. In D. K. Snyder, J. A. Simpson, & J. N. Hughes (Eds.), *Emotion regulation in families: Pathways to dysfunction and health* (pp. 13–55). Washington, DC: American Psychological Association.

Grossman, P., Niemann, L., Schmidt, S., & Walach, H. (2004). Mindfulness-based stress reduction and health benefits. A meta-analysis. *Journal of Psychosomatic Research, 57*, 35–43.

Grzywacz, J. G., & Bass, B. L. (2003). Work, family and mental health: Testing different models of work-family fit. *Journal of Marriage and Family, 62*, 248–62.

Guy, M. E., Newman, M. A., & Mastracci, S. H. (2008). *Emotional labor: Putting the service in public services*. Armonk, NY: M. E. Sharper.

Hakanen, J. J., Bakker, A. B., & Schaufeli, W. B. (2006). Burnout and work engagement among teachers. *Journal of School Psychology, 43*(6), 495–513.

Halbesleben, J. R. B. (2006). Sources of social support and burnout: A meta-analytic test of the conservation of resources model. *Journal of Applied Psychology, 91*(5), 1134–45.

Hammen, C. (2005). Stress and depression. *Annual Review of Clinical Psychology, 1*, 293–319.

Hargreaves, A. (1998a). The emotional politics of teaching and teacher development: With implications for educational leadership. *International Journal of Leadership in Education, 1*(4), 315–36.

Hargreaves, A. (1998b). The emotional practice of teaching. *Teaching and Teacher Education, 14*(8), 835–54.

Hargreaves, A. (2000). Mixed emotions: Teachers' perceptions of their interactions with students. *Teaching and Teacher Education, 16*(8), 811–26.

Hargreaves, A. (2001). Emotional geographies of teaching. *Teachers College Record, 103*(6), 1056–80.

Hargreaves, A. (2004). Inclusive and exclusive educational change: Emotional response of teachers and implications for leadership. *School Leadership & Management, 24*(3), 287–309.

Hargreaves, A., & Tucker, E. (1991). Teaching and guilt: Exploring the feelings of teaching. *Teaching and Teacher Education, 7*(5–6), 491–505.

Harris, A., & Thoresen, C. (2005). Forgiveness, unforgiveness, health and disease. In E. Worthington (Ed.), *Handbook of forgiveness* (pp. 321–34). New York: Routledge.

Harris, G. E. (2003). Progressive muscle relaxation: Highly effective and often neglected. *Guidance and Counseling, 18*(4), 142–48.

Hart, L. (1983). *Human brain, human learning.* New York: Longman.

Harvey, J. (1988). *The quiet mind: Techniques for transforming stress.* Honesdale, PA: Himalayan International Institute.

Hastings, R. P., & Bham, M. S. (2003). The relationship between student behaviour patterns and teacher burnout. *School Psychology International, 24*(1), 115–27.

Hausser, J. A., Mojzisch, A., Niesel, M., & Schulz-Hardt, S. (2010). Ten years on: A review of recent research on the job demand-control (-support) model and psychological well-being. *Work & Stress, 24*(1), 1–35.

Helmstetter, S. (1990). *What to say when you talk to yourself.* New York: Pocket Books.

Herrald, M. H., & Tomaka, J. (2002). Patterns of emotion-specific appraisal, coping, and cardiovascular reactivity during an ongoing emotional episode. *Journal of Personality and Social Psychology, 83*, 434–50.

Hobfoll, S. E., & Freedy, J. (1993). Conservation of resources: A general stress theory applied to burnout. In W. B. Schaufeli, C. Maslach, & T. Marek (Eds.), *Professional burnout: Recent developments in theory and research* (pp. 115–29). Washington, DC: Taylor & Francis.

Hochschild, A. R. (1983/2003/2012). *The managed heart: Commercialization of human feeling.* Berkeley, CA: University of California Press.

Holmes, E. (2005). *Teacher well-being: Looking after yourself and your career in the classroom.* New York: Routledge.

Holzel, B. K., Carmody, J., Vangel, M., Congleton, C., Yerramsetti, S. M., Gard, T., & Lazar, S. W. (2011). Mindfulness practice leads to increases in regional brain gray matter density. *Psychiatry Research: Neuroimaging, 191*(1), 36–43.

Houkes, I., Janssen, P. P. M., de Jonge, J., & Bakker, A. B. (2003). Personality, work characteristics and employee well-being: A longitudinal analysis of additive and moderating effects. *Journal of Occupational Health Psychology, 8*(1), 20–38.

Houkes, I., Janssen, P. P. M., de Jonge, J., & Nijhuis, F. J. N. (2001). Work and individual determinants of intrinsic work motivation, emotional exhaustion, and turnover intention: A multi-sample analysis. *International Journal of Stress Management, 8*(4), 257–83.

Humphrey, J. H. (1992). *Stress among women in modern society.* Springfield, IL: Charles C. Thomas.

Huttenlocher, P. (2002). *Neural plasticity: The effects of environment on the development of the cerebral cortex (Perspectives in cognitive neuroscience).* Cambridge, MA: Harvard University Press.

Imazeki, J. (2005). Teacher salaries and teacher attrition. *Economics of Education Review, 24*, 431–49.

Ingersoll, R. M. (2001). Teacher turnover and teacher shortages: An organizational analysis. *American Educational Research Journal, 38*(3), 499–534.

Ingersoll, R. M., & Smith, T. M. (2003). The wrong solution to the teacher shortage. *Educational Leadership, 60*(8), 30–33.

Ingersoll, R. M., & Strong, M. (2011). The impact of induction and mentoring programs for beginning teachers: A critical review of the research. *Review of Educational Research, 81*(2), 201–33.

Intrator, S. (2006). Beginning teachers and emotional drama in the classroom. *Journal of Teacher Education, 57*(3), 232–39.

Jackson, P. (1968). *Life in classrooms.* New York: Holt, Rinehart & Winston.

Jacobson, E. (1938). *You must relax.* New York: McGraw-Hill.

Jain, S., Shapiro, S. L., Swanick, S., Roesch, S. C., Mills, P. J., Bell, I., & Schwartz, G. E. (2007). A randomized controlled trial of mindfulness meditation versus relaxation training: Effects on distress, positive states of mind, rumination, and distraction. *Annals of Behavioral Medicine, 33,* 11–21.

Jennings, P. A., & Greenberg, M. T. (2009). The prosocial classroom: Teacher social and emotional competence in relation to student and classroom outcomes. *Review of Educational Research, 79*(1), 491–525.

Jennings, P. A., Snowberg, K., Coccia, M., & Greenberg, M. (2012, April). Refinement and evaluation of the Cultivating Awareness and Resilience in Education for teachers program. Paper presented at the Annual Meeting of the American Educational Research Association, Vancouver.

Jha, A. P., Krompinger, J., & Baime, M. J. (2007). Mindfulness training modifies subsystems of attention. *Cognitive, Affective, & Behavioral Neuroscience, 7*(2), 109–19.

Johnson, J. V., & Hall, E. M. (1988). Job strain, work place social support, and cardiovascular disease: A cross-sectional study of a random sample of the Swedish working population. *American Journal of Public Health, 78,* 1336–42.

Johnson, S. L., & Roberts, J. E. (1995). Life events and bipolar disorder: Implications from biological theories. *Psychological Bulletin, 117*(3), 434–49.

Joseph, P. B., & Burnaford, G. E. (2001). *Images of schoolteachers in America* (2nd ed.). Mahwah, NJ: Lawrence Erlbaum.

Kabat-Zinn, J. (1994). *Wherever you go, there you are.* New York: Hyperion.

Kabat-Zinn, J. (2003). Mindfulness-based interventions in context: Past, present and future. *Clinical Psychology Science and Practice, 10,* 144–56.

Kabat-Zinn, J. (2006). *Coming to our senses: Healing ourselves and the world through mindfulness.* New York: Hyperion.

Kagan, J. (1989). *Unstable ideas: Temperament, cognition, and self.* Cambridge, MA: Harvard University Press.

Kahn, J. H., Schneider, K. T., Jenkins-Henkelman, T. M., & Moyle, L. L. (2006). Emotional social support and job burnout among high-school teachers: Is it all due to dispositional affectivity? *Journal of Organizational Behavior, 27*(6), 793–807.

Karasek, R. A. (1979). Job demands, job decision latitude, and mental strain: Implications for job redesign. *Administrative Science Quarterly, 24,* 285–308.

Karasek, R. A., Brisson, C., Kawakami, N., Houtman, I., Bongers, P., & Amick, B. (1998). The job content questionnaire (JCQ): An instrument for intentionally comparative assessment of psychological job characteristics. *Journal of Occupational Health Psychology, 3,* 322–55.

Kashdan, T. B., Uswatte, G., & Julian, T. (2006). Gratitude and hedonic and eudaimonic well-being in Vietnam war veterans. *Behaviour Research and Therapy, 44*(2), 177–99.

Kauffman, C. (2006). Positive psychology: The science at the heart of coaching. In D. R. Stober & A. M. Grant (Eds.), *Evidence-based coaching handbook: Putting best practices to work for your clients* (pp. 219–53). Hoboken, NJ: Wiley.

Kelchtermans, G., & Strittmatter, A. (1999). Beyond individual burnout: A perspective for improved schools. Guidelines for the prevention of burnout. In R. Vandenberghe & A. M. Huberman (Eds.), *Understanding and preventing teacher burnout: A sourcebook of international research and practice* (pp. 304–14). Cambridge, UK: Cambridge University Press.

Keltner, D., & Bonnano, G. A. (1997). A study of laughter and dissociation: Distinct correlates of laughter and smiling during bereavement. *Journal of Personality and Social Psychology, 73,* 687–702.

Keltner, D., Ellsworth, P. C., & Edwards, K. (1993). Beyond simple pessimism: Effects of sadness and anger on social perception. *Journal of Personality and Social Psychology, 64,* 740–52.

Kemper, T. D. (2000). Social models in the explanation of emotions. In M. Lewis & J. M. Haviland-Jones (Eds.), *Handbook of emotions* (2nd ed., pp. 45–58). New York: Guilford Press.

Kempton, S. (2011). *Meditation for the love of it: Enjoying your own deepest experience.* Boulder, CO: Sounds True.

Keyes, C. L. M. (2002). The mental health continuum: From languishing to flourishing in life. *Journal of Health and Social Behavior, 43,* 207–22.

Keyes, C. L. M. (2005). Mental illness and/or mental health? Investigating axioms of the complete state model of health. *Journal of Consulting and Clinical Psychology, 73*(3), 539–48.

Kijai, J., & Totten, D. L. (1995). Teacher burnout in small Christian school: A national study. *Journal of Research on Christian Education, 4,* 195–218.

Kinnunen, U., & Salo, K. (1994). Teacher stress: An eight-year follow-up study on teachers' work, stress, and health. *Anxiety, Stress, and Coping, 7,* 319–37.

Kirby, S. N., Berends, M., & Naftel, S. (1999). Supply and demand of minority teachers in Texas: Problem and prospects. *Educational Evaluation and Policy Analysis, 21,* 47–66.

Klatt, M. D., Buckworth, J., & Malarkey, W. B. (2008). Effects of low-dose mindfulness-based stress reduction (MBSR-ld) on working adults. *Health Educational Behavior, 36*(3), 601–14.

Kokkinos, C. M. (2007). Job stressors, personality and burnout in primary school teachers. *British Journal of Educational Psychology, 77*(1), 229–43.

Kossek, E. E., & Ozeki, C. (1998). Work-family conflict, policies and the job-life satisfaction relationship: A review and directions for organizational behavior-human resources research. *Journal of Applied Psychology, 83,* 139–399.

Krantz, D. S., & McCeney, M. K. (2002). Effects of psychological and social factors on organic disease: A critical assessment of research on coronary heart disease. *Annual Review of Psychology, 53,* 341–69.

Kruml, S. R., & Geddes, D. (2000). Exploring the dimensions of emotional labor: The heart of Hochschild's work. *Management Communication Quarterly, 14*(1), 8–49.

Kubzansky, L., Sparrow, D., Vokonas, P., & Kawachi, I. (2001). Is the glass half empty or half full? A prospective study of optimism and coronary heart disease in the Normative Aging Study. *Psychosomatic Medicine, 63,* 910–16.

Kuhlmann, S., Kirschbaum, C., & Wolf, O. T. (2005). Effects of oral cortisol treatment in healthy young women on memory retrieval of negative and neutral words. *Neurobiology of Learning and Memory, 83,* 158–62.

Kuppens, P., Van Mechelen, I., Smits, D. J. M., & de Boeck, P. (2003). The appraisal basis of anger: Specificity, necessity and sufficiency of components. *Emotion, 3,* 254–69.

Kyriacou, C., & Sutcliffe, J. (1978). A model of teacher stress. *Educational Studies, 4*(1), 89–96.

Ladson-Billings, G. (1995). Toward a theory of culturally relevant pedagogy. *American Educational Research Journal, 32*(3), 465–91.

Langer, E. J. (1989). *Mindfulness.* Reading, MA: Addison-Wesley.

Lantieri, L., Kyse, E. N., Harnett, S., & Malkmus, C. (2011). Building inner resilience in teachers and student. In G. M. Reevy & E. Frydenberg (Eds.), *Personality, stress, and coping: Implications for education* (pp. 267–92). Charlotte, NC: Information Age Publishing.

Larrivee, B. (1996). *Moving into balance.* Santa Monica, CA: Shoreline.

Larrivee, B. (2006a). *An educator's guide to teacher reflection.* Boston: Houghton Mifflin.

Larrivee, B. (2006b). The convergence of reflective practice and effective classroom management. In C. Evertson & C. Weinstein (Eds.), *Handbook of classroom management: Research, practice, and contemporary issues* (pp. 983–1001). Mahwah, NJ: Lawrence Erlbaum.

Larrivee, B. (2009). *Authentic classroom management: Creating a learning community and building reflective practice* (3rd ed.). Upper Saddle River, NJ: Pearson.

Larrivee, B. (2010). What we know and don't know about teacher reflection. In E. G. Pultorak (Ed.), *The purposes, practices, and professionalism of teacher reflectivity: Insights for twenty-first-century teachers and students* (pp. 137–61). Lanham, MD: Rowman & Littlefield.

Lasky, S. (2000). The cultural and emotional politics of teacher-parent interactions. *Teaching and Teacher Education, 16*(8), 843–60.

Lawton, M. P., DeVoe, M. R., & Parmelee, P. (1995). Relationship of events and affect in the daily life of an elderly population. *Psychology and Aging, 10,* 469–77.

Lazarus, R. S. (1991). *Emotion and adaptation*. New York: Oxford University Press.

Lazarus, R. S. (1993). From psychological stress to the emotions: A history of changing outlooks. *Annual Review of Psychology, 44*(1), 1–21.

Lazarus, R. S. (2000). Toward better research on stress and coping. *American Psychologist, 55*(6), 665–73.

Lazarus, R. S. (2001). Relational meaning and discrete emotions. In K. R. Scherer, A. Schorr, & T. Johnstone (Eds.), *Appraisal processes in emotion: Theory, methods, and research* (pp. 37–67). New York: Oxford University Press.

Lazarus, R. S., & Folkman, S. (1984). *Stress, appraisal, and coping*. New York: Springer.

LeDoux, J. (1996). *The emotional brain: The mysterious underpinnings of emotional life*. New York: Simon & Schuster.

LeDoux, J. (2002). *The synaptic self: How our brains become who we are*. New York: Penguin Books.

Lee, R. T., & Ashforth, B. E. (1990). On the meaning of Maslach's three dimensions of burnout. *Journal of Applied Psychology, 75*(6), 743–47.

Lee, R. T., & Ashforth, B. E. (1996). A meta-analytic examination of the correlates of the three dimensions of job burnout. *Journal of Applied Psychology, 81*(2), 123–33.

Leiter, M. P. (1993). Burnout as a development process: Consideration of models. In W. B. Schaufeli, C. Maslach, & T. Marek (Eds.), *Professional burnout: Recent developments in theory and research* (pp. 237–50). Washington, DC: Taylor & Francis.

Leiter, M. P., & Maslach, C. (2000). *Preventing burnout and building engagement: A complete program for organizational renewal*. San Francisco: Jossey-Bass.

Leung, D. Y. P., & Lee, W. W. S. (2006). Predicting intention to quit among Chinese teachers: Differential predictability of the components of burnout. *Anxiety, Stress and Coping, 19*(2), 129–41.

Liljestrom, A., Roulston, K., & deMarrais, K. (2007). "There is no place for feeling like this in the workplace": Women teachers' anger in school settings. In P. A. Schutz & R. Pekrun (Eds.), *Emotion in education* (pp. 275–91). San Diego, CA: Academic Press.

Linnenbrink, E. A. (2007). The role of affect in student learning: A multidimensional approach to considering the interaction of affect, motivation and engagement. In P. A. Schutz & R. Pekrun (Eds.), *Emotion in education* (pp. 101–18). San Diego, CA: Academic Press.

Linston, D., & Garrison, J. (2003). *Teaching, learning, and loving: Reclaiming passion in educational practice*. New York: Routledge Falmer.

Little, E. (2003). *Kids behaving badly: Teacher strategies for classroom behaviour*. Frenchs Forest, Australia: Pearson Education.

Long, N. (1996). The conflict cycle paradigm on how troubled students get teachers out of control. In N. Long & W. Morse (Eds.), *Conflict in the classroom: The education of at-risk and troubled students* (5th ed., pp. 244–65). Austin, TX: Pro-Ed.

Lopez, S., & Snyder, C. (2003). *Positive psychology assessment: Handbook of models and measures*. Washington, DC: American Psychological Association.

Lopez, S., Snyder, C., & Pedrotti, J. (2003). Hope: Many definitions, many measures. In S. Lopez & C. Snyder (Eds.), *Positive psychology assessment: Handbook of models and measures* (pp. 91–106). Washington, DC: American Psychological Association.

Losada, M. (1999). The complex dynamics of high performance teams. *Mathematical and Computer Modeling, 30*, 179–92.

Luskin, F., & Pelletier, K. (2005). *Stress free for good: 10 scientifically proven life skills for health and happiness*. New York: HarperOne.

Lutz, A., Brefczynski-Lewis, J., Johnstone, T., & Davidson, R. J. (2008). Regulation of the neural circuitry of emotion by compassion mediation: Effects of meditative expertise. *PloS One, 3*(3), 1–10.

Lutz, A., Slagter, H. A., Dunne, J., & Davidson, R. J. (2008). Attention regulation and monitoring in meditation. *Trends in Cognitive Sciences, 12*(4), 163–69.

Lyubomirsky, S. (2007). *The how of happiness: A scientific approach to getting the life you want*. New York: Penguin Press.

Lyubomirsky, S. (2011). Hedonic adaptation to positive and negative experiences. In S. Folkman (Ed.), *The Oxford handbook of stress, health, and coping* (pp. 201–24). New York: Oxford University Press.

Lyubomirsky, S., Dickerhoof, R., Boehm, J. K., & Sheldon, K. M. (2011). Becoming happier takes both a will and a proper way: An experimental longitudinal intervention to boost well-being. *Emotion, 11*(2), 391–402.

Lyubomirsky, S., King, L. A., & Diener, E. (2005). The benefits of frequent positive affect: Does happiness lead to success? *Psychological Bulletin, 131*(6), 803–55.

Lyubomirsky, S., Sheldon, K. M., & Schkade, D. (2005). Pursuing happiness: The architecture of sustainable change. *Review of General Psychology, 9*(2), 111–31.

Lyubomirsky, S., Sousa, L., & Dickerhoof, R. (2006). The costs and benefits of writing, talking, and thinking out life's triumphs and defeats. *Journal of Personality and Social Psychology, 90*(4), 692–708.

Maag, J. W. (2008). Rational-emotive therapy to help teachers control their emotions and behavior when dealing with disagreeable students. *Intervention in School and Clinic, 44*(1), 52–57.

MacDonald, E., & Shirley, D. (2009). *The mindful teacher.* New York: Teachers College Press.

Malach-Pines, A. (2000). Treating career burnout: A psychodynamic existential perspective. *Journal of Clinical Psychology, 56*(5), 633–42.

Manning, B. H., & Payne, B. D. (1996). *Self-talk for teachers and students: Metacognitive strategies for personal and classroom use.* Boston: Allyn & Bacon.

Marzano, R. J., Marzano, J. S., & Pickering, D. J. (2003). *Classroom management that works: Research-based strategies for every teacher.* Alexandria, VA: Association for Supervision and Curriculum Development.

Mashburn, A. J., Hamre, B. K., Downer, J. T., & Pianta, R. C. (2006). Teacher and classroom characteristics associated with teachers' ratings of pre-kindergartners' relationships and behaviors. *Journal of Psychoeducational Assessment, 24*(4), 367–80.

Maslach, C. (1982). *Burnout: The cost of caring.* Englewood Cliffs, NJ: Prentice Hall.

Maslach, C., Jackson, S. E., & Leiter, M. P. (1996). *Maslach Burnout Inventory manual* (3rd ed.). Palo Alto, CA: CPP.

Maslach, C., & Leiter, M. P. (1997). *The truth about burnout.* San Franscisco: Jossey-Bass.

Maslach, C., Leiter, M. P., & Schaufeli, W. B. (2008). Measuring burnout. In C. L. Copper & S. Cartwright (Eds), *The Oxford handbook of organizational well-being* (pp. 86–108). New York: Oxford University Press.

Maslach, C., Schaufeli, W. B., & Leiter, M. P. (2001). Job burnout. *Annual Review of Psychology, 52,* 397–422.

Maslow, A. (1954/1970). *Motivation and personality.* New York: Harper & Row.

Matthews, K. A., & Gump, B. B. (2002). Chronic work stress and marital dissolution increase risk of post-trial mortality in men from the Multiple Risk Factor Intervention Trial. *Archives of Internal Medicine, 162*(3), 309–315.

Matthiesen, S. B., Aasen, B., Holst, G., Wie, K., & Einarsen, S. (2003). The escalation of conflict: A case study of bullying at work. *International Journal of Management and Decision Making, 4,* 96–112.

Maxfield, D. (2009, October). Running into the fire: Survival tips for education's first-responders. *Education Week, 29*(6), 28–29.

Mazur, P. J., & Lynch, M. D. (1989). Differential impact of administrative, organizational, and personality factors on teacher burnout. *Teaching and Teacher Education, 5,* 337–53.

McCarthy, C. J., Kissen, D., Yadley, L., Wood, T., & Lambert, R. G. (2006). Relationship of teachers' preventive coping recourses to burnout symptoms. In R. G. Lambert & C. J. McCarthy (Eds.), *Understanding teacher stress in an era of accountability* (Vol. 3, pp. 179–96). Greenwich, CT: Information Age.

McCarthy, C. J., Lambert, R. G., O'Donnell, M., & Melendres, L. T. (2009). The relation of elementary teachers' experience, stress, and coping resources to burnout symptoms. *Elementary School Journal, 109*(3), 282–300.

McEwen, B. (1998). Contradiction, paradox, and irony: The world of classroom management. In R. E. Butchart & B. McEwan (Eds.), *Classroom discipline in American schools: Problems and possibilities for democratic education* (pp. 135–45). Albany, NY: SUNY.

McKay, M., Davis, M., & Fanning, P. (2012). *Thoughts and feelings: Taking control of your moods and your life* (4th ed.). Oakland, CA: New Harbinger.

McKay, M., & Sutker, C. (2007). *Leave your mind behind: The everyday practice of finding stillness amid rushing thoughts.* Oakland, CA: New Harbinger.

McNeely, C. A., & Falci, C. (2004). School connectedness and the transition into and out of health risk behavior among adolescents: A comparison of social belonging and teacher support. *Journal of School Health, 74*(7), 284–92.

Meichenbaum, D. (1977). *Cognitive-behavior modification: An integrative approach*. New York: Plenum.

Meichenbaum, D. (1985). *Stress-inoculation training*. Elmsford, NY: Pergamon.

MetLife. (2004). *The MetLife survey of the American teacher: Transitions and the role of supportive relationships*. New York: Author.

Michie, G. (2011). Fire and water: Reflections on teaching in the city. In A. A. Friedman & L. Reynolds (Eds.), *Burned in: Fueling the fire to teach* (pp. 60–66). New York: Teachers College Press.

Middleton, M., & Midgley, C. (1997). Avoiding the demonstration of lack of ability: An underexplored aspect of goal theory. *Journal of Educational Psychology, 89*(4), 710–18.

Midgley, C., Feldlaufer, H., & Eccles, J. S. (1989). Change in teacher efficacy and student self- and task-related beliefs in mathematics during the transition to junior high school. *Journal of Educational Psychology, 81*, 247–58.

Miller, A. (1995). Teachers' attributions of causality, control and responsibility in respect to difficult pupil behaviour and its successful management. *Educational Psychology, 15*(4), 457–71.

Miller, T. (1986). *The unfair advantage*. Skaneateles, NY: Lakeside.

Mills, L., & Huebner, E. (1998). A prospective study of personality characteristics, occupational stressors, and burnout among school psychology practitioners. *Journal of School Psychology, 36*(1), 103–20.

Mills, R. A., Powell, R. R., & Pollack, J. P. (1992). The influence of middle level interdisciplinary teaming on teacher isolation: A case study. *Research in Middle Level Education, 15*(2), 9–25.

Modinos, G., Ormel, J., & Aleman, A. (2010). Individual differences in dispositional mindfulness and brain activity involved in reappraisal of emotion. *Social Cognitive & Affective Neuroscience, 5*(4), 369–77.

Montgomery, A. J., Panagopolou, E., de Wildt, M., & Meenks, E. (2006). Work-family interference, emotional labor and burnout. *Journal of Managerial Psychology, 21*(1), 36–51.

Montgomery, C., & Rupp, A. A. (2005). Meta-analysis for exploring the diverse causes and effects of stress in teachers. *Canadian Journal of Education, 28*(3), 458–86.

Moon, J. A. (2006). *Learning journals: Handbook for reflective practice and professional development*. New York: Routledge.

Moore, A., Gruber, T., Derose, J., & Malinowski, P. (2012). Regular, brief mindfulness meditation practice improves electrophysiological markers of attentional control. *Frontiers in Human Neuroscience, 6*, 18–29.

Morrison, F. J., & Connor, C. M. (2002). Understanding schooling effects on early literacy: A working research strategy. *Journal of School Psychology, 40*(6), 493–500.

Moskowitz, J. T. (2011). Coping interventions and the regulation of positive affect. In S. Folkman (Ed.), *The Oxford handbook of stress, health, and coping* (pp. 407–27). New York: Oxford University Press.

Mroczek, D. K., & Almeida, D. M. (2004). The effect of daily stress, personality, and age on daily negative affect. *Journal of Personality, 72*, 356–76.

Murdock, T. B., & Miller, A. (2003). Teachers as sources of middle school students' motivational identity: Variable-centered and person-centered analytic approaches. *Elementary School Journal, 103*(4), 383–99.

Murphy, M., & Donovan, S. (1997). *The physical and psychological effects of meditation* (2nd ed.). Petaluma, CA: Institute of Noetic Sciences.

Näring, G., Briët, M., Brouwers, A. (2006). Beyond demand-control: Emotional labour and symptoms of burnout in teachers. *Work and Stress, 20*(4), 303–15.

National Commission on Teaching and America's Future (NCTAF). (2003). *No dream denied: A pledge to America's children.* Washington, DC: Author.

Nezlek, J. B., & Gable, S. L. (2001). Depression as a moderator of relationships between positive daily events and day-to-day psychological adjustment. *Personality and Social Psychology Bulletin, 27*, 1692–1704.

Nias, J. (1996). Thinking about feeling: The emotions in teaching. *Cambridge Journal of Education, 26*(3), 293–306.

Nielsen, N. R., Kristensen, T. S., Schnohr, P., & Gronbaek, M. (2008). Perceived stress and cause-specific morality among men and women: Results from a prospective cohort study. *American Journal of Epidemiology, 168*(5), 481–96.

Noddings, N. (2005). *The challenge to care in schools: An alternative approach to education.* New York: Teachers College, Columbia University.

Noor, N. M. (2004). Work-family conflict, work-and family-role salience, and women's well-being. *Journal of Social Psychology, 144,* 389–405.

Oakes, J., & Lipton, M. (2003). *Teaching to change the world* (2nd ed.). Boston: McGraw-Hill.

Ochsner, K. N., & Gross, J. J. (2004). Thinking makes it so: A social cognitive neuroscience approach to emotion regulation. In K. D. Vohs & R. F. Baumeister (Eds.), *Handbook of self-regulation: Research, theory, and applications* (pp. 229–55). New York: Guilford Press.

O'Connor, E. E., Dearing, E., & Collins, B. A. (2011). Teacher-child relationship and behavior problem trajectories in elementary school. *American Educational Research Journal, 48*(1), 120–62.

Oman, D., Shapiro, S. L., Thoresen, C. E., Plante, T. G., & Flinders, T. (2008). Meditation lowers stress and supports forgiveness among college students: A randomized controlled trial. *Journal of American College Health, 56,* 569–78.

Ong, A. D., Bergeman, C. S., Bisconti, T. L., & Wallace, T. (2006). Psychological resilience, positive emotions and successful adaptation to stress in later life. *Journal of Personality and Social Psychology, 91,* 730–49.

Osher, D., Sprague, J., Weissberg, R. P., Axelrod, J., Keenan, S., Kendziora, K., & Zins, J. E. (2007). A comprehensive approach to promoting social, emotional, and academic growth in contemporary schools. In A. Thomas & J. Grimes (Eds.), *Best practices in school psychology* (Vol. 5, 5th ed., pp. 1263–78). Bethesda, MD: National Association of School Psychologists.

Osterman, K. F. (2000). Students' need for belonging in the school community. *Review of Educational Research, 70*(3), 323–67.

Ozdemir, Y. (2007). The role of classroom management efficacy in predicting teacher burnout. *International Journal of Social Sciences, 2*(4), 257–63.

Pagnoni, G., & Cekic, M. (2007). Aging effects on gray matter volume and attentional performance in Zen meditation. *Neurobiology of Aging, 28,* 1623–27.

Palmer, P. J. (1998). *The courage to teach: Exploring the inner landscape of a teacher's life.* San Francisco: Jossey-Bass.

Park, N., Peterson, C., & Seligman, M. E. P. (2004). Strengths of character and well-being. *Journal of Social and Clinical Psychology, 23*(5), 603–19.

Parrott, W. G., & Spackman, M. P. (2000). Emotion and memory. In M. Lewis & J. M. Haviland-Jones (Eds.), *Handbook of emotions* (2nd ed., pp. 476–90). New York: Guilford Press.

Patrick, H., Anderman, L. H., Ryan, A. M., Edelin, K. C., & Midgley, C. (2001). Teachers' communication of goal orientations in four fifth-grade classrooms. *Elementary School Journal, 102*(1), 35–58.

Pekrun, R., & Schutz, P. A. (2007). Where do we go from here? Implications and further directions for inquiry on emotions in education. In P. A. Schutz & R. Pekrun (Eds.), *Emotion in education* (pp. 303–21). San Diego, CA: Academic Press.

Pellerin, L. A. (2005). Student disengagement and the socialization styles of high schools. *Social Forces, 84,* 1161–79.

Pennebaker, J. W. (1993). Putting stress into words: Health, linguistics, and therapeutic implications. *Behavior Research and Therapy, 31,* 539–48.

Pennebaker, J. W. (1997). *Opening up: The healing power of expressing emotion.* New York: Guilford Press.

Pennebaker, J. W., & Chung, C. K. (2007). Expressive writing, emotional upheavals, and health. In H. S. Friedman & R. C. Silver (Eds.), *Foundations of health psychology* (pp. 263–84). New York: Oxford University Press.

Pennebaker, J. W., Mayne, T. J., & Francis, M. E. (1997). Linguistic predictors of adaptive bereavement. *Journal of Personality and Social Psychology, 72,* 863–71.

Pennebaker, J. W., & Seagal, J. D. (1999). Forming a story: The health benefits of narrative. *Journal of Clinical Psychology, 55,* 1243–54.

Perry, B. D. (2006). *Maltreated children: Experience, brain development and the next generation.* New York: Norton.

Pert, C. (1997). *Molecules of emotion.* New York: Scribner.

Peterson, C., & Park, N. (2003). Positive psychology as the evenhanded positive psychologist views it. *Psychological Inquiry, 14*, 141–46.

Peterson, C., Park, N., & Seligman, M. E. P. (2005). Orientations to happiness and life satisfaction: The full life versus the empty life. *Journal of Happiness Studies, 6*(1), 25–41.

Peterson, C., & Seligman, M. (2004). *Character strengths and virtues: A handbook and classification.* Washington, DC: American Psychological Association.

Phelps, E. A., & LeDoux, J. E. (2005). Contributions of the amygdala to emotion processing: From animal models to human behavior. *Neuron, 48*, 175–87.

Pines, A. M. (1993). Burnout: An existential perspective. In W. B. Schaufeli, C. Maslach, & T. Marek (Eds.), *Professional burnout: Recent developments in theory and research* (pp. 33–52). Washington, DC: Taylor & Francis.

Pines, A. M. (2002). Teacher burnout: A psychodynamic existential perspective. *Teachers and Teaching, 8*, 121–41.

Pines, A. M., Aronson, E., & Kafry, D. (1981). *Burnout: From tedium to personal growth.* New York: Free Press.

Pintrich, P. R. (2000). The role of goal orientation in self-regulated learning. In M. Boekaerts, P. R. Pintrich, & M. Zeidner (Eds.), *Handbook of self-regulation: Theory, research, and application* (pp. 451–502). San Diego, CA: Academic Press.

Prawat, R., Byers, J., & Anderson, A. H. (1983). An attributional analysis of teachers' affective reactions to student success and failure. *American Educational Research Journal, 20*(1), 137–52.

Provasnik, S., & Dorfman, S. (2005). *Mobility in the teacher workforce* (NCES 2005–114). Washington, DC: U.S. Department of Education, National Center for Education Statistics.

Pugliesi, K. (1999). The consequences of emotional labor: Effects on work stress, job satisfaction, and well-being. *Motivation and Emotion, 23*, 125–54.

Quartz, K. H., Thomas, A., Anderson, L., Masyn, K., Lyons, K. B., & Olsen, B. (2008). Careers in motion: A longitudinal retention study of role changing among early-career urban educators. *Teachers College Record, 110*(1), 218–50.

Quinn, A. J. (2003). Organizational culture, school leadership and teacher stress: The relationship to referral rates for student misbehavior. *Australian Journal of Psychology, Supplement, 55*, 205–05.

Ramel, W., Goldin, P. R., Carmona, P. E., & McQuaid, J. R. (2004). The effects of mindfulness mediation on cognitive process and affect in patients with past depression. *Cognitive Therapy and Research, 28*, 433–55.

Reivich, J. J., & Shatte, A. (2003). *The resilience factor: Seven essential skills for overcoming life's inevitable obstacles.* New York: Random House.

Ria, L., Sève, C., Saury, J., Theureau, J., & Durand, M. (2003). Beginning teachers' situated emotions: A study of first classroom experience. *Journal of Education for Teaching, 29*, 219–33.

Richards, J. M., & Gross, J. J. (2000). Emotion regulation and memory: The cognitive costs of keeping one's cool. *Journal of Personality and Social Psychology, 79*, 410–24.

Rimm-Kaufman, S. E., La Paro, K. M., Downer, J. T., & Pianta, R. C. (2005). The contribution of classroom setting and quality of instruction to children's behavior in kindergarten classrooms. *Elementary School Journal, 105*(4), 377–94.

Rogers, C. R. (1951). *Client-centered therapy: Its current practice, implications, and theory.* Boston: Houghton Mifflin.

Rogers, C. R. (1961). *On becoming a person.* Boston: Houghton Mifflin.

Roorda, D. L., Koomen, H. M. Y., Spilt, J. L., & Oort, F. L. (2011). The influence of affective teacher-student relationships on students' school engagement and achievement: A meta-analytic approach. *Review of Educational Research, 81*(4), 493–529.

Roseman, I. R. (2001). A model of appraisal in the emotion system. In K. R. Scherer, A. Schorr, & T. Johnstone (Eds.), *Appraisal processes in emotion: Theory, methods, research* (pp. 68–91). New York: Oxford University Press.

Roseman, I. R., & Smith, C. A. (2001). Appraisal theory: Overview, assumptions, varieties, controversies. In K. R. Scherer, A. Schorr, & T. Johnstone (Eds.), *Appraisal processes in emotion: Theory, methods, research* (pp. 3–19). New York: Oxford University Press.

Roseman, I. R., Wiest, C., & Swartz, T. S. (1994). Phenomenology, behaviors, and goals differentiate discrete emotions. *Journal of Personality and Social Psychology, 67,* 206–21.

Rosengren, A., Orth-Gomer, K., Wedel, H., & Wilhelmsen, L. (1993). Stressful life events, social support, and morality in men born in 1933. *British Medical Journal, 307*(6912), 1102–05.

Rosiek, J. (2003). Emotional scaffolding: An exploration of the teacher's knowledge at the intersection of student emotion and the subject matter. *Journal of Teacher Education, 54*(5), 399–412.

Roth, G., Assor, A., Kanat-Maymon, Y., & Kaplan, H. (2007). Autonomous motivation for teaching: How self-determined teaching may lead to self-determined learning. *Journal of Educational Psychology, 99*(4), 761–74.

Roush, D. (1984). Rational-emotive therapy and youth: Some new techniques for counselors. *Personnel and Guidance Journal, 62,* 414–17.

Ruini, C., Belaise, C., Brombin, C., Caffo, E., & Fava, G. A. (2006). Well-being therapy in school settings: A pilot study. *Psychotherapy and Psychosomatics, 75,* 331–36.

Russell, D. W., Altmaier, E., & Van Velzen, D. (1987). Job-related stress, social support and burnout among classroom teachers. *Journal of Applied Psychology, 72,* 269–74.

Rutter, M., & Maughan, B. (2002). School effectiveness findings 1979–2002. *Journal of School Psychology, 40*(6), 451–75.

Ryan, A. M., & Patrick, H. (2001). The classroom social environment and changes in adolescents' motivation and engagement during middle school. *American Educational Research Journal, 38*(2), 437–60.

Saltzman, A. (in press). *A still quiet place: Manual for teaching mindfulness-based stress reduction to children.* Available at www.stillquiet place.com.

Saltzman, A., & Goldin, P. (2008). Mindfulness-based stress reduction for school-age children. In S. C. Hayes & L. A. Greco (Eds.), *Acceptance and mindfulness interventions for children, adolescents and families* (pp. 139–61). Oakland, CA: Context Press/New Harbinger.

Santavirta, N., Solovieva, S., & Theorell, T. (2007). The association between job strain and emotional exhaustion in a cohort of 1,028 finish teachers. *British Journal of Educational Psychology, 77*(1), 213–28.

Sapolsky, R. M. (1998). *Why zebras don't get ulcers: An updated guide to stress, stress-related diseases, and coping.* New York: Freeman.

Schaufeli, W. B., & Bakker, A. B. (2004). Job demands, job resources and their relationship with burnout and engagement: A multi-sample study. *Journal of Organization Behavior, 25,* 293–315.

Schaufeli, W. B., & Buunk, B. P. (2003). Burnout: An overview of 25 years of research and theorizing. In J. Schabracq, J. A. M. Winnubst, & C. L. Cooper (Eds.), *The handbook of work and health psychology* (2nd ed., pp. 383–425). New York: Wiley.

Schaufeli, W. B., & Enzmann, D. (1998). *The burnout companion to study and practice: A critical analysis.* London: Taylor & Francis.

Schaufeli, W. B., & Salanova, M. (2008). Enhancing work engagement through the management of human resources. In K. Naswall, M. Serke, & J. Hellgren (Eds.), *The individual in the changing working life* (pp. 380–404). Cambridge, UK: Cambridge University Press.

Schaufeli, W. B., Salanova, M., Gonzales-Roma, V., & Bakker, A. B. (2002). The measurement of engagement and burnout: A two sample confirmatory factor analytic approach. *Journal of Happiness Studies, 3,* 71–92.

Scherer, K. R. (2001). Appraisal considered as a process of multi-level sequential checking. In K. R. Scherer, A. Schorr, & T. Johnstone (Eds.), *Appraisal processes in emotion: Theory, methods, research* (pp. 92–120). New York: Oxford University Press.

Schlichte, J., Yssel, N., & Merbler, J. (2005). Pathways to burnout: Case studies in teacher isolation and alienation. *Preventing School Failure, 50,* 1–16.

Schneiderman, N., Ironson, G., & Siegel, S. D. (2005). Stress and health: Psychological, behavioral, and biological determinants. *Annual Review of Clinical Psychology, 1,* 607–28.

Schoeberlein, D., & Sheth, S. (2009). *Mindful teaching and teaching mindfulness: A guide for anyone who teaches anything.* Boston: Wisdom Publications.

Schonert-Reichl, K. A., & Lawlor, M. S. (2010). The effects of a mindfulness-based education program on pre- and early adolescents' well-being and social and emotional competence. *Mindfulness, 1*(3), 137–51.

Schutz, P. A., Cross, D. I., Hong, J. Y., & Osbon, J. N. (2007). Teachers' identities, beliefs, and goals related to emotions in the classroom. In P. A. Schutz & R. Pekrun (Eds.), *Emotion in education* (pp. 223–39). San Diego, CA: Academic Press.

Schutz, P. A., DiStefano, C., Benson, J., & Davis, H. A. (2004). The development of a scale for emotional regulation during test taking. *Anxiety, Stress and Coping: An International Journal, 17*, 253–69.

Schutz, P. A., & Lanehart, S. (Eds.). (2002). Emotions in education [Special Issue]. *Educational Psychologist, 37*(2), 67–134.

Schwartz, J., & Begley, S. (2002). *The mind and the brain: Neuroplasticity and the power of mental force.* New York: HarperCollins.

Schwarzer, R., & Knoll, N. (2003). Positive coping: Mastering demands and searching for meaning. In S. J. Lopez & C. R. Snyder (Eds.), *Positive psychological assessment: A handbook of models and measures* (pp. 393–409). Washington, DC: American Psychological Association.

Schwarzer, R., & Taubert, S. (2002). Tenacious goal pursuits and striving toward personal growth: Proactive coping. In E. Frydenberg (Ed.), *Beyond coping: Meeting goals, visions and challenges* (pp. 19–35). New York: Oxford University Press.

Schwerdtfeger, A., Konermann, L., & Schonhofen, K. (2008). Self-efficacy as a health-protective resource in teachers? A biopsychological approach. *Health Psychology, 27*(3), 358–68.

Segerstrom, S. C., & Miller, G. E. (2004). Psychological stress and the human immune system: A meta-analytic study of 30 years of inquiry. *Psychological Bulletin, 130*(4), 601–30.

Seligman, M. E. P. (2002). *Authentic happiness.* New York: Free Press.

Seligman, M. E. P. (2006). *Learned optimism: How to change your mind and your life* (2nd ed.). New York: Pocket Books.

Seligman, M. E. P. (2011a). *Flourish: A visionary new understanding of happiness and well-being.* New York: Free Press.

Seligman, M. E. P. (2011b). Building resilience. *Harvard Business Review, 89*(4), 100–06.

Seligman, M. E. P., & Csikszentmihalyi, M. (2000). Positive psychology. *American Psychologist, 55*(1), 5–14.

Seligman, M. E. P., Rashid, T., & Parks, A. C. (2006). Positive psychotherapy. *American Psychologist, 61*(8), 774–88.

Seligman, M. E. P., Steen, T. A., Park, N., & Peterson, C. (2005). Positive psychology progress: Empirical validation of interventions. *American Psychologist, 60*(5), 410–21.

Selye, H. (1956). *The stress of life.* New York: McGraw-Hill.

Selye, H. (1974). *Stress without distress.* New York: J. B. Lippincott.

Semmer, N. K. (2003). Job stress interventions and organization of work. In J. C. Quick & L. E. Tetrick (Eds.), *Handbook of occupational health psychology* (pp. 325–53). Washington, DC: American Psychological Association.

Shapiro, S. L., Brown, K., & Biegel, G. (2007). Self-care for health care professionals: Effects of MBSR on mental well-being of counseling psychology students. *Training and Education in Professional Psychology, 1*, 105–15.

Shapiro, S. L., Carlson, L. E., Astin, J. A., & Freedman, B. (2006). Mechanisms of mindfulness. *Journal of Clinical Psychology, 62*, 373–86.

Shapiro, S. L., Schwartz, G. E. R., & Bonner, G. (1998). The effects of mindfulness-based stress reduction on medical and pre-medical students. *Journal of Behavioral Medicine, 21*, 581–99.

Sharp, J. J., & Forman S. G. (1985). A comparison of two approaches to anxiety management for teachers. *Behavior Therapy, 16*, 370–83.

Sheldon, K. M., & Lyubomirsky, S. (2004). Achieving sustainable new happiness: Prospects, practices, and prescriptions. In A. Linley & S. Joseph (Eds.), *Positive psychology in practice* (pp. 127–45). Hoboken, NJ: John Wiley & Sons.

Sheldon, K. M., Ryan, R., & Reis, H. T. (1996). What makes for a good day? Competence and autonomy in the day and in the person. *Personality and Social Psychology Bulletin, 22*, 1270–79.

Siegel, D. J. (2010). *Mindsight: The new science of personal transformation.* New York: Bantam Books.

Silver, R. B., Measelle, J. R., Armstrong, J. M., & Essex, M. J. (2005). Trajectories of classroom externalizing behavior: Contributions of child characteristics, family characteristics, and the teacher-child relationship during the school transition. *Journal of School Psychology, 43*(1), 39–60.

Simbula, S. (2010). Daily fluctuations in teachers' well-being: A diary study using the job demands-resources model. *Anxiety, Stress and Coping, 23*(5), 563–84.

Sin, N. L., & Lyubomirsky, S. (2009). Enhancing well-being and alleviating depressive symptoms with positive psychology intervention: A practice-friendly meta-analysis. *Journal of Clinical Psychology, 65*(5), 467–87.

Singer, T., & Lamm, C. (2009). The social neuroscience of empathy. *Annals of the New York Academy of Sciences, 1156*(1), 81–96.

Singh, N. N., Lancioni, G. E., Singh, J., Winton, A. S. W., Sabaawi, M., & Wahler, R. G. (2007). Adolescents with conduct disorder can be mindful of their aggressive behavior. *Journal of Emotional and Behavioral Disorders, 15*(1), 56–63.

Singh, N. N., Singh, A. N., Lancioni, G. E., Singh, J., Winton, A. S. W., & Adkins, A. D. (2010). Mindfulness training for parents and their children with ADHD increases children's compliance. *Journal of Child and Family Studies, 19*(2), 157–66.

Smalley, S. L., & Winston, D. (2010). *Fully present: The science, art, and practice of mindfulness.* New York: Da Capo Press.

Smith, C. A., & Kirby, L. D. (2004). Appraisal as a pervasive determinant of anger. *Emotion, 4,* 133–38.

Smith, C. A., & Lazarus, R. S. (1990). Emotion and adaptation. In L. A. Pervin (Ed.), *Handbook of personality theory and research* (pp. 609–37). New York: Guilford.

Smith, J. C. (1985). *Relaxation dynamics: A cognitive-behavioral approach to relaxation.* Champaign, IL: Research Press.

Smith, J. C. (2005). *Relaxation, meditation, & mindfulness: A mental health practitioner's guide to new and traditional approaches.* New York: Springer.

Smylie, M. A. (1999). Teacher stress in a time of reform. In R. Vandenberghe & A. M. Huberman (Eds.), *Understanding and preventing teacher burnout* (pp. 59–84). Cambridge, UK: Cambridge University Press.

Smyth, J. (1992). Teacher's work and the politics of reflection. *American Educational Research Journal, 29*(2), 267–300.

Smyth, J. (1998). Written emotional expression: Effect sizes, outcome types, and moderating variables. *Journal of Consulting and Clinical Psychology, 66,* 174–84.

Snyder, C. R., & Lopez, S. J. (2009). *The Oxford handbook of positive psychology* (2nd ed.). New York: Oxford University Press.

Sonnentag, S. (2001). Work, recovery activities, and individual well-being: A diary study. *Journal of Occupational Health Psychology, 3,* 196–210.

Sousa, D. A. (2006). *How the brain learns* (3rd ed.). Thousand Oaks, CA: Corwin Press.

Stinebrickner, T. R. (1998). An empirical investigation of teacher attrition. *Economics of Education Review, 17,* 127–36.

Stinebrickner, T. R. (2002). An analysis of occupational change and departure from the labor force: Evidence of the reasons that teachers leave. *Journal of Human Resources, 37,* 192–216.

Stone, A. A., Kennedy-Moore, E., Neale, J. M. (1995). Association between daily coping and end-of-day mood. *Health Psychology, 14,* 341–49.

Sutton, R. E. (2004). Emotional regulation goals and strategies of teachers. *Social Psychology in Education, 7,* 379–98.

Sutton, R. E. (2007). Teachers' anger, frustration, and self-regulation. In P. A. Schutz and R. Pekrun (Eds.), *Emotion in education* (pp. 259–74). San Diego, CA: Academic Press.

Sutton, R. E., Genovese, J., & Conway, P. F. (2005). *Anger and frustration episodes of teachers: Different emotions or different intensity?* Paper presented at the Annual Meeting of the American Educational Research Association, Montreal, Canada.

Sutton, R. E., & Knight, C. C. (2006). Teachers' emotion regulation. In A. V. Mitel (Ed.), *Trends in educational psychology* (pp. 107–35). Hauppauge, NY: Nova Publishers.

Sutton, R. E., Mudrey-Camino, R., & Knight, C. C. (2009). Teachers' emotion regulation and classroom management. *Theory into Practice, 48*(2), 130–37.

Sutton, R. E., & Wheatley, K. E. (2003). Teachers' emotions and teaching: A review of the literature and directions for future research. *Educational Psychology Review, 15*(4), 327–58.

Swider, B. W., & Zimmerman, R. D. (2010). Born to burnout: A meta-analytic path model of personality, job burnout, and work outcomes. *Journal of Vocational Behavior*, *76*(3), 487–506.

Sylwester, R. (2003). *A biological brain in a cultural classroom* (2nd ed.). Thousand Oaks, CA: Corwin Press.

Tang, Y. Y., Ma, Y., Wang, J., Fan, Y., Feng, S., Lu, Q., Yu, Q., Sui, D., Rothbart, M. K., Fan, M., & Posner, M. I. (2007). Short-term meditation training improves attention and self-regulation. *Proceedings of the National Academy of Sciences*, *104*(43), 17152–56.

Taylor, S. (2012). Transformation through suffering: A study of individuals who have experienced positive psychological transformation following periods of intense turmoil. *Journal of Humanistic Psychology*, *52*(1), 30–52.

Taylor, S. E. (2007). Social support. In H. S. Friedman & R. S. Silver (Eds.), *The Oxford handbook of health psychology* (pp. 145–71). New York: Oxford University Press.

Taylor, S. E., Klein, L. C., Lewis, B. P., Gruenewald, T., Gurung, R. A. R., & Updegraff, J. A. (2000). Biobehavioral responses to stress in females: Tend-and-befriend, not fight-or-flight. *Psychological Review*, *107*, 411–29.

Tedeschi, R. G., & Calhoun, L. G. (2004). Posttraumatic growth: Conceptual foundations and empirical evidences. *Psychological Inquiry*, *15*, 1–18.

Teven, J. J. (2007). Teacher temperament: Correlates with teacher caring, burnout, and organizational outcomes. *Communication Education*, *56*(3), 382–400.

Theobald, N. D., & Laine, S. W. M. (2003). The impact of teacher turnover on teacher quality: Findings from four states. In M. L. Plecki & D. H. Monk (Eds.), *School finance and teacher quality: Exploring the connections* (pp. 33–54). Larchmont, NY: Eye on Education.

Thompson, G. L. (2004). *Through ebony eyes: What teachers need to know but are afraid to ask about African American students*. San Francisco: Jossey-Bass.

Thomsen, K. (2002). *Building resilient students: Integrating resiliency into what you already know and do*. Thousand Oaks, CA: Corwin Press.

Thoresen, C. J., Kaplan, S. A. Barsky, A. P., Warren, C. R., & DeChermont, K. (2003). The affective underpinnings of job perceptions and attitudes: A meta-analytic review and integration. *Psychological Bulletin*, *129*, 914–45.

Tickle, L. (1991). New teachers and the emotions of learning teaching. *Cambridge Journal of Education*, *21*(3), 319–29.

Tindle, H., Chang, Y. F., Kuller, L., Manson, J. E., Robinson, J. G., Rosal, M. C., Siegle, G. J., & Matthews, K. A. (2009). Optimism, cynical hostility, & incident coronary heart disease and mortality in the Women's Health Initiative. *Circulation*, *118*, 1145–46.

Totterdell, P., & Holman, D. (2003). Emotion regulation in customer service roles: Testing a model of emotional labor. *Journal of Occupational Health Psychology*, *8*(1), 55–73.

Travers, C. J., & Cooper, C. L. (1996). *Teachers under pressure: Stress in the teaching profession*. New York: Routledge.

Troman, G., & Woods, P. (2001). *Primary teachers' stress*. New York: Routledge/Falmer.

Truch, S. (1980). *Teacher burnout and what to do about it*. Novato, CA: Academic Therapy.

Tschannen-Moran, M., Woolfolk Hoy, A., & Hoy, W. K. (1998). Teacher efficacy: Its meaning and measure. *Review of Educational Research*, *68*(2), 202–48.

Tsouloupas, C. N., Carson, R. L., Matthews, R., Grawitch, M. J., & Barber, L. K. (2010). Exploring the association between teachers' perceived student misbehavior and emotional exhaustion: The importance of teacher efficacy beliefs and emotion regulation. *Educational Psychology*, *30*(2), 173–89.

Turk, D. C., Meeks, S., & Turk, L. M. (1982). Factors contributing to teacher stress: Implications for research, prevention, and remediation. *Behavioral Counseling Quarterly*, *2*(1), 3–25.

Turner, J. E., & Waugh, R. M. (2007). A dynamical systems perspective regarding students' learning processes: Shame reactions and emergent self-organizations. In P. A. Schutz and R. Pekrun (Eds.), *Emotion in education* (pp. 119–39). San Diego, CA: Academic Press.

Turrell, G., Lynch, J. W., Leite, C., Raghunathan, T., & Kaplan, G. A. (2007). Socioeconomic disadvantage in childhood and across the life course and all-cause morality and physical function in adulthood: Evidence from the Alameda County Study. *Journal of Epidemiology & Community Health*, *61*(8), 723–30.

Unterbrink, T., Hack, A., Pfeifer, R., Buhl-Griebhaber, V., Muller, U., Wesche, H., Frommhold, M., Scheuch, K., Seibt, R., Wirsching, M., & Bauer, J. (2007). Burnout and effort-reward-imbalance in a sample of 949 German teachers. *International Archives of Occupational & Environmental Health, 80*(5), 433–41.

Updegraff, J. A., & Marshall, G. N. (2005). Predictors of perceived growth following direct exposure to community violence. *Journal of Social and Clinical Psychology, 24*(4), 538–60.

Usher, E. L., & Pajares, F. (2008). Sources of self-efficacy in school: Critical review of the literature and future directions. *Review of Educational Research, 78*(4), 751–96.

Vandenberghe, R., & Huberman, A. M. (1999). *Understanding and preventing teacher burnout: A source-book of international research and practice.* Cambridge, UK: Cambridge University Press.

Van der Doef, M., & Maes, S. (1999). The job demand-control (-support) model and psychological well-being: A review of 20 years of empirical research. *Work and Stress, 13,* 87–114.

Van der Klink, J. J. L., Blonk, R. W. B., Schene, A. H., & Van Dijk, F. J. H. (2001). The benefits of interventions for work-related stress. *American Journal of Public Health, 91,* 270–76.

Vanslyke-Briggs, K. (2010). *The nurturing teacher: Managing the stress of caring.* Lanham, MD: Rowman & Littlefield.

Van Veen, K., & Lasky, S. (2005). Emotion as a lens to explore teacher identity and change: Different theoretical approaches. *Teaching and Teacher Education, 21*(8), 917–34.

Vitaliano, P. P., Zhang, J., & Scanlan, J. M. (2003). Is caregiving hazardous to one's physical health? A meta-analysis. *Psychology Bulletin, 129*(6), 946–72.

Wallenstein, G. (2003). *Mind, stress and emotions: The new science of mood.* Boston: Commonwealth Press.

Wang, M., & Holcombe, R. (2010). Adolescents' perceptions of school environment, engagement, and academic achievement in middle school. *American Educational Research Journal, 47*(3), 633–62.

Ware, F. (2006). Warm demander pedagogy: Culturally responsive teaching that supports a culture of achievement for African American students. *Urban Education, 41*(4), 427–56.

Watson, D., Clark, L. A., & Harkness, A. R. (1994). Structures of personality and their relevance to psychopathology. *Journal of Abnormal Psychology, 108,* 18–31.

Watson, D. L., & Tharp, R. G. (2012). *Self-directed behavior: Self-modifications for personal adjustment* (10th ed.). Pacific Grove, CA: Brooks/Cole.

Watson, M., & Battistich, V. (2006). Building and sustaining caring communities. In C. Evertson & C. Weinstein (Eds.), *Handbook of classroom management: Research, practice, and contemporary issues* (pp. 253–79). Mahwah, NJ: Lawrence Erlbaum.

Weber, S., & Mitchell, C. (1995). *That's funny, you don't look like a teacher.* London: Falmer.

Weil, A. (1997/2006). *Eight weeks to optimum health: A proven program for taking full advantage of your body's natural healing power.* New York: Alfred A. Knopf.

Weissberg, R. P., Dymnicki, J. A., Taylor, R. D., & Shellinger, A. B. (2008). Promoting social and emotional learning enhances school success: Implications of a meta-analysis. Unpublished report.

Welwood, J. (1990). *Journey of the heart.* New York: HarperCollins.

Wentzel, K. R. (1997). Student motivation in middle school: The role of perceived pedagogical caring. *Journal of Educational Psychology, 89*(3), 411–19.

Wentzel, K. R. (1998). Social relationships and motivation in middle school: The role of parents, teachers, and peers. *Journal of Educational Psychology, 90*(2), 202–09.

Westman, M. (2001). Stress and strain crossover. *Human Relations, 54,* 717–51.

Whitaker, S. D. (2000). What do first-year special education teachers need? *Teaching Exceptional Children, 33*(1), 28–36.

Whitehead, A. J., & Ryba, K. (1995). New Zealand teachers' perceptions of occupational stress and coping strategies. *New Zealand Journal of Educational Studies, 30,* 177–88.

Whitlock, J. L. (2006). Youth perceptions of life in school: Contextual correlates of school connectedness in adolescence. *Applied Developmental Science, 10*(1), 13–29.

Wilhelm, K., Dewhurst-Savellis, J., & Parker, G. (2000). Teacher stress? An analysis of why teachers leave and why they stay. *Teachers and Teaching, 6,* 291–304.

Wilson, T. D., & Gilbert, D. T. (2005). Affective forecasting: Knowing what to want. *Current Directions in Psychological Science, 14*(3), 131–34.

Wilson, T. D., & Gilbert, D. T. (2008). Explaining away: A model of affective adaptation. *Perspectives on Psychological Science, 3*(5), 370–86.

Winner, J. (2008). *Take the stress out of your life.* New York: Da Capo Press.

Winograd, K. (2003). The functions of teacher emotions: The good, the bad, and the ugly. *Teachers College Record, 105*(9), 1641–73.

Winzelberg, A. J., & Luskin, F. M. (1999). The effects of meditation training in stress levels in secondary school teachers. *Stress Medicine, 15*(2), 69–77.

Wisniewski, L., & Gargiulo, R. (1997). Occupational stress and burnout among special educators: A review of the literature. *Journal of Special Education, 31*(3), 235–46.

Witte, H. (1985). *Coping effectively with life.* Omaha, NE: University of Nebraska Medical Center.

Wolters, C., Yu, S., & Pintrich, P. (1996). The relation between goal orientation and students' motivational beliefs and self-regulated learning. *Learning and Individual Differences, 8*, 211–38.

Wood, M. M., Quirk, C. A., & Swindle, F. L. (2007). *Teaching responsible behavior: Developmental therapy-developmental teaching for troubled children and adolescents* (4th ed.). Austin, TX: Pro-Ed.

Woods, P., & Carlyle, D. (2002). Teacher identities under stress: The emotions of separation and renewal. *International Studies in Sociology of Education, 12*(2), 169–89.

Woolfolk Hoy, A. W., & Weinstein, C. S. (2006). Student and teacher perspectives on classroom management. In C. Evertson & C. Weinstein (Eds.), *Handbook of classroom management: Research, practice, and contemporary issues* (pp. 181–219). Mahwah, NJ: Lawrence Erlbaum.

Xanthopoulou, D., Bakker, A. B., Demerouti, E., & Schaufeli, W. B. (2009). Work engagement and financial returns: A diary study on the role of job and personal resources. *Journal of Organizational and Occupational Psychology, 82*, 183–200.

Yavuz, M. (2009). An investigation of burnout levels of teachers working in elementary and secondary educational institutions and their attitudes to classroom management. *Educational Research and Reviews, 4*(12), 642–49.

Zammuner, V. L., & Galli, C. (2005). Well-being: Causes and consequences of emotion regulation in work settings. *International Review of Psychology, 17*, 355–64.

Zellars, K. L., Hochwarter, W. A., Perrewé, P. L., Hoffman, N., & Ford, E. W. (2004). Experiencing job burnout: The roles of positive and negative traits and states. *Journal of Applied and Social Psychology, 34*(5), 887–911.

Zellars, K. L., Perrewé, P. L., & Hochwarter, W. A. (2000). Burnout in health care: The role of the five factors of personality. *Journal of Applied Social Psychology, 30*, 1570–98.

Zembylas, M. (2003). Caring for teacher emotion: Reflections on teacher self-development. *Studies in Philosophy & Education, 22*(2), 103–25.

Zembylas, M. (2007). Theory and methodology in researching emotions in education. *International Journal of Research & Methods in Education, 30*(1), 57–72.

Zhang, Q., & Zhu, W. (2008). Exploring emotion in teaching: Emotional labor, burnout, and satisfaction in Chinese higher education. *Communication Education, 57*(1), 105–22.

Zylowska, L., Ackerman, D. L., Yang, M. H., Futrell, J. L., Horton, N. L., Hale, T. S., Pataki, C., & Smalley, S. L. (2008). Mindfulness meditation training in adults and adolescents with ADHD. *Journal of Attention Disorders, 11*(6), 737–46.